18'th Annual Tcl Association Tcl/Tk Conference Proceedings

Manassas, VA

October 24-28, 2011

TclA Publications

TCL Association Publications

Proceedings of the 18'th Annual Tcl/Tk Conference
ISBN: 978-0-578-09801-2

Cover and section art courtesy of the Civil War Trust.

Special thanks to Dawson Cowals for designing the Tcl Association logo.
For graphic design or web development consult-ing please visit him on the web at
http://www.dawsoncowals.com/

TclA Publications

Table Of Contents

Tcl 2011
Manassas, VA
October 24-28, 2011

Keynote Talk

NaTcl : Native Client Tcl Port

NaTcl : Native Client Tcl Port

Alexandre Ferrieux, France Telecom

1. What is Native Client ?

In 2010, Google started the NativeClient, aka "NaCl" project, which is a new sandboxing paradigm for browser expansion. The idea is to get the best of two worlds: the speed of (nearly) native code, and the safety of sandboxed environments. The various trust boundaries are illustrated below:

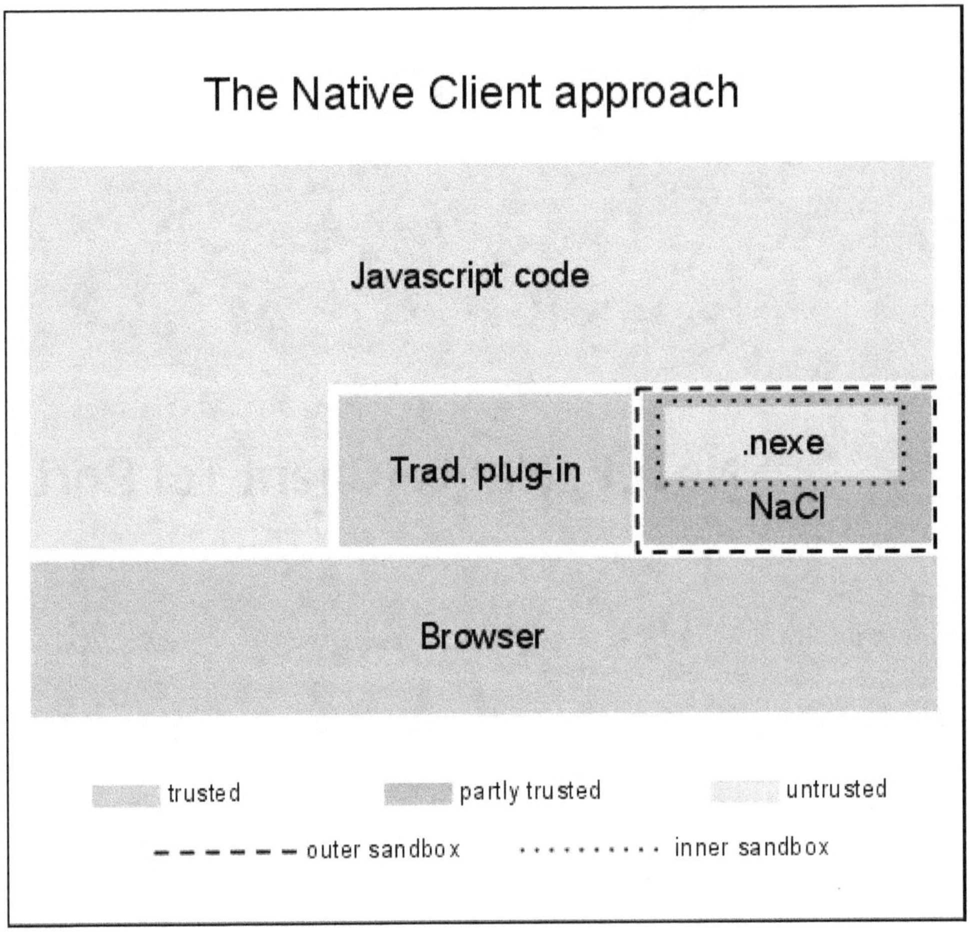

This little miracle is achieved by jailing the native code (".nexe") inside two sandboxing layers:

- the outer sandbox:

  This is a traditional process-level sandboxing (chroot, ulimit, etc). It encloses the entire NaCl plugin-process.
- the inner sandbox:

  This one is the real jewel inside NaCl. It is a machine-code-level verification pass and execution context that is run when loading the .nexe, applying an extensive list of checks, among which:
    - no dangerous instructions (like the one invoking syscalls)
    - all constant jumps fall on N-byte boundaries and in allowed range

- ♦ all computed jumps are preceded by an AND operation restricting them to N-byte boundaries and allowed range
- ♦ the runtime narrows the addressable memory (x86 segment registers)

These constraints together make it impossible for malevolent code to hide syscalls, either in shifts of the instruction decoding frame, or in data (which are necessarily not executable).

For code to be eligible as an .nexe, it must be compiled and linked with a modified gnu toolchain guaranteeing the invariants above. Any violation implies instant rejection at load time.

The N-byte boundary scheme does impact both code size (padding by NOPs) and speed (L1i cache). The NaCl team says they are moderate though. Our own Tcl case demonstrates that the performance loss (wrt truly native Tcl) is indeed bearable.

This double safety legitimates Google's boasting a bulletproof plugin architecture; moreover, the complete isolation from the OS implies that .nexes are only processor-specific: all exchanges with the outside world (the Chrome browser) are done through a new API (aptly named "Pepper" in this salty context). So an x86 .nexe will run unmodified on Windows, Linux, and x86-MacOS.

The Pepper API, which is still in fast expansion, progressively opens up various goodies to the .nexe:

- exchanges with the Javascript context
- sound
- direct access to the frame buffer
- (soon) access to accelerated 2D and 3D graphics

However, some things will by definition never be allowed within NaCl:

- naked sockets
- access to the whole local filesystem

This is obviously the price to pay for the absolute trust that NaCl aims to deserve.

2. NaTcl

2.1 Why ?

In April 2011, Google opened NaCl to outside developers. The motivation for porting Tcl to it stemmed from a general frustration about not (easily) having Tcl in browsers. To the non-JS world, NaCl comes across as an opening to alternate languages.

(for other -- and promising ! -- methods to bring Tcl into the browser landscape, see Steve Landers' paper.)

But the real trigger was Colin Mc Cormack's unwinking enthusiasm and support, backed by his deep knowledge of the whole field (WubTk in perspective).

2.2 Wait a minute

The salient issue that comes to mind when thinking about an NaCl port of Tcl is clearly the isolation from the OS. First, one may ask, How are we supposed to do interesting things in such a neutered environment ?

The answer is, of course: use the browser (and its JS context) as a proxy to the real world. Despite the limitations mentioned above, it can still do many things: GUI (of course); fetch intra-domain URLs; access app-restricted local config or user-selected normal files.

Bottom line: we don't need those missing syscalls anyway !

2.3 How ?

Given the unavailibility of syscalls at link level, two approaches were considered:

- cut "high" : separate Tcl's language and data manipulation core from more peripheral OS-related primitives;
- cut "low" : take it as a whole, faking syscalls.

While the first approach is cleaner, it implies a fair amount of code surgery, which in turn makes it hard to keep in sync with the mainstream codebase. Cutting "low", on the other hand, means a very small set of changes, at the expense of error message clarity ('no such file or directory' instead of 'invalid command name "open"').

After a couple of nanoseconds weighing the options, cutting low sounded like the way to go. This means that the starting point of the porting effort is a list of trivial syscall/libc definitions, typically setting errno to something not-too-alien, and returning the adequate value for failure (NULL or -1). See naclMissing.c.

Once syscall plugging was done, a few ancillary adaptations followed:

- Compatibility headers defining the (unused) structs passed to the emulated syscalls, not provided by the NaCl toolchain's includes. See naclCompat.h
- Toplevel bootstrapping glue calling Tcl_CreateInterp(), wrapping init.tcl, and passing data back and forth to JS. See naclMain.c
- JS support code. See loader.js.
- Incremental build system adaptations: parameterize and call ../unix/configure; patch the generated Makefile.

The bootstrapping code circumvents the absence of local filesystem access by stringifying the contents of init.tcl. This was preferred over a full-fledged VFS by the same reasoning as above: to keep it incremental, refrain from pulling in a significant mass of code.

Note that init.tcl is the only file needing this special handling, because once the interp is initialized, Tcl scripts can take over. For example, [source] is emulated (in init.tcl) by a Tcl coroutine that yields back to JS while the requested URL is fetched by the browser (with a vanilla XHR).

A further motivation for this approach is size and modularity: .nexes tend to be hefty, so as soon as at least two NaTcl-based applications exist (wishful thinking), it is best to share the generic Tcl .nexe in the browser's cache and let the individual apps [source] their specific code (which may be cached too) at init time.

2.4 Putting the pieces together

Once we have a working Tcl interpreter, properly adapted to the peculiar syscall-less link environment, the next step is to integrate it into the JS context's lifecycle. This task is outstandingly easy when Everything Is A String ;-). To be fair, JS also takes part in this, with its own eval() function. Indeed, we can set up a very simple "JS trampoline":

- ```
  (JS) String result = natcl.eval("some Tcl code");
  (JS) eval(result);
  ```

It is important to note that these two lines are not in a tight "while(true)" loop; instead, they are typically invoked from within a JS event handler, which in turn may be set up by (a side effect of) the "eval(result)" line. As a consequence, as long as "some Tcl code" takes a small time to complete (or to [yield]), the JS interpreter and associated browser-borne GUI stay responsive. The coupling between NaTcl and the browser is thus identical to the Tcl/Tk one.

2.5 First real example: the "balls" demo

One of the many showcases of HTML5 features is the Google "balls" demo at

http://www.html5canvastutorials.com/labs/html5-canvas-google-bouncing-balls

It is a modest JS script simulating bouncing balls relaxing to fixed positions drawing a Google logo, and disturbed by the hovering mouse:

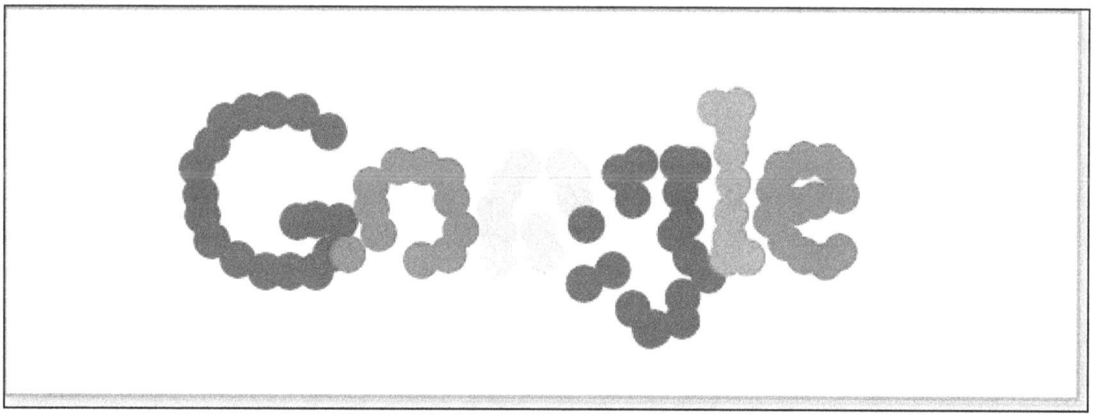

It is an interesting porting exercise for NaTcl, because:

- it features quickly-moving graphics (at 30fps)
- it also involves a bit of physics calculations
- it leverages the browser's beautiful antialiased circles

An additional self-imposed constraint was to use a Tk-like API in the NaTcl script. This is at variance with the natural JS canvas API, which is lower-level (exposes a Repaint callback and immediate-mode graphics). But as it turns out, bridging this gap is fairly simple. Basically, it amounts to mapping the current state (items, coordinates) of the Tcl-level canvas to a JS data structure used in the JS Repaint function.

This setup allows the interactive loop to only exchange with Tcl a (stringified) array of integers, feeding them into a Repaint function that was typically JIT-compiled once for all. The resulting speed is adequate, in that 30fps can still be held on an average-powered laptop.
  ```

2.6 Performance analysis

(to be completed with current Nacl+Chrome)

Bottom line:

- the NaTcl balls demo uses roughly thrice the CPU used by the original pure-Javascript code at the same frame rate.
- pure Tcl code, not hampered by the I/O with the JS context, runs marginally slower than native Tcl on the same platform.

One thing about the string I/O bottleneck: the NaCl team promised the advent of TypedArrays in the Pepper API, which will allow to populate JS data with native values (like lists and integers) from within NaCl. This points to a promising optimization of the transmission of a bunch of coordinates, directly from Tcl's Lists and Integers to JS's. TBC, when Google delivers.

2.7 NaTk

The "balls" demo shows that, with NaTcl in hand, a JS newbie (like me) can whip up a non-ridiculous coupling with the HTML5 canvas. The fundamental reason is that while the String is a handy common ground, each side knows to back it with more efficient representations.

Now, within this general string-coupling strategy, many forms of Tcl-side syntax and JS-side tricks are obviously possible. In particular, if you replace the JS newbie with a JS+Tcl expert like Colin, you get NaTk (based on ideas from WubTk). Learn more about it in Steve's paper.

3. Ecosystem

Despite the OS agnosticism, the portability dream is a bit spoilt by having NaCl only on Chrome (or Chromium) right now. Though the project is opensource, and Google initially targeted it as a multi-browser plugin, the reaction from competing browsers has been, as could be expected, lukewarm to say the least. Tough.

Still, NaCl retains some headroom in two areas:

- The Chrome App Store: there, dependency on Chrome is by design. Moreover, the download size is also part of the tradition, since the apps are installed locally (in a more persistent form of cache). Find a killer app, write it in NaTcl, publish, reach fame, then don't forget to mention "Powered by Tcl" ;-)
- The Android browser. The NaCl inner sandbox also exists for ARM CPUs (though in a less polished state than x86 and x86_64), and the NaCl team is committed to integrating it into the Android browser as soon as the x86 branches' bugcount reaches zero.

4. Afterword

When we were all mulling over Tcl and browsers in the Spring 2011, various ideas were discussed, among which Steve's amazing ones. In hindsight, NaTcl is less sexy than them, especially with its position under fire in the browser war. Still, it strikes a different balance between effort (minimal) and outcome (medium). And anyway, the observation of intimate contact between Tcl and Javascript was personally enriching.

ACKs

- Colin McCormack, for the initial spark, many good ideas and optimizations, and NaTk.
- Cameron Laird, for patient proofreading and key side-questions
- Brad Chen (from Google), for his sheer skills at taming rogue instructions on any processor
- Steve Landers, for exploring the opposite approach and succeeding !

Bibliography

- NaCl page on Google Code: https://sites.google.com/a/chromium.org/dev/nativeclient
- NaCl inner sandbox concepts by Brad Chen: http://www.youtube.com/watch?v=L8m9U7p_Ntk&feature=related
- NaTcl branch on core.tcl.tk: http://core.tcl.tk/tcl/timeline?r=ferrieux-nacl
- Wiki page by Colin et al, to get started with NaTcl: http://wiki.tcl.tk/28211

Tcl 2011
Manassas, VA
October 24-28, 2011

Tcl and Browsers

A History of 'Tcl in the Browser'

(and a new, perhaps even better, approach)

Steve Landers

steve@digitalsmarties.com

Abstract

Tcl has been running in browsers since the early days of the Internet. And yet this deployment model is still not mainstream in the Tcl world. With the dominance of the iPad in tablet computing, and the well known limitations on scripting languages in the iOS computing environment, the need for a browser-based Tcl solution is becoming greater.

This talk will survey the various approaches to implementing Tcl in a browser, including historical solutions such as WebRouser and the venerable Tcl Plugin, Java-based solutions such as Æjaks, Javascript solutions such as IncrTcl in Javascript, and native code solutions such as NaTcl. The pros and cons of each approach will be compared, along with other approaches such as implementing the TEBC in Javascript. Finally, the talk will introduce a new effort involving the use of LLVM and the Emscripten technology to translate a Tcl interpreter (in this case, Jim Tcl) to optimized Javascript.

The Motivation

The need to run Tcl in a browser has been apparent since the early days of the Internet. But the motivation for doing so has changed over time.

In 1993 there was no scripting language for the available browsers, and it was soon recognized that Tcl could fill the void.

A team led by Mike Doyle at the Center for Knowledge Management at the University of California, San Francisco, began discussing the first web application architecture in 1993. One of the team, David Martin, knew John Ousterhout from his student days at University of California, Berkeley. Martin suggested they look at creating a Tcl interpreter (with socket communications and security added) as one of the first plug-ins, so as to provide an easy means for creating interactive content. That ultimately turned into WebWish, which was developed to run on Eolas' WebRouser in 1995 [1].

So the initial motivation was to get a scripting language in the browser, and arguably Tcl was the first. With a bit of luck and a lot less politics Tcl could have been ubiquitous. As it was, Javascript became the default scripting language when the first version of Javascript (then called LiveScript) shipped in the beta releases of Netscape Navigator in September 1995.

While Javascript is a capable language, Tcl had the added attraction of wide portability from embedded systems through to mainframe computers. It wasn't just the potential for portability of code that was the attraction, perhaps more importantly it was the portability of skills.

> Anyway I know only one programming language worse than C and that is Javascript. [...] I was convinced that we needed to build-in a programming language, but the developers, Tim first, were very much opposed. It had to remain completely declarative. Maybe, but the net result is that the programming-vacuum filled itself with the most horrible kluge in the history of computing: Javascript.
>
> Robert Cailliau[2]

And so the emphasis changed from getting "a" scripting language to getting "our" scripting language in the browser. Doing so would have benefits beyond portability, including increased productivity and new deployment options.

It is the experience of many in the Tcl/Tk community that the productivity available from Tcl-related technology is significantly more than that available from Javascript. In particular, from Tcl's string handling and Tk's development model that includes the command-based objects, the gridded geometry manager and asynchronous events with call-backs.

Deployment through a browser offers the hope of "zero install", or "minimal install" applications. In large system installations getting approval for inclusion of a new application in the Standard Operating Environment (SOE) can take years of effort, so this can be the difference between a product from a smaller developer being ignored or adopted.

But in recent years there is another, perhaps ultimately more significant, motivation: relevancy in a world increasingly focussed on mobile applications. Mobile computing has been the fastest growing area of IT for the last few years and is dominated by two platforms – Apple's iOS and Google's Android.

As has been widely reported, there are significant barriers (including technical, legal and merely perceived) to implementing applications in scripting languages on iOS. Put differently, Apple's clear preference is for native (i.e. compiled) applications to be implemented in Objective-C and scripted applications in Javascript. To that extent, the iOS Webkit-based browser (Mobile Safari) is optimized to support Javascript through technologies such as the Nitro engine [3].

It is the opinion of this author that a Tcl port to iOS is technically feasible (although significant ongoing effort would be required to implement and maintain bindings to the iOS APIs). And it would not break Apple licensing agreements to deploy applications as a Starpack [4] providing that Tcl's ability to run arbitrary code was disabled.

But even if this effort were practical (as opposed to merely feasible), there is still the issue that deployment of every application would need to go through the iTunes App Store. And herein is a significant problem: many Tcl/Tk applications are custom built for specific customers. This just doesn't fit with the App Store model.

So it seems that in the case of iOS, the only practical solution is to find a way to deploy Tcl/Tk applications in a browser.

The situation on Android is a less restrictive. The preferred application language is Java but C is supported, and there is the Scripting Layer for Android, which has allowed a number of languages to be ported. There was a port of Tcl to the Android [5] however there was no GUI support, no interface to native APIs and the installation was complicated (requiring a jail broken device). Unfortunately it appears the Tcl Android port no longer works with later Android releases.

To summarise, the motivation for Tcl in a browser, even from the earliest days of the Internet, were:

- portability (both of code and skills)
- productivity (and, in particular, the benefits of Tk)
- deployment

And to this we add the elephant in the room – mobile applications, in particular on the iPad.

The Timeline

This timeline will look at the more significant implementations of Tcl in the browser. Perhaps it would be more accurate to say deploying "Tcl applications through a browser", because a number of these solutions still run Tcl on the server. This has implications for offline operation, which is increasingly important for mobile applications.

1995 – Eolas WebRouser

In 1995 Eolas released a version of WebRouser, an applet-enabled web browser based on Eolas' enhanced version of NCSA Mosaic that could run Tcl/Tk scripts using Eolas' WebWish Tcl plugin. WebRouser and WebWish were presented in the cover story in the February 1996 issue of Dr Dobb's Journal [6]. WebWish was the first Web Tcl implementation and one of the first plugins supported in a browser.

Pros

- Tcl and Tk
- security model
- web application support

Cons

- installation requires a plugin
- no longer available (Mosaic based)

1996 – The Tcl Plugin

In 1996 Jeff Hobbs produced a "proof of concept" Tcl plugin for Netscape following a visit to the Tcl group that was then at SunLabs. Jacob Levy (part of that group) produced the first Tcl/Tk plugin for Netscape and Laurent Demailly worked on the 2.0 implementation [7]. Version 3.0 [8] can still be installed in Firefox and Internet Explorer.

The Tcl Plugin made use of the Safe-Tcl [9] interpreter to provide a sandboxed security model. Safe-Tcl disables the Tcl commands that could potentially be harmful to the underlying system, but provides a mechanism by which these can be re-enabled in a controlled way by suitably authorised personnel.

On the positive side, the plugin still works and can be used to deploy applications on Firefox and Internet Explorer, although the installation isn't straightforward.

Pros
- Tcl and Tk
- Safe-Tcl security model
- still available on Firefox and IE

Cons
- installation – requires a plugin
- no WebKit (Safari, Chrome) port
- not available on mobile devices

1998 – Proxy Tk

In 1998 Mark Roseman and his team at TeamWave software implemented ProxyTk, a Java applet user interface toolkit for Tcl [10]. The small Java applet (50k bytes in size) ran in a browser to provide the user interface, and communicated with a Tk-like API running in a Tcl web server. Unlike the two previous browser plugin examples, in ProxyTk the application was split between the user interface running in the browser and the application Tcl code running on the server, with an efficient protocol connecting the two. The Tk commands on the server were "translated" into Java widgets in the client.

ProxyTk was ahead of its time but unfortunately it was swallowed in a corporate takeover and never reached its full potential.

Pros
- Tcl and Tk
- client / server
- real Tcl on the server

Cons
- subset of Tk features
- installation – requires a plugin
- requires Java to be enabled
- no longer available

2003 - TkWeb

In 2003 Roy Keene wrote TkWeb [11], an attempt at rendering Tcl/Tk scripts using HTML. And around the same time Wilfred J. Hansen published a technical note about Rendering Tcl/Tk

Windows as HTML [12]. Both of these were experiments aimed at proving the practicality of retaining the Tk API while rendering Tk widgets in a browser by generating HTML.

TkWeb took unmodified Tcl/Tk code and produced a Tcl/CGI application that could be run in a browser, without the need of a plugin. As such, it could be considered as the "logical" ancestor to more recent projects such as WubTk, discussed later.

Pros	Cons
• Tcl and Tk	• subset of features
• Javascript, potential iOS support	• experimental
	• no offline support

2006 – Æjaks

In 2006 Tom Poindexter developed Æjaks [13] – which "combines the server-side Ajax-based windowing system, Echo2, with the powerful simplicity of the Tcl language". Æjaks is a thin layer over Echo2 [14], a Java and Javascript-based platform for building interactive web-based applications. It translates Echo2 objects into Tcl objects, accessible behind a Tk-like object interface.

Æjaks used the Jacl interpreter [15] (an alternative implementation of Tcl 8.0 written in Java) so many recent Tcl features aren't available. The plan is to update Æjaks to JTcl [16], a modernised version of Jacl which provides a high degree of compatibility with Tcl 8.4.

A consideration with Æjaks is that, although Echo2 provides excellent cross-browser compatibility and uses modern Javascript techniques, it doesn't have the same amount of community acceptance or contributed widgets as other Javascript Web frameworks – in particulary jQuery [17] and jQueryUI [18].

Æjaks is a very capable system, and definitely one to consider for Tk-based web development. But being client/server it can't fully address the iPhone / iPad market.

Pros	Cons
• Tcl + Tk-like	• subset of features
• Javascript, potential iOS support	• no offline support

2007 – JsTcl

In 2007 Stéphane Arnold implemented JsTcl [19], a Tcl implementation in Javascript. JsTcl was a transliteration of Picol [20], a Tcl interpreter in 550 lines of C code by Salvatore Sanfilippo.

While very limited, it did demonstrate that a Tcl interpreter in Javascript is practical.

Pros	Cons
• Javascript, potential iOS support	• experimental, with limited features

2010 – WubTk

In 2010 Colin McCormack developed WubTk, a Tk-like API that maps Tk commands run in a Tcl interpreter on a server to jQueryUI widgets running in a browser.

jQuery is a cross-browser JavaScript library designed to simplify the client-side scripting of HTML. jQueryUI is a library that "provides abstractions for low-level interaction and animation, advanced effects and high-level, themeable widgets" built on top of jQuery.

WubTk combined the approach of TkWeb (i.e. generating html) with the power and simplicity of jQueryUI.

WubTk is (as the name indicates) implemented on top of the Wub [21] pure-Tcl web server, although it isn't tied to Wub. It supports a gridded geometry manager and many common widgets. Each WubTk instance has a persistent state which is retained between requests from the browser.

WubTk has been used to deploy custom commercial applications, and was used to demonstrate a Tcl/Tk application deployed on an iPad and iPhone during August 2010: most likely the first time this occurred.

As demonstrated at the Tcl2010 conference [22], WubTk allows the integration Tcl, Tk, jQuery, HTML5 [23] and CSS3 [24]. This allows Tcl/Tk developers to use modern web features such as multimedia and 3D graphics without losing the productivity that Tk is well known for.

Pros	Cons
• Tcl and Tk	• subset of Tk
• Javascript, iOS support	• no offline use
	• Tcl only on the server-side

2011 – NaTcl

Developed in 2011 by Alexandre Ferrieux, NaTcl [25] is Tcl running in the Native Client (NaCl) [26] sandbox of the Google Chrome browser [27]. This allows the Tcl interpreter to run securely within the browser environment at speeds similar to the standard Tcl interpreters on the same platform, with full access to the Chrome DOM [28].

NaTcl was one of the first scripting language running on the Native Client. As noted in the original announcement, it is the first whose name fits well with the Google naming conventions (sodium chloride and sodium tetrachloride) [29].

NaTcl is a significant development in running Tcl within a browser. And although currently limited to Chrome, there is potential for ubiquity if the Native Client becomes accepted as a standard in the WebKit-based browser world (which includes Safari and Chrome). But that is definitely not guaranteed, given Apple's desire to control what goes on iOS.

Pros	Cons
• speed	• no Tk binding
• full Tcl	• Chrome only, so no iOS
• interface with the DOM	• plugin (of sorts)

2011 – incrTcl in Javascript

Also developed during 2011 has been incrTcl in Javascript [30], by Arnulf Wiedemann. Starting life as an enhanced version of JsTcl, it is an attempt to have a more complete version of a Tcl interpreter written in Javascript.

As well as supporting more basic Tcl features, it supports incr Tcl features and more recent features such as namespaces, dicts and the expand operator. In addition, a number of Tk widgets are supported, including implementations of TkTable, BWidget tree and the paned window.

This is an impressive effort, starting with the original 1000 lines of code in JsTcl it is currently (as of October 2011) around 22,000 lines of code.

Pros	Cons
• Tcl and Tk	• partial implementation
• Javascript, potential iOS support	• speed

2011 – NaTk

Not only does Tk provide a compelling abstraction for specifying user interfaces in native applications, as WubTk demonstrated the Tk model is also beneficial for web applications. But WubTk was tied to the client/server Wub-based architecture, so in 2011 Colin McCormack re-implemented the WubTk concepts and produced a "Tk over HTML/CSS" called NaTk, the goal being to demonstrate it with NaTcl.

While still a "proof of concept", NaTk shows a way forward. In theory, it could be used to provide a Tk implementation for any browser-based Tcl implementation such as NaTcl or incrTcl in Javascript.

And, as has been noted previously, it goes beyond Tk allowing the development of hybrid applications that allow more advanced HTML5 features such as multimedia, CSS transformations and 3D to be used from Tcl via a Tk-like API.

Summary

So in 2011 we are left with several options for deploying Tcl applications via a browser:

- the Venerable Plug-in - not easy to deploy and is restricted to Netscape/Mozilla/Firefox or Internet Explorer (so no iOS deployment)
- Æjaks - requires a server so no offline use and no client-side Tcl
- WubTk, also requires a server but with the advantage of HTML5 integration and iOS deployment
- NaTcl - restricted to Chrome (so no iOS deployment) and no Tk (yet)
- incrTcl in Javascript, which is still under development

Arguably none are ready for prime time, albeit they are close.

Oh no, not again[1]

With this in mind, in mid 2011 Gerald Lester, Steve Huntley and Steve Landers began discussing ways to provide Tcl/Tk on the iPad. All agreed that the only practical way is to use Javascript and map Tk onto HTML5, since a port of Tcl (let alone Tk) isn't likely to be practical.

Three basic approaches to providing Tcl were identified:

- translate application Tcl code to Javascript
- implement the TEBC engine in Javascript
- implement Tcl in Javascript

Lester was to address the first, Landers the second and all three considered the last, especially in the light of incrTcl in Javascript. This paper addresses the second approach and an unexpected development that introduced a new option for the third.

TEBC in Javascript

TEBC is an abbreviation for TclExecuteByteCode – the part of the Tcl interpreter that actually executes the Tcl Bytecodes.

1 "Curiously enough, the only thing that went through the mind of the bowl of petunias as it fell was 'Oh no, not again'. Many people have speculated that if we knew exactly why the bowl of petunias had thought that we would know a lot more about the nature of the universe than we do now" - Douglas Adams, The Hitch Hiker's Guide To The Galaxy

This approach is initially quite attractive, because it would (in theory) allow any arbitrary Tcl byte-code to be compiled using a real Tcl interpreter and then run in a browser.

After discussions with Miguel Sofer, it became apparent that there are real difficulties with this option, and it isn't worth pursuing. Perhaps that is understating the forcefulness of Miguel's argument.

The first problem is the complexity of the TEBC code. To quote Donal Fellows, '... an example of how to not write your code — TEBC currently looks like a bomb exploded in it .. but hard to do in any other way; optimized bytecode executors usually are huge balls of spaghetti' [31].

Leaving aside this complexity, there is another practical consideration: not all Tcl commands are byte-coded, and so Javascript implementations would still be needed for those. This in itself pushes the TEBC solution closer to the "Tcl in Javascript" approaches.

And finally, there is the intangible but nevertheless real concern about the constraints upon developing (or even replacing) the TEBC engine that would result from having a second widely deployed implementation "in the wild".

The Unexpected Development

In May 2011 Fabrice Bellard announced a PC emulator written in Javascript that was fast enough to run Linux in a browser [32] "I did it for fun, just because newer JavaScript engines are fast enough to do complicated things" Bellard said [33].

The emulator is available at on Ballard's home page at http://bellard.org. Once Linux is downloaded it boots in a surprisingly fast 5 seconds when run on Safari 5.1 on a 2.8 GHz iMac i7. The Javascript code for the emulator weighs in at around 120KB. An outstanding achievement by any standard.

The technique used by Bellard was hand-coded Javascript using W3C Typed Arrays. A discussion on Stack Overflow goes into more details about the technical aspects [34].

While this development isn't directly related to the topic of Tcl in a browser, it did show that a modern Javascript interpreter is fast enough to emulate PC hardware. And if that is the case, then surely it would be fast enough to run a Tcl interpreter?

But implementing a Tcl interpreter in Javascript from scratch would be a significant project.

Fortunately, there is an alternative.

Emscripten

Steve Huntley had already flagged Emscripten [35] (a C to Javascript translator) and Steve Landers began looking into it as a way to take an existing Tcl interpreters written in C and translate it to Javascript.

The goal of the Emscripten project is simple: to allow any C/C++ code to run on the web.

Emscripten is a compiler that converts LLVM [36] bitcodes into Javascript. It can use either the llvm-gcc or clang compilers, and so supports both C and C++ (or any other language supported by these compilers).

The performance of the generated code is acceptable, without being stellar. Currently it is around 10 times slower than gcc -O3. But this will almost certainly get better with improvements over time to LLVM, Emscripten, Javascript optimisers and Javascript engines.

Already a number of languages have been ported to Javascript using Emscripten, including Python, Ruby and Lua. The goal became to add Tcl to that list.

The first decision was which Tcl to use. While the core Tcl release is an obvious choice, there are a number of potential problems in using it for this project:

- it is a relatively large code base
- it contains feature that are not relevant to a browser environment (e.g. threads, file I/O)
- it isn't easily modularised

One of the small Tcl interpreters like Picol would have also been an option, but this would have been too limiting.[2]

But there is an alternative that is modular, small and with most key Tcl features: Jim Tcl.

Jim Tcl

Originally developed by Salvatore Sanfilippo, and now maintained by Steve Bennett, Jim is a small footprint re-implementation of Tcl that is particularly suited for embedded environments [37].

Jim implements a large subset of Tcl and adds many advanced features like references with garbage collection, closures, a built-in Object Oriented programming system, functional programming commands, and first class arrays.

Jim is also quite small, around 10k lines of code and a binary size of between 100-200 kB depending on the modules used.

Jim passes many Tcl unit tests, and many Tcl programs run unmodified, but it is best to think of Jim's relationship with Tcl as one of programmer portability than necessarily program portability.

So the plan became to treat the browser as an embedded system and to compile Jim Tcl to Javascript using Emscripten.

2 the author has subsequently found that Tom Poindexter built Picol using Emscripten at about the same time

Jim JS

Clearly the project needs a better name than Jim JS but (in a move somewhat atypical for an open source project) the decision was made to actually get the software working instead of investing time and effort in a cute name or flashy website. But I digress …

Emscripten requires specific versions of LLVM and Clang or LLVM-GCC, along with one or both of the SpiderMonkey or V8 Javascript engines. Given these specific requirements an Ubuntu virtual machine was created to avoid clashes with existing compiler toolchains, and also to facilitate sharing the development environment. As an aside, the ability to check-point and restart the virtual machine (a feature of VMware and other products) greatly facilitated the testing of the configuration.

Once installed, it was a matter of selecting the Jim Tcl modules, creating a build script that calls the Jim Tcl Makefile as appropriate, then waiting for it to break.

And break it did. But fortunately there are good examples in the Python build system, plus Emscripten includes a make proxy tool that converts normal build commands to those appropriate for Emscripten. The result was 2.4 MB of rather dense and obtuse Javascript.

Invoking the generated Javascript in a browser is relatively straight forward: define an html form containing an input field for the Tcl code, along with two Javascript functions: one to evaluate the entered text by passing it to a predefined function in the generated Javascript, one to print the results.

```
function execute(text) {
  printed = false;
  Module.run(text);
  if (!printed) {
    print('<small><i>(no output)</i></small>');
  }
}

function print(text) {
  console.log(text);
  var output = document.getElementById('output');
  if (output) output.innerHTML += text + '<br>';
  printed = true;
}
```

In a typical application (rather than a test environment) the Module.run() function would be invoked from Javascript, either directly or as the result of an AJAX operation. The generated Javascript can make calls to any Javascript function, and so it would be straightforward to add a facility to make DOM calls from Tcl.

In early tests it was found that simple commands like "set i 10" worked, but compound commands like "set i 10 ; set j 20" did not, nor did expr and many other commands. The root cause seemed to be memory management issues, as a diagnostic from the Emscripten runtime support code flagged that something was trying to allocate zero btyes.

A discussion with Steve Bennett quickly identified the problem: rather than test that the requested allocation size is not zero, Jim Tcl relies on the memory management library to return zero bytes if it is. Once this was identified it was easily fixed in the Jim JS runtime code.

The next issue was that many commands worked, but others such as expr caused Jim to exit with no error message. The solution was found by enabling various DEBUG_SHOW options within the Jim Tcl C headers. This caused Jim to display debugging information:

For example:

```
command = expr 1
==== Tokens ====
[ 0]@1 ESC 'expr'
[ 1]@1 SEP ' '
[ 2]@1 ESC '1'
[ 3]@1 EOF ''
==== Script ====
[ 0] LIN
[ 1] ESC expr
[ 2] ESC 1
==== Expr Tokens ====
[ 0]@0 INT '1'
[ 1]@0 EOL ''
_strtoull is not a function                   jim.js:32571
```

This shows that a C library function (strtoull) has not been implemented in the Emscripten Javascript runtime, but by undefining HAVE_LONG_LONG when building Jim the equivalent (and implemented) strtoul is generated.

Futher testing showed there were several runtime functions that were partially implemented. For example, not all strtol(3) parameters are supported. The solution is to implement a wrapper function in Javascript that accepts the calls used by Jim Tcl and maps them to the appropriate Emscripten runtime function.

This shows the basic steps in finishing the port of Jim Tcl to Javascript:

- run a test and look for the missing Javascript functions
- adjust the Jim configuration to avoid generating missing functions
    - or implement a wrapper function in Javascript to convert to existing but incompatible runtime functions
    - or implement a new function in Javascript

At this point in time (October 2011) this is an ongoing activity.

Performance and Optimization

Anecdotally, performance is quite acceptable. For example, testing on an iMac 2.8 GHz i7 results in the following using ActiveTcl 8.6b1.2 and Jim in the browser:

time {set a 10} 100000

ActiveTcl 8.6b1.2	0.25151566 microseconds per iteration
Jim/Firefox	18 microseconds per iteration
Jim/Safari	16 microseconds per iteration

time {set a 10; set b $a} 100000

ActiveTcl 8.6b1.2	0.42748254 microseconds per iteration
Jim/Firefox	30 microseconds per iteration
Jim/Safari	27 microseconds per iteration

So that's 60-80 times slower than "native" (let's say an order of magnitude) on a simple operation, with essentially no optimization.

As mentioned, the generated Jim Javascript code is around 2.4 Mb in size. Whilst this isn't outrageous, it can be improved significantly by running it through a Javascript optimizer such as Google's Closure compiler []. The resulting jim.js is around 650 kB, it obviously loaded more quickly but was not measurably faster to execute. Other Javascript optimizers are yet to be tried.

Summary and Conclusions

The need for Tcl/Tk deployment in a browser is no less now than it was in the early nineties.

And in spite of several efforts over the years the average Tcl developer is still not in a position to deploy an application in a browser. But with the growth in mobile computing, and in particular iOS, the need has never been greater.

There are at least three projects underway that could meet this need in varying degrees (NaTcl, Jim JS and incrTcl in Javascript). And in many ways all three are complementary.

If one was to crystal-ball gaze, there is a scenario where Jim JS is used to get ubiquity, NaTcl for the case when performance is needed, with parts of incrTcl in Javascript for it's excellent widget support.

But dreaming even more, imagine a hand-crafted, fast Javascript implementation of Tcl (that took the lead from the Linux in a Browser project) combined with a more complete NaTk (providing Tk over HTML and HTML5/CSS3 integration).

And not just for deploying applications in a browser. As shown by Entice [38] and other tools, desktop applications with embedded browsers are both viable and attractive. So perhaps the next generation of Tk should not be based on X11, Windows or Cocoa, but on Javascript, HTML and CSS.

Tk9 anyone?

References

[1] WebRouser Announcement – http://1997.webhistory.org/www.lists/www-talk.1995q3/0566.html

[2] Interview with Robert Cailliau - http://en.wikinews.org/wiki/Wikinews:Story_preparation/Interview_with_Robert_Cailliau

[3] Javascript Engine - http://en.wikipedia.org/wiki/JavaScript_engine

[4] Starpack – http://wiki.tcl.tk/3663

[5] Tcl Android – http://wiki.tcl.tk/27643

[6] WebRouser – Dr Dobb's Journal, Issue #244, February 1996

[7] Levy, J. A *Tk Netscape Plugin.* Proceedings of the Fourth Annual Tcl/Tk Workshop. July, 1996. http://www.usenix.org/publications/library/proceedings/tcl96/full_papers/levy/index.html

[8] Tcl/Tk Plugin Version 3 – http://www.tcl.tk/software/plugin/

[9] Safe-Tcl – http://labs.oracle.com/techrep/1997/smli_tr-97-60.pdf

[10] Roseman, Mark *Proxy Tk: A Java applet user interface toolkit for Tcl.* Proceedings of the Seventh Annual Tcl/Tk Conference, February 2000, http://www.usenix.org/events/tcl2k/full_papers/roseman/roseman_html/

[11] TkWeb – http://www.rkeene.org/projects/tkweb/

[12] Hansen, Wilfred J. *Rendering Tcl/Tk Windows as HTML.* Proceedings of the Tenth Annual Tcl/Tk Conference, July 2003 http://www.tcl.tk/community/tcl2004/Tcl2003papers/rendering.doc

[13] Æjaks – http://aejaks.sourceforge.net/Aejaks_Home

[14] Echo2 – http://echo.nextapp.com/site/echo2

[15] Jacl – http://wiki.tcl.tk/1637

[16] JTcl – http://jtcl.kenai.com/

[17] JQuery – http://jquery.com

[18] JQueryUI – http://jqueryui.com

[19] JsTcl – http://wiki.tcl.tk/17972

[20] Picol – http://wiki.tcl.tk/17893

[21] Wub – http://wiki.tcl.tk/wub

[22] Landers, Steve *WubTk - Tcl/Tk Apps Anywhere.* Proceedings of the Seventeenth Annual Tcl/Tcl Conference, October 2010, http://www.tclcommunityassociation.org/wub/proceedings/Proceedings-2010/SteveLanders/WubTk/wubtk.pdf

[23] HTML5 – http://en.wikipedia.org/wiki/HTML5

[24] CSS3 – http://en.wikipedia.org/wiki/CSS3

[25] NaTcl – http://wiki.tcl.tk/28211

[26] Google Native Client – http://en.wikipedia.org/wiki/Google_Native_Client

[27] Google Chrome – http://www.google.com/chrome

[28] DOM – http://en.wikipedia.org/wiki/Document_Object_Model

[29] Google native code browser plug-in gets tickled – The Register, April 14, 2011 http://www.theregister.co.uk/2011/04/14/tcl_on_native_client/

[30] incrTcl in Javascript – http://wiki.tcl.tk/28293

[31] TEBC – http://wiki.tcl.tk/22133

[32] Fabrice Bellard – Javascript PC Emulator – Technical Notes - http://bellard.org/jslinux/tech.html

[33] cnet News - Javascript: Now powerful enough to run Linux, May 17, 2011, http://news.cnet.com/8301-30685_3-20063563-264.html

[34] StackOverflow discussion on Bellard's performance tricks – http://stackoverflow.com/q/6245191
[35] Emscripten – http://github.com/kripken/emscripten/wiki
[36] LLVM - http://llvm.org/
[37] Jim Tcl – http://jim.berlios.de/
[38] Landers, Steve *Entice – Embedding Firefox in Tk* . Proceedings of the Thirteenth Annual Tcl/Tcl Conference, October 2006 - http://www.tcl.tk/community/tcl2007/papers/Steve_Landers/Entice.pdf

Itcl in Javascript

An implementation of Tcl/Itcl using Javascript.

A paper for the Eighteenth Annual Tcl/Tk Conference

Abstract

Incr Tcl in Javascript (also called: itcl in Javascript) is a work in progress, which started about February 2011. It's intention is to extend the existing [Tcl in Javascript] an interpreter for the Tcl language written in Javascript with a lot of additional features and commands as well as an implementation of itcl in Javascript. During implementation there was the need for optimizing parsing and evaluation of Tcl statements, which resulted in a partial parsing strategy.

Contact information

Arnulf Wiedemann

Lechstr. 10

D-86931 Prittriching

Email: arnulf@wiedemann-pri.de

Inhaltsverzeichnis

1The Idea

During looking for a suitable tool to run Tcl in a browser I found [Tcl in Javascript] also named JsTcl. I found it interesting but with too few features from Tcl, so I decided to enhance that. JsTcl is an implementation of a Tcl interpreter written in Javascript and the parser is based on [Picol]. An implementation in Javascript has the big advantage, that it is running on most browsers, also there are some incompatibilities to take care of between the browsers. One advantage is, that you don't need to compile and link and besides the browser incompatibilities you don't have to worry about the platform you are running on.

2How it started

When looking for a frontend/client for [ATWF] and [Reporting Tools with Tcl] I did spend some time checking all the available stuff. For a [Tcl] client it was easy there I decided to use a [Tclkit]/[Starkit], but in a browser, the only existing possibility is the [Tcl/Tk plugin], but there I knew that there were some problems and it was not much updated in the past.

So I was thinking about generating [HTML] code on the server side with [Tcl]. At that time I was also checking what of the existing [javascript] based libraries could be used especially [jQuery] and [YUI]. Both had a lot of interesting features. I also found [Tcl in Javascript] and was thinking about using that as an interface for making either [jQuery] or [YUI] functionality available with a [Tcl] wrapper.

When looking closer at that and playing with it I did like it a lot, but was soon missing [Tcl] functionality I wanted to use.

That was the start of the [incr Tcl in Javascript] project. At the beginning I was only adding some (from my point of view) functionality, which I was missing most.

The general idea already used/implemented by Stéphane Arnold was to have TclObjects (TclObj) implemented as [javascript Object]s ([TclObject js Object]), which hold a [Tcl] value that can be converted into the different types needed like:

- string
- integer
- real
- boolean
- list

I have added to these types:

  - dict
  - stmt
  - word
  - word_part

The „dict" type holds - as in the Tcl C-implementation - the internal representation of a Tcl dictionary.

I started with implementing [namespace]s. This was done by having a [javascript Object] [TclNamespace js Object] that did have properties for the relevant information and was used in a similar way as the TclNamespace struct in the C implementation. It contains references to the parent [namespace] and a list of the child namespace references. There was some basic implementation of a callframe available, I modified that to use a [TclCallframe js Object], which had additional properties like the currently executed statement for introspection, the used [namespace] for that callframe etc.

For [namespace]s also the [Tcl] parser ([TclParser js Object]) had to be extended to understand the [namespace] syntax for command and variable names.

The [TclNamespace js Object] was designed to allow different types of namespace:

- Tcl.NAMESPACE a "normal" [Tcl] [namespace]
- Tcl.ITCL_CLASS an [itcl] class [namespace]
- Tcl.ITCL_EXTENDED_CLASS an [itcl] extendedclass [namespace]
- Tcl.TYPE_CLASS an [itcl] type [namespace]

For the [itcl] namespace types there was designed a resolve_commands reference for allowing implementation of namespace command resolvers.

This Object includes method for registering class commands and for registering subcommands, which is used for implementing namespace ensembles. A list of superclasses is provided here as well as entries for a class constructor and a class destructor.

Later on there was added support for namespace variables which are handled with a reimplementation in [javascript] of the equivalent C-functions lookupVariableEx, lookupSimpleVariable, GetNamespaceForQualName and FindNamespaceVar.

3Design Goals for Implementation of Itcl in Javascript

The internal types of a [TclObject js Object] (in the C-Implementation a TclObj) are:

- OBJECT_TYPE_TEXT
- OBJECT_TYPE_LIST
- OBJECT_TYPE_INTEGER
- OBJECT_TYPE_REAL
- OBJECT_TYPE_BOOL
- OBJECT_TYPE_DICT
- OBJECT_TYPE_STMTS
- OBJECT_TYPE_STMT
- OBJECT_TYPE_WORD
- OBJECT_TYPE_WORD_PART
- OBJECT_TYPE_EXPR_TREE

Parsing rules for Tcl script input are corresponding to the [Dodekalog].

The reason for partially parsing the Tcl input is mostly performance and to some extent later on easier handling of the execution of a statement. Partially parsing is done in the following way: all the tokenizing for Tcl is done, but no variables are expanded, no bracket commands are executed and braced parts are handled as one token. And also within quoted strings the parts, which have later on to be expanded are parsed into separate "word_part" [TclObject js Object]s. Same is done for array names and array references.

Tokens returned from parsing are:

- TOKEN_WORD_SEP
- TOKEN_STR
- TOKEN_EOL
- TOKEN_EOF
- TOKEN_ESC
- TOKEN_CMD
- TOKEN_VAR
- TOKEN_EXPAND
- TOKEN_PAREN

- TOKEN_BRACE
- TOKEN_VAR_ARRAY
- TOKEN_VAR_ARRAY_NAME
- TOKEN_ARRAY_NAME
- TOKEN_VAR_COMPOSED
- TOKEN_BRACED_VAR
- TOKEN_QUOTED_STR
- TOKEN_COMMENT
- TOKEN_DECIMAL
- TOKEN_INTEGER
- TOKEN_REAL
- TOKEN_BOOLEAN
- TOKEN_HEX
- TOKEN_OCTAL
- TOKEN_MINUS
- TOKEN_PLUS
- TOKEN_MUL
- TOKEN_DIV
- TOKEN_MOD
- TOKEN_LT
- TOKEN_GT
- TOKEN_LE
- TOKEN_GE
- TOKEN_NE
- TOKEN_EQ
- TOKEN_NOT
- TOKEN_RP
- TOKEN_AND
- TOKEN_OR
- TOKEN_EXOR
- TOKEN_AND_IF
- TOKEN_OR_IF
- TOKEN_STR_EQ
- TOKEN_STR_NE
- TOKEN_STR_IN
- TOKEN_STR_NI

•TOKEN_STR_PARAM

•TOKEN_STR_CMD

•TOKEN_NO_WORD_SEP

•TOKEN_EXPR

•TOKEN_STMTS

For "normal" Tcl code the tokens from TOKEN_WORD_SEP to TOKEN_COMMENT are returned

Tokens TOKEN_DECIMAL to TOKEN_STR_NI are returned for expression like parts in if, while and in the expr command. The last few ones are used internally for partially parsed statements.

Examples:

String	Token	Value
$abc	TOKEN_VAR	abc
${abc def}	TOKEN_BRACED_VAR	
	■TOKEN_BRACE	
	■TOKEN_STR	abc
${abc def}	TOKEN_BRACED_VAR	
x(y)	TOKEN_ARRAY_NAME	x0x01y
$x(y)	TOKEN_VAR_ARRAY	
${x}(y)	TOKEN_VAR_ARRAY_NAME	
[set a 1]	TOKEN_CMD	
{a y}	TOKEN_BRACE	a y
“abc”	TOKEN_QUOTED_STRING	abc
“abc[x a]$y{d e f}yyy”	TOKEN_QUOTED_STRING	
	■TOKEN_STR	abc
	■TOKEN_CMD	x a
	■TOKEN_VAR	y
	■TOKEN_BRACE	d e f
	■TOKEN_STR	yyy
xyz	TOKEN_STR	xyz
{*}	TOKEN_EXPAND	“”

Some commands use a statement part as en expression to be evaluated and to return a value of true or false like if and while for the condition or the Tcl expr command. For these the condition is parsed to an expression tree existing of nodes ([TclNode js Object]). When tokenizing an expression string first all parts are put into nodes objects and these [TclNode js Object]s are placed in a tree with the operator as the parent node and the operands as the child nodes. A paren "(" is also a parent node. The nodes are first put in parsing order in the expression tree and afterward the expression tree is reorganized according to the precedence rules o the operators.

Operators are:

- + TOKEN_PLUS
- \- TOKEN_MINUS
- * TOKEN_MUL
- / TOKEN_DIV
- % TOKEN_MOD
- < TOKEN_LT
- > TOKEN_GT
- <= TOKEN_LE
- >= TOKEN_GE
- != TOKEN_NE
- == TOKEN_EQ
- ! TOKEN_NOT
- (TOKEN_PAREN pseudo operator used for precedence handling
-) TOKEN_RP pseudo operator used for precedence handling
- & TOKEN_AND
- | TOKEN_OR
- ^ TOKEN_EXOR
- && TOKEN_AND_IF
- || TOKEN_OR_IF
- eq TOKEN_STR_EQ
- ne TOKEN_STR_NE
- in TOKEN_STR_IN
- ni TOKEN_STR_NI

Precedence rules are (as in C):

Token	Precedence
TOKEN_OR_IF	1
TOKEN_AND_IF	2
TOKEN_OR	3
TOKEN_EXOR	4
TOKEN_AND	5
TOKEN_EQ	6
TOKEN_NE	6
TOKEN_LT	7
TOKEN_GT	7
TOKEN_LE	7
TOKEN_GE	7
TOKEN_PLUS	9
TOKEN_MINUS	9
TOKEN_MUL	10
TOKEN_DIV	10
TOKEN_MOD	10
TOKEN_PAREN	12
TOKEN_STR	99

Reorganizing is done in flipping nodes that have a higher precedence:

if precedence of node is greater than the precedence of the left node and the node is not a TOKEN_PAREN flip nodes.

- set the parent->child_left to child_left of the node
- set parent of the node to child_left
- set child_left of the node to child_left->child_right
- set child_left->child_right to the node
- reorganize child_left

Some tokens are used only internal during parsing:

TOKEN_EOL the separator for a Tcl statement either "\r", "\n" or a ";"

TOKEN_WORD_SEP space or tab between words

TOKEN_ESC for signaling the different parts of a word like in yyy[a b]ccc

one part is yyy one part is the TOKEN_CMD "a b" and one

part is ccc. In between TOKEN_ESC is returned to signal

these parts

TOKEN_EOF at the end of the code to parse

Some tokens are only used within expression trees:

TOKEN_INTEGER 1 to n digits 0-9

TOKEN_DECIMAL an integer with a leading unary "+" or "-"

TOKEN_REAL a decimal with a "." as the fraction separator, a fraction and an

exponent with e+/-nnn syntax

TOKEN_BOOLEAN the Tcl values for a boolean, true/false/0/1

...

TOKEN_HEX 0x followed by 0-9A-Fa-f characters

TOKEN_OCTAL 0-7 1 to n characters

4Performance issues

The original implementation of Tcl in Javascript was parsing every statement byte by byte when executing Tcl code.

When starting I used that for a while too, but when trying to implement itcl in Tcl, there were big performance problems. One point was the complete parsing of a statement when executing Tcl code, second problem was having itcl implemented in Tcl, which forced a twice time interpretation when interpreting a class definition once by javascript for running Tcl second by Tcl for parsing itcl.

So I decided to write the itcl interpreter in javascript too and as a second issue for better performance to parse initial Tcl code only once and then keep something like an intermediate code a "partially parsed" form of Tcl statements.

Because of Tcl's dynamic structure, that partially parsed form did not extend variable references or commands in braces etc. but did mostly a tokenizing, so the low level parsing had to be done only once. That did help a lot to increase performance. Nevertheless it would be useful in the future to have something similar to the Tcl bytecode and to have an interpreter for that intermediate format written in javascript. Designing and implementing such an intermediate language and an interpreter for it could perhaps be a future [GSoC] project.

There are three types that are used for a partially parsed Tcl statement. A Tcl statement is mapped to a "stmt" type, the parts of a Tcl statement like the command name and the params are represented as „word" (statement part) and because a statement part can be composed of different sub parts. A sub part - named a "word_part" - is available, that can be:

- a variable reference within a quoted string
- a name constructed form a string part for example an array name
- a command part in brackets etc..

To hold that parsed information there are 3 different [javascript Object]s:

- [TclStatement js Object]
- [TclWord js Object]
- [TclWordPart js Object]

see below for details.

Later on there was another improvement of performance in implementing a cache for variable and command access depending on the callframe and using some epoch mechanism like it is used in TclOO for determining if the cache is still up-to-date. As every command and variable object (javascript Object) has an id in it the maximum id for variables/commands is used to determine, if the cache is still usable, as creating a variable/command modifies that maximum id and renaming/deleting a variable/command has to remove the corresponding cache entries.

Implementing that cache mechanism together with more often using the partially parsed statements gave a performance improvement of 400% for simple setting or getting a variable! “There is still some room for improvements” - as one of my former colleagues used to say - concerning performance.

5Tcl Javascript Objects

5.1 [TclCallframe js Object]

Parameters:

- interp
- type

Container for a Tcl callframe. A callframe is a [javascript Object] which is pushed on a stack built from a [javascript Array] when a proc or method is called. Contains all local variables, these are in a [javascript Object]: variables as [TclVariable js Object]s and the name as the index, and information about a possible [itcl] object, when the command was an [itcl] object. There is also a type of a callframe, which can be – as in the C implementation -

- CALL_TYPE_PROC
- CALL_TYPE_METHOD
- CALL_TYPE_UPLEVEL
- CALL_TYPE_UPVAR
- CALL_TYPE_EVAL

After the call the callframe object is popped from the stack again.

5.2 [TclCommand js Object]

Parameters:

- name
- func
- privdata

A TclCommand represents either a Tcl proc or a Tcl command implemented as a javascript function. The func argument is either javascript implementation of a Tcl command or a Tcl sub command or it is the javascript implementation of the Tcl proc command and in that case the privdata argument contains an array with the arglist and the body. This object also contains a call function, which checks, if there are execution traces and adds the enterstep and leavestep traces, so the interp knows which ones to call and it evaluates the enter trace, if one exists.

Now the functions code is executed with the calling arglist. For javascript functions it just executes them, for a Tcl proc the relevant javascript implementation function is called. This pushes a new callframe onto the callframe stack and prepares the arglist for Tcl including handling of the special args argument. During that part also the contents of the arglist, which can be a braced word is extracted. The the handling of optional arguments is done with filling in default values, if the argument is not there. The arglist is the stored as local variables in the callframe, so one can set and get these variables using the formal parameter names.

Also the level info for the info level command is prepared and pushed onto the callframe. After that evaluation of the body is done.

Now the level_info is popped off the callframe and the callframe is popped off the callframe stack. Following this the leave and leavestep traces are taken of the interpreter and if there is a leave trace that is called with the result of the executed code.

5.3 [TclDict js Object]

Parameters:

- interp

A container for the functions which build the dict ensemble. The dicts itself are [TclObject js Object]s. The implementation is very similar to the C-implementation in that it stores the keys and values for the keys in an associative array and the sequence of the keys in and additional array. Every value can be another dict. Conversion between the dict representation and the string representation and vice versa is done in the [TclObject js Object] when needed.

5.4 [TclEvalStatement js Object]

Parameters:

- Interp
- statement_parser

Javascript functions to evaluate preparsed Tcl statements and words, if the latter for example is a braced command.

5.5 [TclInterpAlias js Object]

Parameters:

- src_path
- src_cmd
- target_path
- target_cmd
- params

A container for holding information on mapping a Tcl command to another Tcl command. Right now the src_path and target_path have to be the same (interpreter) and must be empty for the current interpreter. When looking up a command to call the interpreters alias list is first searched for a relevant command and after that the command is looked up in the namespace etc.

5.6 [TclInterp js Object]

Parameters:

- win
- start_dir

A container which holds all the information necessary for an Tcl interpreter like the stack for the callframes, the stack for the namspaces etc.

5.7 [TclNamespace js Object]

Parameters:

- interp
- ns_name
- privdata

A container for managing all the information for a Tcl namespace including an itcl class. With all the functions for looking up commands and variables and creating and deleting namespaces.

5.8 [TclNode js Object]

Parameters:

- interp
- name
- node_type
- child_left
- child_right

A container for holding a node of an expr tree used in if, while and expr Tcl command

5.9 [TclObject js Object]

Parameters:

- interp
- value
- type

A TclObject holds - as in the C implementation – information about a Tcl values. That can be a string, an integer, a dict and additionally here a statement, a word, an expr tree etc.

The type determines the initial type of the object. This type can change when shimmering.

Possible types are:

- OBJECT_TYPE_TEXT
- OBJECT_TYPE_LIST
- OBJECT_TYPE_INTEGER
- OBJECT_TYPE_REAL
- OBJECT_TYPE_BOOL
- OBJECT_TYPE_DICT
- OBJECT_TYPE_STMTS
- OBJECT_TYPE_STMT
- OBJECT_TYPE_WORD
- OBJECT_TYPE_WORD_PART
- OBJECT_TYPE_EXPR_TREE

5.10 [TclPackage js Obejct]

Parameters:

- interp

Container for holding all information of a Tcl or Tk package like the script for loading the package, the version umber etc. Including functions for the sub commands.

5.11 [TclParser js Object]

Parameters:

- Text

The base container for parsing Tcl statements. Also includes all the functions necessary to parse Tcl statements and get back the words and word parts of a Tcl statement..

5.12 [TclParseStatement js Object]

Parameters:

- interp

Container for parsing a normal Tcl statement or an expr of an if, while or expr Tcl command. It builds as a side effect an expr tree or the statements/statement/word/word_part info when parsing. Both cases use TclParser object to get the input parsed into tokens.

5.13 [TclResolve js Object]

Parameters:

- interp

- type

A container for resolving variable and function references for itcl classes/objects

5.14 [TclStatement js Obejct]

Parameters:

- interp
- file_name
- line_no
- word_obj

Container for holding info for a parsed Tcl statement. It contains a list of words, which in turn can contain a list of word_parts and both can contain statements (a list of statement info) when the statement contained a word which for example was a proc body.

5.15 [TclTest js Object]

Parameters:

- Interp

A container for the functions for building a tcltest test case and running it.

5.16 [TclTestResult js Object]

Parameters:

- interp
- test_name
- test_description
- expected_result
- result

A container for storing the result of a tcltest tcl test case, including an error message for a failing test etc.

5.17 [TclTrace js Object]

Parameters:

- interp
- type
- name

- ops
- command

A container for holding information for Tcl traces for variable, command and execution traces.

5.18 [TclVariable js Object]

Parameters:

- interp
- name
- type

A container for a Tcl variable contains a [TclObject js Object] and additional information like the type of the variable etc.

5.19 [TclWord js Object]

Parameters:

- interp
- token
- value
- file_name
- last_line_no
- line_no
- stmts

A container for a part of a Tcl statement. Can contain a list of statements, if it is for example the body of a proc.

5.20 [TclWordPart js Object]

Parameters:

- interp
- token
- value
- stmts

A container for information of parts of a TclWord, for example the parts of a string, when the string contains a variable reference or a braced command etc.

6Itcl Javascript Objects for Tcl

Objects used for implementing itcl classes and itcl objects. They hold the information needed to describe the itcl class/object

6.1 [ItclClasses js Object]

Parameters:

- interp

Contains references to all itcl classes/class objects (ItclClass).

6.2 [ItclClass js Object]

Parameters:

- interp
- name
- full_name
- class_type

Contains information about itcl class methods, variables, types, options etc.

6.3 [ItclCommand js Object]

Parameters:

- name
- class_name
- func_type
- protection
- func
- params
- body

This is the container an itcl method, same as TclCommand is for Tcl procs

6.4 [ItclFunction js Object]

Parameters:

- interp

6.5 [ItclFunctionParam js Object]

Parameters:

- interp
- definition
- min_args
- max_args
- have_args_arg
- usage
- default_args

Definition of the parameter signature of an itcl method/proc

6.6 [ItclObject js Object]

Parameters:

- Interp
- name
- class_obj
- constructor_args

Container for an itcl object, contains set of class variables for that object of all classes n inherited classes.

6.7 [ItclOption js Object]

Parameters:

- interp

A container for an itclextended class option (like a Tk option) with all the information about the name and class of the option, a possible default value, a possible script for cget, configure and validate or a possible variable containing a cget, configure or a validate method

6.8 [ItclVariable js Object]

Parameters:

- interp

Container for an itcl variable with the possible protection, init value and config script and the type (variable or common)

6.9 TclItclDict

Parameters:

- interp

still a leftover from the time when itcl basics were in Tcl and parsed from Tcl. Nowadays the itcl parsing is implemented in js too (deprecated should possibly be removed, have to check).

6.10 TclItclHelper

Parameters:

- Interp

still a leftover from the time when itcl basics were in Tcl and parsed from Tcl. Nowadays the itcl parsing is implemented in js too (deprecated should possibly be removed, have to check).

7Status

The interpreter is in the middle of the implementation, there are still a lot of sub commands missing and there is the need for test cases, as I know already about some problems/bugs and there will be a lot of bugs still in there, which have not yet been found because of missing test cases. Right now there has been spent more time to the second topic [Tk Widgets in Javascript] to be able in the near future to have some demos, which show some of the functionality. There is also the need for more examples/demos.

Tk Widgets in Javascript

An implementation of Tk widgets using Javascript.

A paper for the Eighteenth Annual Tcl/Tk Conference

Abstract

Tk in Javascript is a work in progress, which started about May 2011 and is part of the incr Tcl in Javascript project is, which is intended to be one possible frontend/client part of ATWF and Reporting Tools with Tcl. It tries to implement Tk widget using javascript and DOM trees.

That includes a mapping of for example button/label/entry widgets to something which can be done with HTML parts in creating DOM trees and adding properties and attributes to the DOM nodes, that includes mapping of Tk option model to javascript style model and properties of DOM nodes.

Second goal is to map Tk event handling and bind functionality to the javascript event model and the javascript event listeners/handlers. There are also more complex widgets in work like Tree, Tktable, panedwindow, combobox etc.

The selection on which widgets are implemented first is driven by: what is needed for a reporting environment, that includes the decision on which options are implemented first.

Contact information

Arnulf Wiedemann

Lechstr. 10

D-86931 Prittriching

Email: arnulf@wiedemann-pri.de

Inhaltsverzeichnis

1How it started

During the implementation of [incr Tcl in Javascript] there did raise the question, how to get easy and efficient access to the DOM information. First idea was to give a user direct access to javascript DOM commands using a Tcl wrapper, but that would force the user to learn a lot of javascript and its model for widgets and events. So after some thoughts in that direction it seemed better to try to map Tk functionality to javascript DOM and event model. There followed the decision on directly using DOM for the implementation without first using HTML code and let the browser convert that to the DOM info.

Next there was the need to find out how to map basic Tk widgets to the DOM model like:

- button
- entry
- frame
- label
- toplevel

As I had in mind to use that as a client/frontend for [Reporting Tools with Tcl], these were the base widgets for starting.

After some experiments I decided to use <div> for a label widget, <button> for a button widget, <input> for an entry widget and again <div> for a frame widget and a toplevel widget.

2The initially implemented Tk widgets

2.1 [TkWidget js Object]

Parameters:

- interp
- name
- full_name
- type

To hold all the relevant information for a [Tk] [widget] a [TkWidget js Object] was implemented, which stores in it's properties for example the widget name (i.e. .fr.b1), a reference to the DOM node, the type of the widget (for example Tk.WIDGET_TYPE_BUTTON) a reference to a javascript Object with properties for that instance of the widget, a list of allowed options for that widget and a list of bind infos.

The javascript Objects for the above mentioned widget are:

- [TkButton js Object]
- [TkEntry js Object]
- [TkFrame js Object]
- [TkLabel js Object]
- [TkToplevel js Object]

The instances for the widgets are implemented very similar to thc implementation of itcl class objects as new commands, The javascript object used for this is [TkObject js Object]. It contains as properties the path name and a reference to the [TkWidget js Object].

2.2 [TkButton js Object]

Parameters:

- interp
- path_name
- widget_obj

A container for holding information for a Tk button widget instance.

2.3 [TkEntry js Object]

Parameters:

- interp
- path_name
- widget_obj

A container for holding information for an Tk entry widget instance.

2.4 [TkFrame js Obejct]

Parameters:

- interp
- path_name
- widget_obj

A container for holding information for a Tk frame widget instance.

2.2 [TkLabel js Object]

Parameters:

- interp
- path_name
- widget_obj

A container for holding information for a Tk label widget instance.

2.3 [TkToplevel js Object]

Parameters:

- interp
- path_name
- widget_obj

A container for holding information for a Tk toplevel widget instance.

3Implemented Widgets

All Tk widget commands are implemented in namespace ::tk but for compatibility there are interp aliases to be able to use for example button without the ::tk:: namespace prefix for creating a new button instance.

So we have the following commands:

- ::tk::button
- ::tk::entry
- ::tk::frame
- ::tk::label
- ::tk::toplevel

From experiments I found out, that you need a <div> element around most of these widgets to be able to force width and height requirements and also when packing these widgets. So in HTML a button widget would look like so:

```
<div>
   <button>button1</button
</div>
```

The sub commands for a button could not be implemented directly as a namespace ensemble, as the button itself is implemented like an itcl class, so that namespace cannot be additionally be used for a namespace ensemble.

So for example the cget and configure command of a button widget are implemented as ::tk::button::configure and ::tk::button::cget and are handled like itcl class methods. As a result you can use .b1 cget ... and .b1 configure ..., if .b1 has been created as a button widget instance using: button .b1 ...

But be aware: a Tk widget instance is no class object and a sub command of the widget is no class method. It is only handled very similar to these parts, to be able to use common code!

4Tk Options

Now there was the question on how to get all the different standard and widget specific options mapped to the style properties of a DOM element.

4.1 [TkStandardOptions js Object]

Parameters:

- interp

For handling of all the possible options (including Tk standard options), the attachment of the allowed options to a widget type and a mapping between Tk options and javascript options a [TkStandardOptions js Object] has been implemented.

It contains all the possible options of the Tk widgets according to the Tk option model with configure name, option name, option class and default value for an option and for every widget type there is a list containing all the options, which are allowed for a specific widget.

The allowed options are used for checking against illegal options and for producing an error message with the allowed options.

4.2 [TkOptionTemplate js Object]

Parameters:

- interp
- configure_name
- alias_name
- option_name
- option_class
- default_value

To hold information for one specific option a [TkOptionTemplate js Object] is used. It has properties for configure name, option name, option class and the default value as well as a possible alias name for example -background for the -bg option.

4.3 [TkOption js Object]

Parameters:

- interp
- option_template_obj
- option_value

The [TkOption js Object] contains a reference to the [TkOptionTemplate js Object] for the relevant option and a property for the current value (this is used for fast reference instead of looking it up in the DOM tree). Maybe this will change in the future to save space.

5Javascript Objects for Tcl usage

5.1 [JsDomNode js Object]

Parameters:

When working with rhino (a command line javascript interpreter for Linux) it was necessary for being able to test simple DOM related parts easily to implement a dummy javascript Object for at least creating and appending DOM nodes. This has been done with the implementation of [JsDomNode js Object]. It has functions for creating elements and setting attributes and appending elements, as that functionality is not available in rhino.

5.2 [JsOption js Object]

Parameters:

- interp
- configure_name

A container for a javascript option to be mapped to an Tk option.

To hold information for one specific option a [JsOptionTemplate js Object] is used.

5.3 [JsOptionTemplate js Object]

Parameters:

- interp
- configure_name

Used in [JsStandardOptions js Object] to hold information about a specific style property.

It has properties for configure name and a container for sub options, as in javascript options can be structured like border can be set directly identical for all 4 sides or via borderTop, borderLeft, borderRight and borderBottom.

The [TkStandardOptions js Object] contains references to the [TkOptionTemplate js Object] for the relevant option.

5.4 [JsStandardOptions js Object]

Parameters:

- interp

A container which initializes the standard javascript options and has a simple mapping between Tk option and js options (not yet complete)

6Tk Javascript Objects

As a base for the Tk bind command a simple parser for an event sequence has been implemented, which can parse the modifier, type and detail parts. This information is stored in a [TkEventSequence js Object].

6.1 [TkEventSequence js Object]

Parameters:

- interp
- modifier1
- modifier2
- type
- detail

A container for storing information about a [Tk] [event] sequence for use for example by the [Tk] [bind] command.

For positioning widgets within a browser window [Tk] [pack] and [grid] commands have been implemented. [Tk] [grid] command is still very rudimentary and not yet really usable.

6.2 [TkGrid js Object]

Parameters:

- interp
- widget_obj

Container for grid information for example the widgets and the row/column info etc.

6.3 [TkObject js Object]

Parameters:

- interp
- name
- widget_obj

Container for a [Tk] [widget]. This is the instantiated command object, which is created when a [Tk] [widget] like a [button] for example is instantiated. It contains a [TkWidget js Object], which holds the specific info for that instance of the widget. Also all the specific option values for that widget are collected here and can be modified and fetched using the configure and cget sub command of the widget.

When setting an option with the configure command, the option name and value are mapped from the [Tk] values to the the style or attribute name and the appropriate value for javascript.

For example the Tk option -foreground is mapped to the javascript style attribute "color" and the -text option of a Tk button is mapped to the "textContent" field when using Firefox. That is still a different field name for IE, which has yet to be implemented.

6.4 [TkPack js Object]

Parameters:

- interp
- widget_obj

Container for pack information for example the widgets and other related info. The pack command appends DOM nodes created for the different widgets as DOM nodes with no connection to the visible window content to an existing DOM node for example the node of the HTML <body> tag. For a [toplevel] [widget] a HTML <div> node is created and appended to the <body> tag.

The style attributes width and height have to be provided as a "100px" pixel value with "px" at the end and determine the width and height of the toplevel widget/window.

For implementing the -side left and -side right option of the pack command one can use the style attributes {float: left} and {float: right} respectively.

For -side top the style float part is omitted, for -side bottom I have not yet found out how to do that. To avoid wrapping of widgets it is normally necessary to have style attribute display set to {display: table-row}, if you have {float: left} or {float: right} but, what a pitty not always, there are special cases where you also for that case have to use {display: block} I have not yet found out all the rules on how to use that. For the small test cases it works, but I am pretty sure there are still a lot of failing cases.

7BWidget Tk Widgets

7.1 [TkTree js Object]

Parameters:

- interp
- path_name
- widget_obj

A container for holding information for a BWidget Tree widget. That one was rather hard, as in the end it is implemented as an own table for every node in the tree. That is necessary as otherwise you do not easily get all the columns of the tree rendered with the same size.

I have got inspiration from a treeview implementation from GubuSoft and from YUI treeview. The tick is to use little images for the opentree, closetree and for the lines between the nodes and the image for the node. The last field in the table does not handle overflow, so that the text labels can be as long as they are needed.

There is an event handler attached to the opentree and closetree images and another one to the node image and the node text, these can also be different using the Tk bindImage and bindText options.

The opentree and closetree event handlers just set the first level sub nodes style of the selected node to {display: none}, which makes that subtree invisible after rendering (it needs no space any more and looks like the nodes have been removed). When opening the tree again one just has to set the sub nodes style to {display: block} or {display: table-row} and the subtree is visible again.

7.2 [TkLabelEntry js Object]

Parameters:

- interp
- path_name
- widget_obj

A container for holding information for a BWidget LabelEntry widget. It combines a label (a <div>) element with an entry (a <input>) element, surrounded by another <div> element (in principle a frame). You can set the configure options for the label and the entry part.

7.3 [TkScrollableFrame js Object]

Parameters:

- interp
- path_name

- widget_obj

A container for holding information for a BWidget ScrollableFrame widget. It combines a frame (a <div>) element with another frame and for the second frame the style attribute overflow is set to {style: auto}. The sub command getframe returns that inner frame path name (DOM element).

8TkTable Widget

8.1 [TkTable js Object]

Parameters:

- interp
- path_name
- widget_obj

A container for holding information about a TkTable table widget. This one is tricky too. It is built with 5 tables. The outermost is used to hold four other tables:

- top_left_table
- top_right_table
- bottom_left_table
- bottom_right_table

This is necessary for being able to have title rows and title cols which are not scrolled. Top_left_table has the part in the top left corner with the row parts and col parts, which are never scrolled. Top_right_table has the title row parts, which are only scrolled horizontally when the table is scrolled. bottom_left_table has the title cols, which are only scrolled vertically when the table is scrolled, and bottom right table contains the rows and columns which are visible and can be scrolled horizontally and vertically.

Here are also the scrollbars and when scrolling depending on the direction either the top_right_table is scrolled accordingly or the bottom_left_table. This is done by setting the scrollLeft or scrollTop attribute of these tables to the same value as the corresponding value of the bottom_right_table when scrolling the bottom_right_table. With that trick it looks like both tables are scrolling synchronous.

When calculating the position and table of a cell title rows and title cols have to be taken in account on deciding which of the four tables holds the desired cell. And for giving back the index of a cell has to be done the same way for getting the absolute index of the cell.

When the -command option is used, every cell gets attached the click event and in the event handler the command script is called with the pah name of the table and the index of the cell in nn,nn syntax are passed as parameters to the script.

9Advanced Tk Widgets

9.1 TkPanedWindow

Parameters:

- interp
- path_name
- widget_obj

A container for holding information about a panedwindow widget. A panedwindow is built as a <div> element. Every adding of a pane adds two <div> elements, one for the sash, and one for the pane.

The sash element knows about the 2 surrounding <div> elements and changes their sizes when dragging the sash. When more than one sash element exist, the second sash element is also moved, when the first one reaches that and the pane before or after that second sash element (depending on the direction of the moving) is also changed in size.

Two sash elements can touch each other that means the pane in between has size 0. And all the sashes can be moved to the left or right or to the bottom or top border.

The -side option when adding a pane determines – as with the pack command – how the panes are arranged.

10YUI revisited

Because of a lot of still missing base functionality in the Tk implementation in Javascript the YUI Implementation and functionality has been revisited and inspected again. Because of some functionality, which was needed and was available there the decision was made to extract some base functionality to use here. After analyzing YUI to see how to use parts without need for ant build system a solution was found to use parts of YUI without using the build system, which resulted in only 2 lines to be added to a source file for using it here. For easily being able to enhance with Tk specifics there was the decision to do a fork of the sources and start only with limited set of modules from YUI. The name for that fork is TUI (Tcl User Interface), but up to now 90% of original code is still used (for the modules taken over, which is only a smaller part of the full implementation about 20-25%). There have been about 25.000 lines of the source code adapted for TUI usage (not much had to be modified).

After that the implementation of "derived classes" has been started to build a button widget with YUI functionality.

The next part (still in progress) is the implementation of a Tktable widget. There exists a datatable implementation, but that has only title lines and there are always at least one title line. Titlecols functionality is missing completely and also the tag functionality is missing so there has been started an implementation of a Tktable widget based on the TUI functionality and similar to the datatable implementation of YUI. As in YUI scrolling will be done with a plugin attached to Tktable widget.

Other widgets like Tree, panedWindow, ScrollableFrame etc. will follow.

11Status

The implementation is in the middle of the minimal necessary functionality. Work will continue to get a version, which has at least the minimal necessary functionality to be able to serve as a frontend for [Reporting Tools With Tcl] to build a minimal reporting system together with [ATWF]. As with [incr Tcl in Javascript] there are missing tests and demos.

Tcl 2011
Manassas, VA
October 24-28, 2011

Tcl Interpreters

JTcl and Swank: What's new with Tcl and Tk on the JVM

[1]Bruce A. Johnson, [2]Tom Poindexter, & [3]Dan Bodoh

[1] bruce@onemoonscientific.com, One Moon Scientific, Inc, Westfield, NJ and University of Maryland, Baltimore County
[2] tpoindex@gmail.com
[3] dan.bodoh@gmail.com

Abstract

JTcl is an implementation of the Tool Command Language (Tcl) written in Java and is derived from the Jacl project. The current release (2.0) of JTcl implements a large extent of Tcl 8.4 syntax and commands, limited only by the API restrictions of the Java Virtual Machine. Swank is an implementation of the TK GUI toolkit implemented using the Java Swing GUI API. Most Tk 8.4 widgets and commands have been implemented as well as additional ones based on Swing widgets. This paper describes the current state of these projects and gives examples of their use.

Introduction

The Java Virtual Machine [Lind99] has become a platform on which a variety of computer programming languages can be executed. While originally written to execute Java programs that had been compiled into Java byte codes, it is now used to run languages such as Clojure, Groovy, Jacl, JRuby, Jython, Rhino and Scala [WikiJVM]. Some of these, like Scala, appeared originally as a language on the JVM, and others, like Jacl, are JVM implementations of existing languages. Jacl, which is an implementation of Tcl [Ost10], was one of the first non-Java languages on the JVM and appeared shortly after the initial development of Java [Lam97].

While there is an abundance of alternative programming languages on the JVM, there are relatively few implementations of graphical user interface toolkits besides the AWT and Swing toolkits that come standard with most Java distributions. The primary alternatives have been Swank, SWT (the Standard Widget Toolkit), and quite recently JavaFX. While SWT is largely implemented on top of native platform widgets and JavaFX is implemented with its own windowing toolkit, Swank is a layer on top of the Swing widgets that provides an interface to the programmer that is analogous to that of the Tk toolkit [Ost10].

In this paper we'll discuss recent developments in the Tcl and Tk on the JVM, focussing on the language implementation JTcl, and the Tk-style graphical user interface toolkit Swank.

JTcl

JTcl is a fork of Jacl, an implementation of Tcl written in Java [Lam97]. Jacl was written during the period of Tcl/C 8.0 development and contains Java equivalents of many internal data structures, most importantly the notion of Tcl objects to hold binary representation of numeric data types, efficient list and array structures, and implementation of most of Tcl 8.0's commands. Jacl does not implement the Tcl byte code compiler and runtime [Lew96], nor the Tcl fileevent command and supporting event system that allows for event driven I/O. After initial development by the original authors, Jacl development was performed by individuals rather than as an official port of the Tcl Core Team. During this time Jacl development slowed to mostly bug fixes but did result in a few major improvements, a port of the Incr Tcl object system [DeJ05] and the Tcl-to-Java compiler (TJC) [DeJ06]. Development of core Tcl commands and features did not keep synchronized with mainline Tcl development. Despite Jacl's slow progress, it had proved useful in a number of commercial products, open source projects and proprietary internal projects. Jacl was used by IBM in its WebSphere Application Server and One Moon Scientific's NMRView products [John04], as well as the open source Swank and Æjaks projects [Poin07].

Jacl Modernization

Jacl modernization was selected as one of the Tcl Core Team projects during the Google Summer of Code 2009 [Szul09]. The goal of the project was to bring Jacl's language features to the level of Tcl/C 8.4. Tcl 8.4 was chosen as a target level for several reasons. First, it represented a stable base of Tcl compliance that could be achieved by implementing new commands or augmenting existing ones. Second, the project was limited to one student for one summer, so the work product of the GSOC project was limited. Third, current Tcl/C version 8.5 contained many structural changes, such as the expand syntax which would require a considerable amount of interpreter changes. The target of the GSOC project was derived by comparing the current set of Jacl command definitions with the Tcl/C 8.4 definitions. Many of the command implementations required relatively little additional code to support a particular command option, larger code rework was required to implement commands such as [regex] and [regsub]. These commands relied on moving from a custom underlying regular expression library to use the Java **java.util.regexp** package.

While the GSOC 2009 Jacl Modernization project yielded many improvements, it did not reach full Tcl 8.4 compliance. The GSOC project relied on command descriptions based on the Tcl 8.4 manual pages, so while many command options were added or improved, strict compliance to Tcl/C test cases was not tested. The Jacl implementation of [regex] and [regsub] improved significantly to match Tcl 8.4, but many edge cases were not addressed. Addition of a event system and [fileevent] also proved to be too ambitious, requiring more time that was available.

The JTcl project was formed to continue development of Jacl and complete the work of the GSOC Jacl Modernization project. The project founders decided that a fork was the best way to achieve its goals. Jacl was a part of the TclJava project, which produced the the Jacl interpreter as well as TclBlend, a Tcl extension that enables use of Java classes and objects from the the Tcl/C runtime. Much of the TclJava packaging and build system was designed to support the use of the java package in both Jacl and TclBlend environments. JTcl project members had no interest in the TclBlend extension and instead would focus entirely on the Java implementation of Tcl.

In addition to furthering Tcl 8.4 compliance, a number of other improvements were desired. First, Java code development is greatly enhanced by the use of Java-centric Integrated Development Environments (IDEs) such as Eclipse, Netbeans and IntelliJ, so the structure of the JTcl source code should be arranged to support easy use by Java IDEs.. Second, the build system in Jacl using *make* would be replaced with a Java-centric build system. While *make* could be used to compile and package JTcl, Java oriented build systems *ant* and *maven* are better supported by Java IDEs. Third, packaging the JTcl system would be in a single jar file for simple installation, as opposed to the Jacl system packaging in five separate jar files. Lastly, extraneous source code such as the TclBlend extension would be removed entirely.

Tcl Compliance and Test Suite

The Tcl language for any particular version is described in man pages and other documentation, but the definitive source of Tcl compliance is represented by the Tcl test suite. The test suite is usually developed in conjunction with a particular version of Tcl to ensure that the interpreter's result for any give operation matches expected results.

The Jacl project contained a test suite that matched Tcl 8.0 compliance and was enhanced as changes were made to the source code. For JTcl, the Tcl 8.4 test suite was imported and used to measure Tcl compliance. JTcl integrates the Tcl test suite through the JUnit test facility. JUnit is a Java oriented test environment, roughly equivalent to the tcltest Tcl package. When running JUnit in a Java environment, the normal usage is to run a test method that invokes methods on an object under test, and asserts that actual results are equal to expected results. Since JUnit is widely supported by Java IDEs, the Tcl test suite in JTcl is invoked through JUnit classes. This allows testing of JTcl source code directly from the IDE, without requiring a compile/test cycle.

The Tcl test suite contains generic tests that should run the same on any execution platform as well as many tests that are specific to the platform. For example, a particular test may only run on a Windows platform, while an equivalent test may only run on a Unix environment. A Java JVM presents a single virtual machine that (mostly) eliminates machine and platform differences. As a result, only the tests that are labeled as generic are tested in JTcl.

Even with running only the generic Tcl tests in JTcl, many differences in test results were observed and many of which were false negative results. Erroneous test results generally fell into the following categories:

1. **Differences in error messages** – when a test would check for specific error messages, differences between JTcl and Tcl/C would often arise as error callback messages may contain slightly different text. Most of these differences are a result of Tcl/C's byte code compiler, which returns errors stating "...while compiling..." vs. the pure interpreter's error messages "...invoked from within....".
2. **Ordering of results** - many Tcl commands return unordered results, e.g. [info commands]. Due to JTcl's use of native Java libraries for hash maps instead of Tcl's C coded ones, key lists were returned with different orderings.
3. **Unsupported functions of the JVM** – the Java JVM does not support many low level system functions, so Tcl commands such as [file stat] are limited to the operations that can be performed.
4. **Regexp differences** – JTcl makes use of the Java library **java.util.regexp** package for regular expression handling, whereas Tcl uses the Spencer ARE library coded in C. While most common Tcl ARE regular expressions are accepted in JTcl via direct use of **java.util.regexp** or through emulation, some Tcl ARE expressions such as the Basic-RE meta-character ('b') are not supported.

To work around these differences, the JTcl JUnit base class is designed to run a Tcl test suite test file with a list of expected failure cases. Each failure case returned by the test suite is examined to note the type of the failure, and when the difference could be categorized as one of the above cases, that case was added to the expected failure list. The result of the expected failure lists allow the entire test suite to be run, with a better indication of positive or negative results. Numerous Tcl command implementation classes were modified to pass the Tcl test suite.

Code Modernization / IDE support

While the main focus of the JTcl project is to continue the effort of making JTcl conform to the Tcl language 8.4 test suite, and number of other efforts were done to modernize the code. "Modernize" is somewhat a subjective term. The JTcl project's definition of modernization includes reforming the code as if the JTcl code was being developed new by skilled Java programmers using accepted Java development best practices and tools.

The existing Jacl Java code was originally developed to closely mimic the Tcl/C version. This was likely done for ease of the initial port to Java. JTcl has the following changes to the source code, besides those made for test suite compliance:

1. **Source packages** – Java code can be organized into distinct packages (i.e., namespaces). This promotes grouping similar source code classes by function. In JTcl, the package tcl.lang.* is

used for core interpreter classes, tcl.lang.cmd.* for commands, tcl.lang.channel.* for I/O classes, etc. Standard JTcl packages java, itcl, and tjc were moved to tcl.pkg.* packages. Included Tcl library code (e.g., *.tcl files) was moved from Java source code directories to resource directories.

2. **Code formatting** – much Jacl's source code had specific hand-formatted conventions, such as ASCII form-feed characters (^L) to separate methods, comments within method arguments, debug-only code fragments. JTcl code is reformatted using automated tools for consistency, and debug specific code is removed in favor of using the IDE's debug and breakpoint facilities.
3. **Block comments converted to Javadoc comments** – Jacl code contains many block comments that precede methods, but these were not in the format to support the Javadoc tools for creating automated source code documentation. Where practical, source code block comments in JTcl are Javadoc formatted.
4. **IDE/build tool friendly directory layout** – the project directory layout was changed to easily support Java IDEs and build tools. src/main/java contains the Java source code, src/main/resources contain Tcl library code, src/test/java contains Java JUnit code, src/test/resources contain test Tcl code (i.e., the Tcl test suite.) Additional directories contain the project website source code, maven assembly descriptors, runtime startup scripts, etc.

Packaging / Tcllib

Recent Jacl distributions have included the Incr Tcl and Tcl-to-Java compiler packages. Jacl's packaging favored separate jar files for the Jacl core interpreter and each extension. JTcl instead packages all core and extension components into a single jar file. Jacl also includes Tcllib as part of its packaging. Tcllib is a large collection of Tcl coded libraries.. Some modules of Tcllib that only support Tcl versions 8.5 and 8.6 are excluded in the JTcl distribution.

Packaging all core and library components of JTcl into a single jar file allow the interpreter to be started as simply as java -jar jtcl.jar, though a more common usage still utilizes helper scripts. The JTcl startup scripts jtcl (for Linux/Unix/MacOSX/Cygwin/Msys environments) and jtcl.bat (Windows) allow for additional jar files to be included via the normal CLASSPATH environment variable, as well as runtime Java JVM parameters to be easily modified.

The JTcl website is included in the project and is built using the maven build system. The JTcl source Javadoc files are also built during website generation.

RegExp Improvements

The regular expression engine class, tcl.lang.Regex, is new in JTcl and used by [regsub], [regexp] and [lsearch -regexp]. This class brings the full power of TCL 8.4 Advanced Regular Expressions (ARE) to JTcl, with a few caveats. The older Basic Regular Expressions (BREs) and Extended Regular Expressions (EREs) are not supported, although EREs that are identical to AREs and not explicitly requested with the 'e' embedded option are supported.

A primary implementation goal was to make use of **java.util.regex.Pattern** and **java.util.regex.Matcher** [Oracle2004], rather than writing a custom engine based on the C library used in Tcl 8.4. A **tcl.lang.Regex** instance combines the steps of compiling a regular expression and matching it on an input string, and contains all the functionality required to implement [regsub] and [regexp].

The **tcl.lang.Regex.compile()** method is responsible for converting a Tcl regular expression to a Java **Pattern** instance. This method parses the Tcl regular expression, building a Java regular expression in a **Stringbuffer**, and compiles the Java regular expression into a **Pattern** instance.

Many aspects of the conversion of Tcl regular expression syntax to Java syntax are merely direct translations. For example, a static Hashmap is used to translate Tcl's character classes and escape sequences to Java's equivalent, such as [:alnum:], to \pAlnum and [:ESC:] to \\033.

More complex translations are required for those elements that are similar in the two regular expression languages, but differ in minor details or at boundary conditions. For example, an empty Tcl regex matches before every character in the string, and after the last character. Java's empty regex is similar, but does not match after the last character. So a Tcl empty regex is translated to ^|(?!$) for Java. Many similar complex translations are needed for the embedded options, which are similar to but not exactly like the **java.util.regex.Pattern** match flags.

Tcl does contain some regex features that are not available in Java. These are emulated with more complex Java expressions. For example, the Tcl \M (match at the end of a word) has no direct Java equivalent, so it is translated to (?=\W|$)(?<=\w) (look ahead for a word character and behind for non-word character).

The decision to use **java.util.regex.Pattern** led to one incompatibility in JTcl regular expressions. Tcl always attempts to match the longest string starting from the outermost levels to the inner levels of parentheses. With alternation (A|B) Tcl chooses the longest match of all the branches. Java evaluates the regular expression from left to right, and returns the first successful match, even if it's not the longest. This incompatibility will not affect most common uses of [regexp] and [regsub].

Pattern syntax error information returned by Tcl is replicated by translating the message from the **java.util.regex. PatternSyntaxException** thrown by the Java **Pattern.compile().** However, Java is more forgiving about poor regular expression syntax, and therefore some expressions that would generate an error in Tcl may be interpreted as literal characters in JTcl.

Code refactoring was done to collapse the [regexp] and [regsub] common code into **tcl.lang.Regex**. The matched input substring state information used by [regexp

-all] and [regsub -all] was delegated to **java.util.regex.Matcher**, simplifying the code.

An apparent Tcl 8.4 bug was replicated in the JTcl code: a difference between regexp and regsub. The command [regexp -all -inline {a*} {a}] returns one match, {a}. The similar command [regsub -all {a*} {a} {Z}] returns {ZZ}, one Z for the match of {a} with {a}, and a second Z for a zero-length match after the 'a'. The **java.util.regex.Matcher** match groups are used for code simplicity, with a special case in the [regexp] implementation for this inconsistency.

Process Pipelines for [exec] and [open]

Process pipelines for [exec] and [open "| command"] and the Tcl 8.4 [exec] input and output redirection were added to JTcl, using pure Java. The **tcl.lang.Pipeline** class parses an [exec]- or [open]-style pipeline string and builds a chain of **tcl.lang.process.TclProcess** instances for the chain of operating system commands in the pipeline. Each **TclProcess** instance is made aware of its neighbor **TclProcess** (or its redirected input and output) with a **tcl.lang.process.Redirect** instance. The **Pipeline** instance can manage any of the [exec] redirectors The [open "| command"] command uses a channel view of **Pipeline**, **tcl.lang.channel.PipelineChannel**.

The **tcl.lang.process.TclProcess** class is abstract with currently one concrete subclass: **tcl.lang.process.JavaProcess**. **JavaProcess** is a pure Java implementation using **java.lang.Process** and **java.lang.ProcessBuilder**. This code organization allows for future development of platform-specific **TclProcess** subclasses that use native code, or a Java 7 subclass that makes use of the new redirection capabilities of **ProcessBuilder**.

The **tcl.lang.process.TclProcess** subclass is responsible for handling its own input and output redirection. **JavaProcess** is limited by the capabilities of the Java 1.5 and 1.6 API, which does not expose the operating system's pipe and file descriptor inheritance mechanisms. All pipelines and redirection must use **Process.getInputStream()**, **Process.getOutputStream()**, and **Process.getErrorStream().** To create a pipe, a new thread is created with an instance of **tcl.lang.process.TclProcess.Coupler** which reads the upstream **JavaProcess**'s output stream and writes to the downstream **JavaProcess**'s input stream.

These limitations in the Java API create some incompatibilities between a Tcl pipeline and a JTcl pipeline. A pipeline launched in the background by JTcl cannot outlive the JTcl process itself because JTcl, rather than the operating system, is managing the pipe.

The Java Process API use of the **InputStream** class for standard input and the lack of file descriptor inheritance in the API creates problems for JTcl's tclsh emulation, **tcl.lang.Shell,** when using [exec]. With Java's **InputStream**, the only way to detect an end-of-file condition is to do an **InputStream.read().** But doing the read will take at least one byte from the standard input. So the **JavaProcess** instance for an exec'd process can take an extra byte from standard input that it may not need, stealing that byte from the JTcl shell itself. A simple example is shown below.

Contents of the file testStdin.txt:

```
exec head -1
this line should go to head and to stdout
puts {this line should be interpreted by the JTcl shell}
exit
```

This file is sent to the JTcl shell via standard input:

```
$java tcl.lang.Shell < testStdin.txt
```

Two possible cases occur – the first is the expected output:
this line should go to head and to stdout
this line should be interpreted by the JTcl shell

The second case is when the JavaProcess instance for 'head' steals an extra byte
this line should go to head and to stdout
couldn't execute "uts": no such file or directory

These incompatibilities are relatively minor, and could be fixed with the Java 7 capabilities of **ProcessBuilder** which support true file descriptor inheritance at the operating system level.

The [pid fileid] command is supported on Posix systems on at least some JVMs by looking for a field named "pid" in the java.lang.Process instance with a value the same as that returned by **Process.getClass().getDeclaredField("pid")**. If this fails, -1 is returned as the process id.

File Events and the New Channel Subsystem

Significant improvements were made to the channel subsystem for JTcl to support non-blocking I/O, Unicode, and to fix failing tests in the Tcl 8.4 test suite. Both [fcopy] and [fileevent] are supported,

The [fcopy] command simply copies from one channel to another within a separate Java thread, and uses the existing JTcl event queue to execute the callback script when [fcopy] completes. If possible, a byte copy is made to avoid the Unicode encoding and decoding step, and an efficient buffering is enabled.

The [fileevent] command depends on the new non-blocking I/O implemented in the channel subsystem. The fileevent itself is described with two objects, **tcl.lang.channel.FileEventScript** and **tcl.lang.channel.FileEvent**. The instance of **FileEventScript** exists for the lifetime of a fileevent, and schedules new instances of **FileEvent** on the JTcl event queue. Each **FileEvent** instance, when it comes off the queue, tests for readability or writability of the channel and executes the fileevent script as necessary.

As originally coded in Jacl, the **tcl.lang.channel.Channel** abstract class is the root object for all types of channels. Much of the channel code was re-written in a more Java-like fashion, replacing the literal C-to-Java translation. Subclasses of **Channel** are shown in Table 1.

Table 1	
Java Class	**Description**
SeekableChannel	Abstract class that adds seek() and tell()
FileChannel	Extends **SeekableChannel** to implement file I/O
ResourceChannel	Implements reading of a Java resource using a "resource:" prefix on the file name
ReadInputStreamChannel	Bridges a Tcl channel to a Java **InputStream**
AbstractSocketChannel	Abstract class that has common code for socket channels
ServerSocketChannel	Implements Tcl server sockets
SocketChannel	Implements Tcl sockets
TclByteArrayChannel	Used internally to bridge Tcl channels to Tcl byte arrays

In order to support the JTcl enhancements and fixes, Jacl's **TclInputStream** and **TclOutputStream** classes were replaced with a chain of subclasses of **java.io.InputStream**, **java.io.Reader**, **java.io.OutputStream**, and **java.io.Writer**.

The input side of a Channel uses the following chain of **InputStreams** and **Readers**:

Channel.getInputStream() presents an **InputStream** view of the data on the channel. For example, a **FileChannel** uses **java.io.FileInputStream**.

EofInputFilter reads bytes from **Channel.getInputStream()** and adds the end-of-file byte configured by the channel.

InputBuffer reads bytes from the EofInputFilter, provides a resizable read buffer and implements non-blocking reads. It performs non-blocking reads by performing **EofInputFilter.read()** in a separate thread. All byte read operations on the channel are taken from this **InputStream**.

MarkableInputStream reads bytes from the **InputBuffer** and allows for look-ahead in the stream.

UnicodeDecoder reads bytes from the **MarkableInputStream** and converts to Unicode using the encoding configured by the channel.

EolInputFilter reads characters from **UnicodeDecoder** and performs the configured end-of-line translation on the channel. All character read operations on the channel are taken from this **Reader**.

The output side of a **Channel** uses the following chain of **OutputStreams** and **Writers**:

EolOutputFilter is written to by the channel when it performs character writes. It performs the configured end-of-line translation on the channel.

UnicodeEncoder is written to by **EolOutputFilter**, and translates Unicode characters to bytes according to the encoding configured on the channel.

OutputBuffer is written to by **UnicodeEncoder** as well as by the channel when it performs byte writes. It provides a resizable buffer, but unlike **InputBuffer**, does not handle non-blocking writes.

EofOutputFilter is written to by **OutputBuffer** and adds the end-of-file character that the channel is configured to use.

NonBlockingOutputStream is written to by **EofOutputFilter**, and performs its **OutputStream.write()** and **OutputStream.flush()** in a separate thread for non-blocking writes.

Channel.getOutputStream() is written to by NonBlockingOutputStream, and provides an OutputStream view of the channel data.

Testing Sockets and File Events

A hallmark of Tcl is its event system that allows writing of servers with a minimal amount of code. An example of this is the DustMote script [Kapl02] that implements a web server in merely 41 lines of code. We found that DustMote running under JTcl could readily serve a web site (the document root was set to the content of the www.onemoonscientific.com site) indicating that the fileevent and server socket code functions as expected.

As a further test, multiple simultaneous instances of JTcl were set up calling a script using the [http::geturl] command to pull a file from the DustMote server. As described above the fcopy command initiates a separate Java thread to do the file copy to the clients socket and we indeed observed that the Thread usage by DustMote increased proportionally to the number of clients accessing it.

Swank

The success of Tcl as a programming language comes not only from the intrinsic value of Tcl, but its companion Graphical User Interface Toolkit, Tk. Tk has become so successful that it is used not only as the GUI toolkit for Tcl, but also with other languages such as Python. Without a Java implementation of Tk, JTcl would not be able to fill many of the programming niches accessible to Tcl. Tk widgets are, however, programmed with low level calls to each platforms native graphics system and replicating this in Java would be a large task.

Developing Swank

Two key factors allowed for the feasibility of developing Swank ("Tk in Java") in a reasonable period of time. Swing, the primary Java user interface toolkit, provides a rich variety of widgets with similar functionality to Tk widgets. For example, the Tk toplevel widget is similar to the Swing

Table 2			
Swing	**Tk**	**Swing**	**Tk**
JButton	button	JRadioButtonMenuItem	radiobutton (on menus)
JCheckBox	checkbutton	JScrollBar	scrollbar
JFrame	toplevel	JSlider	scale
JLabel	label	JSpinner	spinbox
JList	listbox	JTextArea	message
JMenu	menu	JTextField	entry
JMenuBar	menubar	JTextPane	text
JPanel	frame	JFrame (composite)	labelframe
JRadioButton	radiobutton	JPanel (customized)	canvas

JFrame widget, the button to JButton, the menu to JMenu, etc. Using the Swing widgets meant that the behavior of Swank would not be as similar to Tk as it would if the Swank widgets were developed with lower level Java graphic operations. On the other hand, adopting Swing meant that a great deal of coding work could be skipped. Furthermore,using the Swing widgets provides a richer set of behaviors than the original Tk widgets.

The second key factor was the introspection capabilities of the JTcl language. Much of the code that forms the basis of Swank is generated by JTcl scripts that determine the fields and methods of each Swing component and then automatically produce Java code that provides a Tk-like interface to the components. This generates a large number of configuration options for each widget. Some of these map

Table 3			
Swing	**Tk**	**Swing**	**Tk**
JDesktopPane	jdesktoppane	JProgressBar	jprogressbar
JComboBox	jcombobox	JScrollPane	jscrollpane
JDialog	jdialog	JSplitPane	panedwindow
JEditorPane	html	JTabbedPane	jtabbedpane
JInternalFrame	JInternalframe	JTable	jtable
JOptionPane	joptionpane	JToolBar	jtoolbar
JPasswordField	jpasswordfield	JTree	jtree
JPopupMenu	jpopupmenu	JWindow	jwindow

coincidentally to the names and functions of Tk configuration options. In other cases, JTcl code is used to specifically generate Java code for Tk options. In some of these cases it is only necessary to generate code that parses the appropriate Tk option and maps it to an existing Java Swing method. In other cases specific Java code is written to enable the correct action in response to the specified option. This Java code is inserted in the generated Java file.

In earlier versions of Swank we made available nearly all configuration options of the Swing widgets as Tk-style configuration options. Starting with version 3.0 the code generator has been changed to limit the options to a predefined list that leaves out many of the more obscure Swing configuration options. This leads to a simpler toolkit that presents options more consistent with that of the Tk toolkit.

Swank Widgets

Swing widgets and the Tk style commands used with Swank to create them are listed in Table 2. These are the widgets that have a particularly close correspondence between the Tk widget and the Tk-style widget as implemented in Swank.

Some Swing widgets don't have a direct correspondence to existing Tk widgets, but were deemed useful enough that they should have a Tk style command in Swank. These are listed in Table 3. Some of them do have analogous Tk commands that are available in extensions like the table and combobox widgets. Others, like the panedwindow, exist in Tk, but the Swank implementation has significant differences.

The behavior of most of the widgets in these tables is largely a product of that of the underlying Swing widget. The two most complex Tk widgets, text and canvas, required substantial Java code to reproduce the behavior of the Tk widgets. The canvas widget, in particular, is almost entirely implemented by Swank specific Java code. This widget is based on the Swing **JPanel**, which essentially provides an empty screen area on which to draw by overriding its **paintComponent** method.

Swank Canvas Widget

The Swank canvas widget provides most all of the features of the Tk canvas, plus some additional capabilities. Colors are one area where the Swank canvas is distinguished from that of Tk. In Swank, objects like rectangles and ovals can have gradient or texture fills, and the colors for all Swank canvas items can be transparent.

Configuration Options

Additional configuration options are available for Swank canvas items. For example, while Tk lines can have arrows at one or both ends of the line, lines on the Swank canvas allow for different styles (arrow, square, circle, diamond or nothing) at each end. All Swank canvas items also support a -rotate configuration item. A common style when generating diagrams is the placing of a text label on a shape. To facilitate this, rectangles and ovals on the Swank canvas can be configured with a text option (and corresponding font and text color options).

Additional Canvas Items

Several additional canvas item types are present in Swank. In addition to normal text items, the Swank canvas adds htext items. These support many HTML tags and some CSS styles (as implemented by Java Swing HTML endowed text widgets). For example, an htext item could have an H2 header, superscripts, bold and italic text or be laid out as a table using HTML table tags.

Connection items are unique in that their coordinates are specified in terms of a fraction of the bounds of two other items on the canvas. In this way it is easy to produce diagrams where dragging one item around maintains a displayed connector to a second item without needing to write Tcl level code to reposition the connector. Annotation items combine a line with an arrow at one end and a text string at the other.

Affine Transforms

All Swank canvas items can have an Affine transform associated with them. The standard Swank canvas includes fractional transforms that allow canvas drawing in fractional positions of the canvas, allowing, for example, a rectangle to fill the top half of a canvas, no matter how the canvas is resized. This capability is extensively used in the NMR analysis program dataChord where custom canvas items add transforms to the canvas that allow items to be drawn relative to the first items position. In this way labels and annotations positioned near features of the NMR spectrum remain positioned relative to the NMR feature, no matter how the whole spectrum is zoomed or panned. Additionally, the whole Swank canvas has an Affine Transform associated with it, the scale of which is changed with the canvas "zoom" subcommand. This allows one to zoom the view of the entire canvas in or out.

Handle Selection

A standard feature of many programs for creating diagrams or illustrations is the ability to select, move and resize items on the drawing canvas using various mouse actions. This can be implemented in a Tk program by drawing selection indicators and handles with explicit canvas items, but it seemed such a common paradigm that we added low level support to the Swank canvas for these actions.

All items can be selected using an "hselect" subcommand. Any items that are selected are displayed with selection handles. When the mouse enters a handle the cursor is changed to an "appropriate" resize cursor. The handles are not implemented as separate canvas items, but are fundamentally displayed by the underlying Java code at appropriate positions on the bounds of the item. Moving and resizing selected items is the responsibility of "user code" and is not part of Swank, but is easily implemented.

Scene Graph

Advanced graphics applications often arrange the display items as a collection of nodes in a graph structure known as a Scene Graph. Rendering of the items is then done by traversing the scene graph and rendering each viewable item. Whether or not items are rendered in front of or behind other items depends on their relative position in the scene graph. A scene graph is being developed for the Swank canvas. As currently implemented the Swank canvas scene graph is implemented by adding a new "-node" configuration option for each item on the canvas and adding a new node item type. Each traditional item on a canvas (arc, rectangle, line etc.) exists as leaf node on the graph and can not have other items attached. Only the new node item can have descendants, which may be traditional display items, or additional nodes.

If nodes are not specified the canvas acts as the traditional Tk canvas, effectively being a scene graph with one root node and zero or more visual items that are rendered in order of their attachment to the root node. The scene graph is rendered in a depth-first (post-ordered) fashion with children at each node rendered from left to right (first to last added). The bounding box (returned with the "canvas bbox" command) is the union of the bounds of all the items below that node. Node items are also rendered if they have a non empty fill or outline parameter. They are rendered as rectangles whose size is the same as the bounding box described above. Note that if the fill parameter is set, and is not transparent, all items below that node will be obscured as the node is drawn after the items below it on the graph.

The raise and lower canvas subcommands have a modified behavior with respect to scene graphs that have more than one node. A raise command issued without a "aboveThis" argument will move the specified items to be the last items of the node to which they are attached. If an "aboveThis" argument is specified, the aboveThis item must be attached to the same node as any items to be moved. Thus raise (and the comparable holds for lower) will only change the display order of items relative to other items attached to the same node (but, note that node items themselves can be raised or lowered).

Charts

Charts are implemented using JFreeChart [Gilb11]. In the Swank implementation they are essentially just another item that can be placed on the canvas. The chart shown in Figure 1, for example, is not implemented by using a multiple individual canvas items, as would be done in Tk, but is instead a single chart item that can readily be resized and repositioned on the canvas.

The canvas charts, illustrate a significant advantage of working in the JVM environment. Working with the C implementation of Tcl/Tk one would need to find a charting library that works on all the major environments (Mac, Windows, Linux, etc.) and then ensure that it compiles, links and runs on these. Integrating such a library might require significant knowledge of the build environment of each operating system. Using such a library also requires an ongoing commitment to update the library and build environment for new operating system releases. With the JVM approach,however, one needs only ensure that the libraries jar files are available on the build and run classpaths and one has a high level of confidence that the application will run on any platform implementing a compatible version of the JVM.

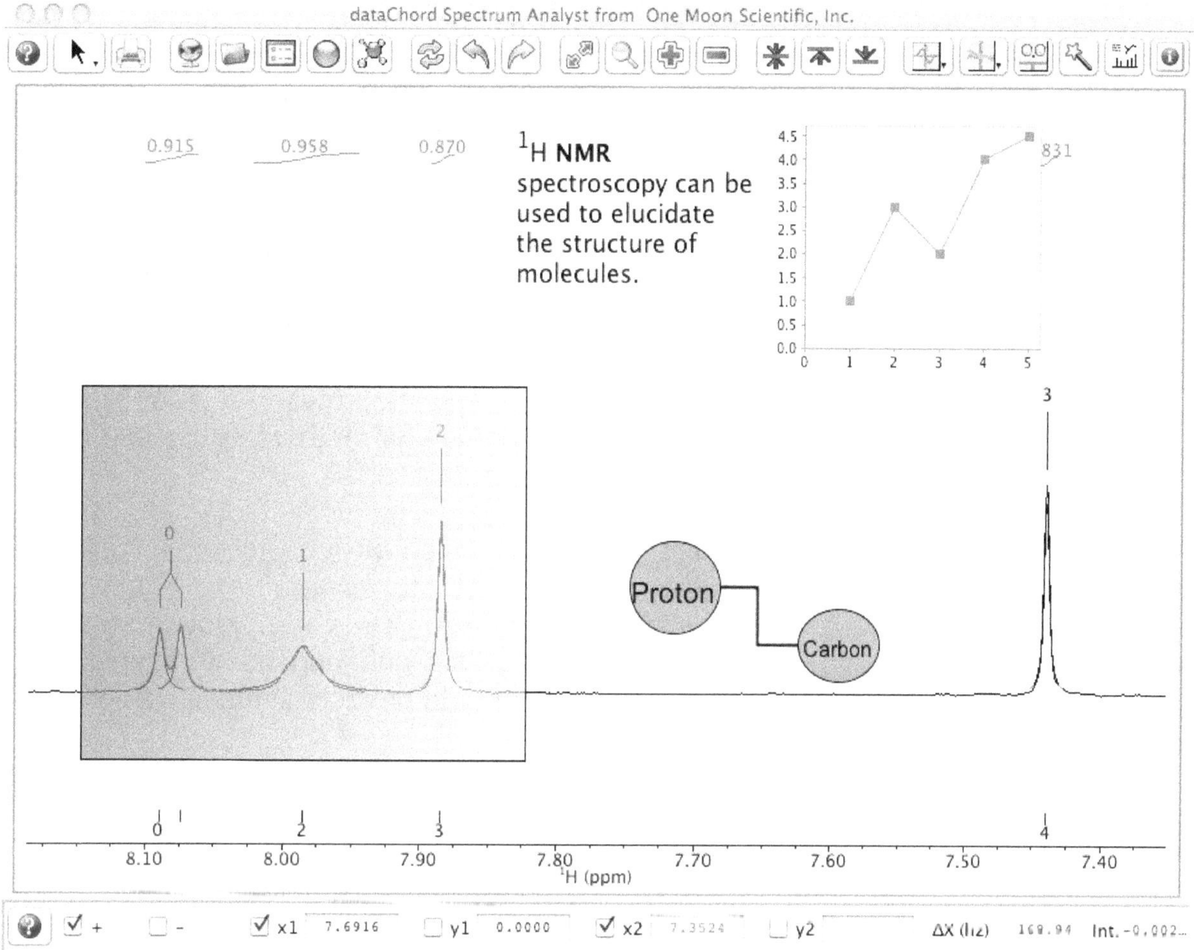

Figure 1. This figure is a screenshot of the program dataChord Spectrum Analyst which is a Java program that integrates JTcl and Swank. The primary window is used for displaying Nuclear Magnetic Resonance (NMR) spectra, but also provides for rich annotation features by the user. The NMR spectra are analyzed, in part, using tools available from the Apache Commons Math libary [ACM11]. The spectra are rendered as custom items on the Swank canvas, so multiple spectra can be rendered in various positions and orientations on the canvas. The screenshot is somewhat contrived to show various Swank canvas items: a rectangle with a transparent, gradient color, two ovals joined by a connector item, an htext item showing the user of superscript and bold text, and a chart item, implemnted using the JFreeChart library.

Much of the data analysis of dataChord Spectrum Analyst is implemented as JTcl scripts, and as a client-server program it relies heavily on the file, channel and socket capababilites of JTcl.

Canvas3D

Besides the standard Tk-like canvas, Swank includes a canvas suitable for displaying 3D objects. The implementation is at present fairly limited, but does provide the ability to draw spheres, cylinders, cones, and text. The actual 3D graphics are implemented using Java3D.

Building and Packaging

Swank is built and packaged using the same maven-based infrastructure as used by JTcl. The primary build result is a zip file that forms a "batteries included" distribution, that includes JTcl (which as discussed above includes incr Tcl, the TJC Tcl to Java Compiler, and much of Tcllib), the chart canvas item code (including JFreeChart jar files), and the canvas3d package.

Helper scripts for starting a Swank environment are included and are analogous to those described above for JTcl. Tk distributions include a program called "wish". Swank provides helper scripts called "wisk" (and wisk.bat on Windows) that start up the same type of environment that "wish" does. Also included are helper scripts, swkcon (and swkcon.bat on Windows). These start up Swank with a Swank implementation of the TkCon console [Hobbs09].

Conclusions

Together, JTcl and Swank, provide an environment for developing applications that is very similar to that of Tcl and Tk. Most programs that will run with Tcl 8.4 will run unchanged on JTcl. Swank has a greater level of differences to Tk, but provides a high level of compatibility along with additional widgets and capabilities, especially with regards to the canvas widget.

A large advantage of developing in the JTcl/Swank environment is the ability to take advantage of other libraries implemented in Java. The developer can have a high level of confidence that the combination of JTcl and Swank with other Java libraries will run unchanged on any platform with the JVM. An example of this is the program, dataChord Spectrum Analyst (Figure 1), which is written to use JTcl and Swank, and integrates in a cross-platform way libraries for math, statistics and charting.

JTcl is hosted at http://jtcl.kenai.com/ and Swank at http://swank.kenai.com/. Installers, source code, documentation, mailing lists and bug trackers are available for both projects at these sites.

References

[ACM11]
Commons Math: The Apache Commons Mathematics Library
http://commons.apache.org/math/

[DeJ05]
Incr Tcl extension for Jacl
TclJava project
http://sf.net/projects/tcljava
http://sourceforge.net/mailarchive/message.php?msg_id=1134245

[DeJ06]
TJC : A Tcl to Java Compiler
Mo DeJong
Thirteenth Annual Tcl/Tk Workshop, 2006
http://modejong.com/publications.html

[Gilb11]
JFreeChart
David Gilbert

http://www.jfree.org/jfreechart

[Hobbs09]
TkCon Project
Jeffrey Hobbs
http://tkcon.sourceforge.net/

[John04]
"From C to Java, Scientific Data Analysis with Java, Jacl and Swank"
Bruce A. Johnson
11'th Annual Tcl/Tk Conference
http://www.tcl.tk/community/tcl2004/Papers/

[Kapl02]
DustMote
http://wiki.tcl.tk/4333

[Lam97]
"Jacl: A Tcl Implementation in Java"
Ioi K. Lam, Brian Smith
Fifth Annual Tcl/Tk Workshop, 1997
http://www.usenix.org/publications/library/proceedings/tcl97/lam.html

[Lew96]
"An On-the-fly Bytecode Compiler for Tcl"
Brian T. Lewis
Fourth Annual USENIX Tcl/Tk Workshop, 1996
http://www.usenix.org/publications/library/proceedings/tcl96/lewis.html

[Lind99]
"The Java™ Virtual Machine Specification, 2nd Ed.", T. Lindholm and F. Yellin, 1999, Prentice Hall.

[Oracle2004]
http://download.oracle.com/javase/1,5.0/docs/api/overview-summary.html

[Ost10]
"Tcl and the Tk Toolkit, 2nd Ed.", John. K. Ousterhout and Ken Jones, 2010, Addison-Wesley.

[Poin07]
Aejaks Project
Tom Poindexter
http://sf.net/projects/aejaks

[Szul09]
Tcl/Tk Community Google Summer of Code 2009
Jacl Modernization Project
http://wiki.tcl.tk/23812

[WikiJVM]
JVM Languages
http://en.wikipedia.org/wiki/JVM_languages

Jim Tcl

A Small Footprint Tcl Implementation

Steve Bennett,
WorkWare Systems
http://www.workware.net.au/
steveb@workware.net.au

July 2011

Abstract

Jim Tcl is a modern implementation of Tcl, designed to be small, modular, easy to build and easy to embed. Along with a high degree of compatibility with Tcl 8.5, Jim Tcl includes a number of innovative features such as lambdas, garbage collection, object-oriented I/O and signal handling. This paper presents a detailed look at some of the most interesting aspects of Jim Tcl.

The Jim Tcl [1] project was begun in 2005 by Salvatore Sanfilippo, largely as a testbed for new features such as functional programming support which were difficult to retrofit to Tcl[1] and required some practical experimentation. Since then, Jim Tcl has acquired many new features, both standard Tcl features and features unique to Jim Tcl and has improved in stability and speed.

1. THE STATE OF JIM TCL

Jim Tcl v0.71, which was released in June 2011;

- Runs on at least: Mac OS X, Linux (many architectures), FreeBSD, QNX, eCos, Solaris, cygwin, msys/mingw and Haiku.
- Includes many C and Tcl optional components, including: glob, tclcompat, tree, rlprompt, oo, binary, load, package, readdir, array, clock, exec, file, posix, regexp, signal, aio, eventloop, pack, syslog, nvp, readline, sqlite, sqlite3, win32
- Passes over 3700 unit tests
- Is between 100KB and 220KB in size depending on selected components, platform and build options
- Has 127 built-in commands

A Short History of Jim Tcl

The Jim Tcl project has been active for over six years.

Date	Who	Description
Feb 2005	antirez	Initial public version
Sep 2005	antirez	Enter low activity maintenance period
Jun 2008	oharboe	Take over as maintainer
Jul 2008	oharboe	Change to FreeBSD license
Nov 2008	steveb	Begin port of missing Tcl functionality
Oct 2009	oharboe	Move to git
Jul 2010	oharboe	Release 0.51
Oct 2010	steveb	Release 0.63 - Merge workware port
Jan 2011	steveb	Release 0.70 - Including utf-8 support
Jun 2011	steveb	Release 0.71

The very first publicly released version of Jim Tcl included support for references and garbage collection as well as a handful of core commands.

Subsequent releases have added many new core commands, optional extensions and significant Tcl compatibility.

The following graph shows the evolution of Jim Tcl in both size (features) and speed. A standard set of performance benchmarks is run for every, single commit to the public repository in order to monitor the size, speed and correctness over time.

[1] In this paper, the term Tcl will be used to refer to the original, official Tcl implementation — http://tcl.sourceforge.net/ while Jim Tcl will be used to refer to the Jim Tcl implementation — http://jim.berlios.de/

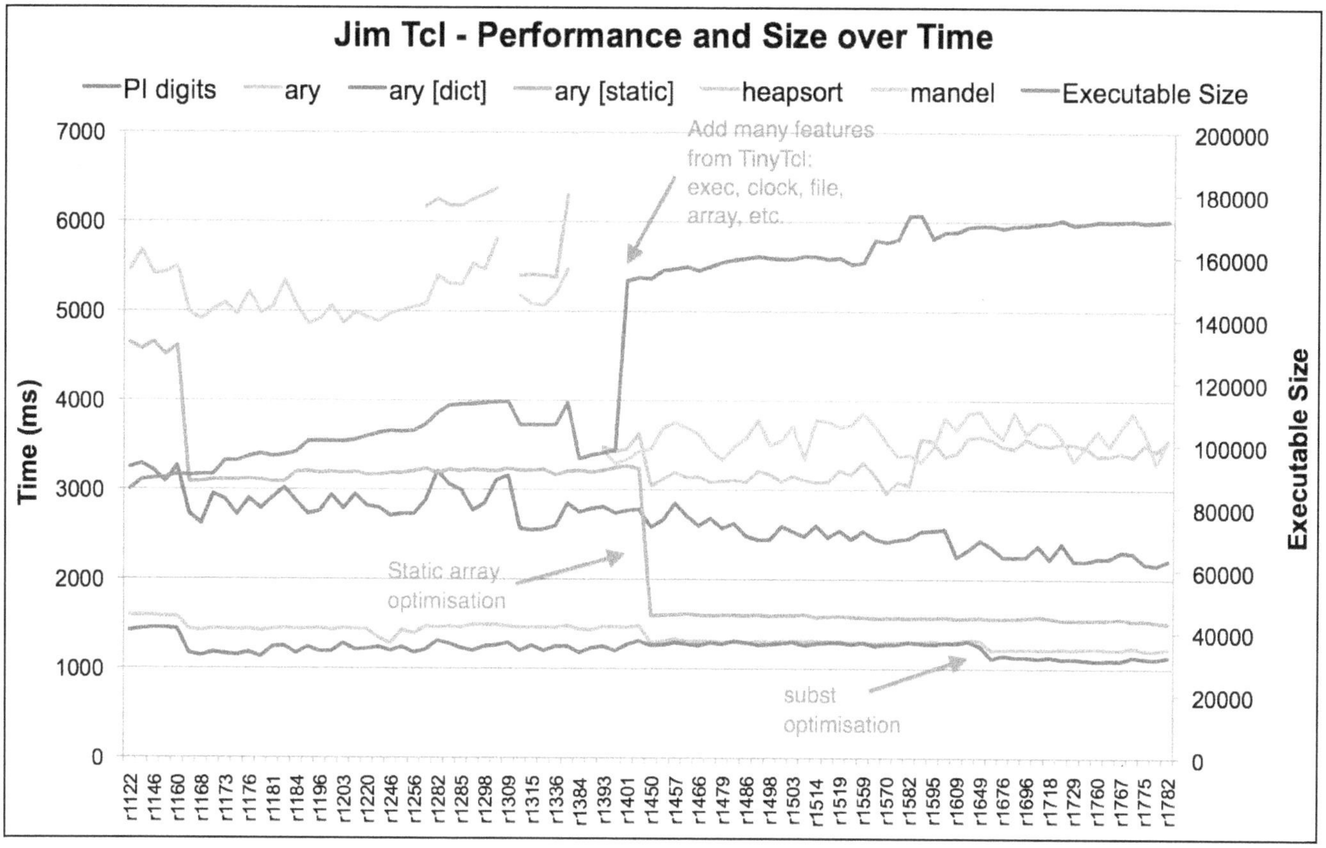

Jim Tcl on Linux, 266MHz ARM, gcc 4.2.4 -Os [2]

The Philosophy of Jim Tcl

When reimplementing an existing system, it can be difficult to balance competing goals of compatibility and whatever is driving the need for a new implementation. Jim Tcl strives to be a small footprint implementation, in both code size and memory usage, however this goal often competes with the goal of Tcl compatibility.

The philosophy of how Jim Tcl balances it's goals can be summarised as:

> *Jim Tcl attempts to avoid gratuitous incompatibilities with Tcl, while being open to the addition of new features which improve the usability and usefulness of Jim Tcl. Any large feature, including Tcl-compatible features, must be optional at compile time.*

The expression of this philosophy can be seen, for example, in the implementation of regular expressions (regexp, regsub) in Jim Tcl. To minimise the footprint, there are three options available (at compile time):

1. Disable regular expression support
2. Use the system-provided POSIX regex support to provide ERE[3] regular expression support. (This is the default)
3. Use the built-in regex support to provide (a significant subset of) ARE[4] regular expression support, including UTF-8.

Note that this approach necessarily leads to some differences between Jim Tcl and Tcl, and even between different configurations of Jim Tcl, but the size difference is significant.

Configuration	Size (bytes)
Jim Tcl, system regex	3500
Jim Tcl, built-in regex	9878
Jim Tcl, built-in regex + utf-8	9929
Tcl 8.5.8	54892

[2] Note that executable size represents the default configuration, which includes additional components over time.

[3] ERE — POSIX Enhanced Regular Expressions (see also BRE — Basic Regular Expressions)

[4] ARE — Advanced Regular Expressions

Jim Tcl does not attempt to present a stable C API. The ability to change the API from release to release allows new features to be added to Jim Tcl far more rapidly than would otherwise be the case. With the primary target for Jim Tcl being embedded scenarios, recompiling applications when upgrading to a later release is an acceptable tradeoff.

Similarities with Tcl

Today, Jim Tcl passes several thousand test cases, most of which are fully compatible with Tcl. Jim Tcl includes support for almost all of the core Tcl commands, including: append, array, switch, catch, break, continue, string, list, llength, lindex, lsort, lsearch, regexp, regsub, upvar, uplevel, foreach, dict, lassign, lset, exec, format, scan, binary and many more. In addition Jim Tcl supports {*}, loadable modules, modifying the environment to exec via the $env array, binary strings, UTF-8 strings, dictionaries and tailcall.

Many Tcl scripts will work unchanged, especially those which avoid the use of namespaces, safe interpreters, threading, traces and, of course, Tk. Jim Tcl implements the Dodekalogue [2].

Developers familiar with Tcl have been able to almost seamlessly make the transition to Jim Tcl.

Missing features and capabilities

Jim Tcl omits support for a number of Tcl features, usually due to one of the following reasons.

1. The functionality has little relevance, or at least is not critical, for an embedded system or embedded application (namespaces, safe interpreters)
2. The functionality is too large and/or complex to consider adding (dynamic encodings, byte code compiler)
3. There has been no interest in the feature by someone willing to work on it (coroutines, Tk)

The following is an abbreviated list of features missing from Jim Tcl compared with Tcl 8.5:

- Namespaces
- Traces (variable traces and execution traces)
- Byte code compilation
- Safe interpreters
- Threads
- Dynamic encodings (fconfigure -translation, etc.)
- Tk

In addition, a number of commands omit certain options and/or subcommands, such as lsort -dictionary -stride -unique, clock add, string wordend, wordstart.

Jim Tcl-specific features and capabilities

The Jim Tcl project started as a platform to experiment with new features, especially those related to functional programming such as closures, references, garbage collection, lambdas and tail calls. The ongoing development of Jim Tcl maintains the philosophy of pushing the boundaries when implementing new features, while still carefully considering the pros and cons with maintaining Tcl compatibility.

The following are some of the unique features of Jim Tcl, the first three of which will be explored in greater depth in the remainder of this paper.

- Functional programming support, including references, closures, lambdas and garbage collection
- Accurate tracking of source locations and source accurate error messages
- Fast, simplified packaging system
- Built-in line editing
- Procs allow default args anywhere (TIP #288)
- Procs support automatic upvar syntax: &ref
- Expression shorthand syntax: $(...)
- Procs can be stacked and invoked with upcall
- Signal handling
- Integers are 64-bit on supported platforms
- Supports 'jimsh -e' for immediate evaluation
- Object Oriented I/O
- Built-in support for syslog, IPv6, UDP, UNIX domain sockets and pipes on supported platforms
- Automatic conversion between list, dict and array
- Very modular with many features such as clock, regexp, binary, exec, glob, package and even I/O being optional
- Very easy to cross compile
- Single source file bootstrap jimsh can be built with just a C compiler.

Jim Tcl is not simply a cut-down version of Tcl. Many of these features are designed to simplify code, simplify deployment and provide a very capable dynamic language, especially for embedded systems.

For example, built-in support for signal handling, UDP, UNIX domain sockets and syslog make it possible to build small, but highly capable scripts and daemons with no additional libraries or components required.

2. SOURCE ACCURATE ERROR MESSAGES

One of the downsides of a language as dynamic as Tcl is that it can be difficult to provide accurate source information in error messages since any string can potentially be evaluated as a script and that string could have been created in arbitrarily many ways.

This issue was significant in our product, µWeb [3] which formerly used TinyTcl [4] (based on Tcl 6.7) as the scripting engine. While TinyTcl provides a small footprint scripting language and allowed for rapid development, it also deferred some errors until runtime. The following was the typical result of a runtime error:

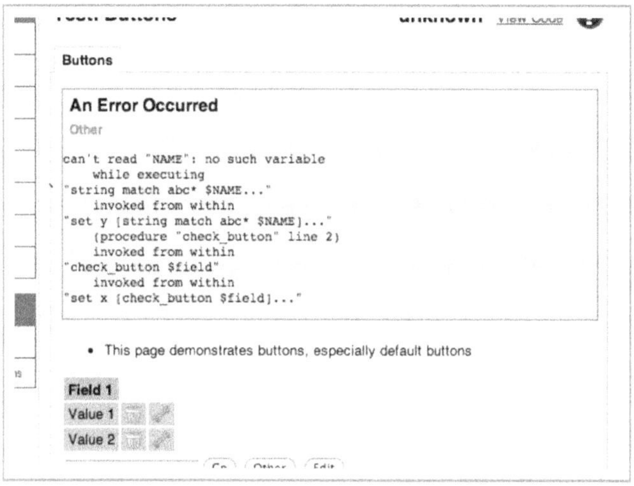

µWeb with TinyTcl — runtime error message

In µWeb, Tcl scripts are defined in "page description files" from which they are parsed and embedded in C code. The stack trace as shown above describes the error, but it can be difficult to match up with the original source.

One of the most compelling reasons to move from TinyTcl to Jim Tcl was the better error reporting. Compare the same error when using Jim Tcl as the scripting engine.

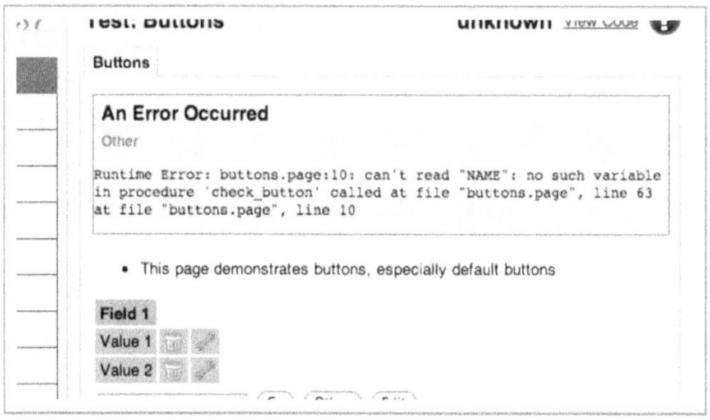

µWeb with Jim Tcl — runtime error message

Notice that the exact line number is identified for each level of the stack trace, even though the original source has been parsed and embedded in C code.

```
 1: title "Test: Buttons"
 2: label "Buttons"
 3:
 4: storage none
 5:
 6: summary {Test submit buttons}
 7:
 8: init -tcl {
 9:     proc check_button {name} {
10:         set y [string match abc* $NAME]
11:     }
12: }
...omitted...
59: button other {
60:     label Other
61:     editmode none
62:     submit -tcl {
63:         set x [check_button $field]
64:         cgi success "Got [cgi get text]"
65:     }
66: }
```

buttons.page

Identification of the exact location of the error makes it significantly easier for our customers, especially those new to the platform or Tcl to find and fix errors.

Below we discuss how Jim Tcl implements source tracking in such a way that it is both accurate in a highly dynamic language, and economical in resource usage.

Accurate Source Tracking — How it Works

In Tcl versions up to approximately 8.3, Tcl_Eval(), the heart of the Tcl interpreter parsed and evaluated scripts for every command. A while loop with 1000 iterations re-parsed the commands in the body of the loop 1000 times. While this made the interpreter simpler and consumed less memory, it had poor performance with some scripts. Starting with Tcl 8.4 and the introduction of the byte code compiler, parsing and execution were separated, resulting in a dramatic increase in performance. While Jim Tcl eschews the complexity and size of a byte code compiler and evaluation engine, it similarly separates parsing and evaluation for a significant performance boost.

The approach to parsing scripts into an internal representation is at the heart of how Jim Tcl manages source location information, and the core structure used is the Jim "Object", or Jim_Obj.

Jim Objects

Similarly to the Tcl_Obj structure in Tcl, Jim uses a reference counted Jim_Obj structure to cache an appropriate internal representation for "objects" in order to improve performance. Simple internal representations are used for (64 bit) integers, floating point values and strings, while more complex internal representations are used for more complex objects such as scripts, expressions, variables and commands.

Consider the following script:

```
incr x 3
```

After parsing and evaluating, these three "words" become the following three Jim_Obj structures:

string	incr
type	command
int-rep	pointer to struct Jim_Cmd
string	x
type	variable
int-rep	pointer to variable value plus scope info
string	3
type	int
int-rep	Integer 3 as a 64 bit value

While the string value is available whenever required, the internal representation acts as a cache for the most recent use of the value. For example if this command is executed in a loop, the command, variable and integer are immediately accessible without parsing or conversion.

Although this approach uses more memory than the simpler re-parsing approach, the additional memory required is modest while the performance gains are significant. It also makes it possible to associate additional information with each "word" or "token".

The following explains how these specialised internal representations are used to carefully track source locations through the interpreter.

Script Parsing

Consider the following simple script.

```
1: set x abc
2: if {[string match -x* $x]} {
3:     puts "$x matches"
4: } else {
5:     puts "$x does not match"
6: }
```

test.tcl

When this script is evaluated via the source command (and thus Jim_EvalFile()), or via Jim_EvalSource() the original source filename and line number are known. A Jim_Obj structure is created for the script with a type of "source" and the filename and line number of the first line of the script are recorded.

string	`set x abc\nif {[string match -x*...`
type	source
int-rep	test.tcl:1

Initial Jim_Obj representation of the script

When this script is evaluated (which will be immediately in this case), the script is parsed and converted to a "script" object with an internal representation as follows:

string	set x abc\nif {[string match -x* $x]}...
type	script
int-rep	test.tcl:1 plus script token list

Jim_Obj representation after conversion to script

Where the token list associated with the script is:

Token Type	string	type, int-rep
`LIN`		scriptline line=1
`ESC`	`set`	source (test.tcl:1)
`ESC`	`x`	source (test.tcl:1)
`ESC`	`abc`	source (test.tcl:1)
`LIN`		scriptline line=2
`ESC`	`if`	source (test.tcl:2)
`STR`	`[string match -x* $x]`	source (test.tcl:2)
`STR`	`\nputs "$x matches"\n`	source (test.tcl:2)
`ESC`	`else`	source (test.tcl:4)
`STR`	`\nputs "$x does not match"\n`	source (test.tcl:4)

Token list after conversion to script

Every token in the script becomes a Jim_Obj, initially of type "source" which records the original source location of that token.

When the script is evaluated, the internal representation of each Jim_Obj in the token list is converted as required from the "source" object.

Token Type	string	type, int-rep
LIN		scriptline line=1
ESC	set	command
ESC	x	variable
ESC	abc	source (test.tcl:1)
LIN		scriptline line=2
ESC	if	command
STR	[string match -x* $x]	expression
STR	puts "$x matches"	source (test.tcl:2)
ESC	else	compared-string
STR	puts "$x does not match"	script (test.tcl:4 plus token list)

Token list after evaluating script

Notice how the object associated with each word of evaluated script has changed internal representation based on how it is used. Most objects have lost the original source location (each object can have only one internal representation). However any "script" objects (such as the "else" arm) retain the source location. Also the "scriptline" object for each command in the script retains the source location.

This continues for each script which is executed, where the source location in the original "source" object is propagated into the token list of the script.

When source tracking is not possible

Now it is possible to create situations where the source information is totally lost, or was never available. For example:

- A script which was entered via a UI element such as a GUI widget or web form (probably a bad idea!)
- A script which was read from a file without the use of 'source' or 'package require'
- A script which was "composed" from strings which have no source information.

All of these scenarios are likely to be less common in practice than scripts which are executed or derived from source files. In some of these situations there is essentially nothing that can be done, however it would be possible to provide a Tcl command to set source information. Consider the following possible approach to adding source information to a string where 'makesource' returns a new string with the given source information added.

```
set f [open script.tcl]
set buf [$f read]
eval [makesource $buf script.tcl 1]
```

Tcl access to source information

In addition to providing for more informative error messages, Jim Tcl makes source information available directly to Tcl scripts through the 'info source' command and through the stack introspection command 'info frame'. Consider the script:

```
# test3.tcl
puts [info source {}]

proc a {} {
}

puts [info source [info body a]]

set b {
   one
   two
   three
}
puts [info source [lindex $b 1]]
```

The 'info source' command examines the given string (object) and returns any source information associated with that string. The above script produces:

```
$ jimsh test3.tcl
test3.tcl 2
test3.tcl 4
test3.tcl 11
```

Whenever a command is evaluated, the current source information is propagated. During proc invocation, this information is stored in the stack frame and is available via the 'info frame' command. The higher level commands 'stacktrace' and 'stackdump' provide access to this "live stack trace" information. The same information is used when an error occurs and the stack is unwound. When an error is caught with 'catch', this stack trace is available via the 'info stacktrace' command as well as via the '-errorinfo' key in the options dictionary.

Case Study — µWeb

The µWeb Embedded Web Framework makes use of Jim Tcl's ability to preserve and access source information both during parsing and at runtime as explained in the following diagram.

Source location is tracked from the original page definition files with Jim Tcl as a Domain Specific Language (DSL) parser, through the generated code where this information is used by the runtime Jim Tcl interpreter to produce accurate error messages which relate back to the original page definition files.

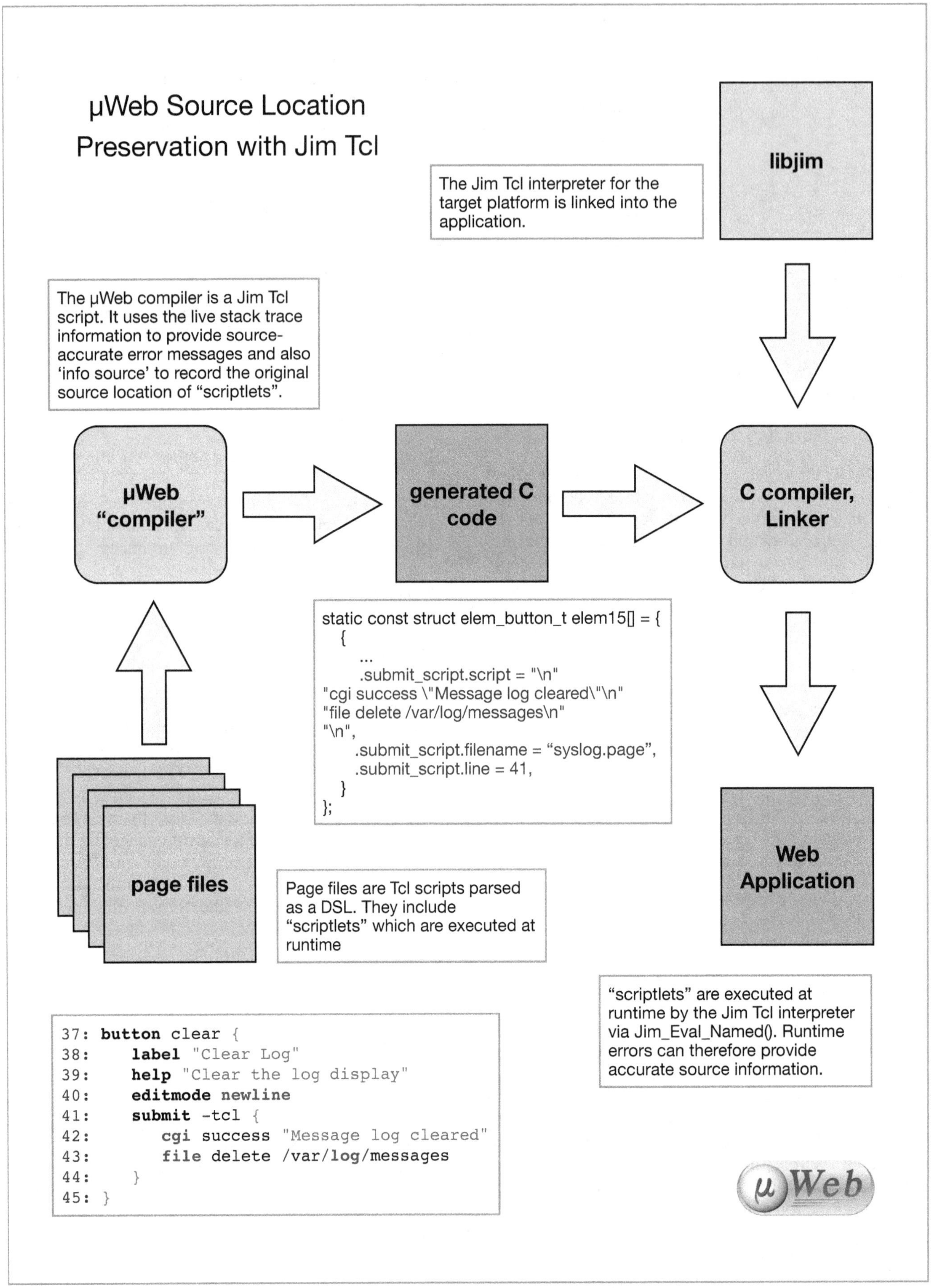
µWeb Source Location Preservation with Jim Tcl
The Jim Tcl interpreter for the target platform is linked into the application.
libjim
The µWeb compiler is a Jim Tcl script. It uses the live stack trace information to provide source-accurate error messages and also 'info source' to record the original source location of "scriptlets".
µWeb "compiler"
generated C code
C compiler, Linker
static const struct elem_button_t elem15[] = {
{
...
.submit_script.script = "\n"
"cgi success \"Message log cleared\"\n"
"file delete /var/log/messages\n"
"\n",
.submit_script.filename = "syslog.page",
.submit_script.line = 41,
}
};
page files
Page files are Tcl scripts parsed as a DSL. They include "scriptlets" which are executed at runtime
Web Application
"scriptlets" are executed at runtime by the Jim Tcl interpreter via Jim_Eval_Named(). Runtime errors can therefore provide accurate source information.
37: button clear {
38: label "Clear Log"
39: help "Clear the log display"
40: editmode newline
41: submit -tcl {
42: cgi success "Message log cleared"
43: file delete /var/log/messages
44: }
45: }
µWeb

Domain Specific Language (DSL) Parser

Early versions of μWeb used Tcl as the DSL parser. However changing to use Jim Tcl as the DSL parser had a number of benefits.

1. Supports identical Tcl-based DSL syntax
2. Error messages from the parser are more informative
3. Source location information is available for passing to the runtime interpreter
4. It is easy to ship the DSL parser as a single executable with Jim Tcl embedded.

Source Location in the Tcl Test Framework

Jim Tcl includes a pure-Tcl implementation of tcltest to run the unit test suite. This implementation takes advantage of the source location information to provide the exact location of unit test failures.

```
$ ./jimsh tests/list.test
list-1.13 ERR basic tests
At       : tests/list.test:32
Expected: 'xa {{}} b'
Got      : 'a {{}} b'
-----------------------------------------
FAILED: 1
  tests/list.test:32 list-1.13
-----------------------------------------
```

The Jim Tcl version of tcltest provides error locations

If a test fails because of a mismatch between the result and the expected result, the location of the test body is given with 'info source'.

If a test fails because it returns an unexpected error, the location of the error is given with 'info stacktrace'.

Experimental code coverage tool

The dynamic nature of Tcl, especially the inability to distinguish code from data can make code coverage analysis difficult. Nonetheless, a simple 50-line Jim Tcl script is able to provide useful code coverage information by simply recording the source location of every command executed.[5]

```
$ ./jcov test.tcl
   1: set x abc
   2: if {[string match -x* $x]} {
####:     puts "$x matches"
   -: } else {
   3:     puts "$x does not match"
   -: }
```

Code coverage output shows which arm was not taken

Experimental Jim Tcl Debugger.

Although not yet available in the official Jim Tcl distribution, a pure-Tcl implementation of an interactive debugger has been developed which uses the source location information to display the source code associated with the currently executing code as well as listing source for any procedure and managing breakpoints by source location.

```
$ ./jimdb test.tcl
Jim Tcl debugger v1.0  -  Use ? for help

@ test.tcl:1 set x abc
>    1 set x abc
     2 if {[string match -x* $x]} {
dbg> n
=> abc
@ test.tcl:2 if {[string match -x* $x]} ...
     1 set x abc
>    2 if {[string match -x* $x]} {
     3     puts "$x matches"
dbg> p $x
abc
dbg> ?
 s        step into     w        where
 n        step over     l [loc]  list source
 r        step out      v        local vars
 c        continue      u        up frame
 p [exp]  print         d        down frame
 b [loc]  breakpoints   t [n]    trace
 ? [cmd]  help          q        quit
dbg> l alias
@ stdlib.tcl
     1 # Create a single word alias (proc)
     2 # e.g. alias x info exists
     3 # if {[x var]} ...
*    4 proc alias {name args} {
     5     set prefix $args
     6     proc $name args prefix {
     7         tailcall {*}$prefix {*}$args
     8     }
     9 }
    10
    11 # Creates an anonymous procedure
    12 proc lambda {arglist args} {
dbg> b puts
Breakpoint at puts (tclcompat.tcl:21)
dbg>
```

Experimental Interactive Debugger

[5] Both the code coverage tool and the debugger rely on an experimental command trace feature

3. THE JIM TCL PACKAGE SYSTEM

Tcl has a sophisticated package system for loading Tcl source and binary modules as packages. This system is also complex and potentially slow as pkgIndex.tcl files are searched and parsed.

Consider the following simple invocation.

```
$ cat pkgtest.tcl
package require blah
$ strace -e strace=open tclsh8.5 t.tcl
open("/usr/share/tcltk/tcl8.5/init.tcl",...
open("t.tcl", ...
open("/usr/share/tcltk/tclIndex", ...
open("/usr/lib/tcltk/tclIndex", ...
open("/usr/local/share/tcltk/tclIndex", ...
open("/usr/local/lib/tcltk/tclIndex", ...
open("/usr/lib/tclIndex", ...
open("/usr/share/tcltk/tcl8.5/tclIndex",...
open("/usr/share/tcltk/tcl8.5/tm.tcl", ...
open("/usr/share/tcltk/tcllib1.12/interp/
pkgIndex.tcl", ...
open("/usr/share/tcltk/tcllib1.12/png/
pkgIndex.tcl", ...
...etc..
```

A total of 115 files are opened and read

The need to create and deploy pkgIndex.tcl files can also be awkward.[6]

Simple Package System

With the focus of Jim Tcl on embedded environments, it is appropriate to take a much simpler approach to packaging[7]. The Jim Tcl packaging system:

- Has no version support. Versions are managed through filenames
- Has no index files and no autoload support
- Is fast
- Is easy to understand
- Is easy to deploy

The Jim Tcl packaging system works as follows:

1. The package subsystem maintains a list of loaded packages.
2. The command 'package require foo' searches each directory in $::auto_path for either foo.so or foo.tcl. If either file is found, the package is deemed to be located (even if loading the package fails).
3. Once the file is found, it is loaded either as a binary module or as a Tcl script.

Some notes:

1. Package names must be lower case — foo not Foo.
2. Binary loadable modules are named foo.so on all platforms.
3. The entry point for the module foo.so is Jim_fooInit
4. Versions are expected to be handled by including the version in the name. For example 'package require foo2'.
5. The $:auto_path list is initialised based on the install prefix (<prefix>/lib/jim) plus the environment variable $JIMLIB, although applications which embed the Jim Tcl interpreter can add additional directories as appropriate.

Static vs dynamic packages

Jim is designed to be modular. This means both being able to omit features not required, but also making it easy to incorporate features. One example is static Tcl extensions. Pure-Tcl extensions such as glob, stdlib, tclcompat and binary can easily be built as static extensions in libjim and jimsh by simply selecting them with ./configure.

```
$ ./configure --with-ext="binary glob"
```

Similarly, C-based extensions can be built either as static extensions or loadable modules.

External loadable extensions

Building loadable modules can be difficult on different platforms. Jim Tcl provides a helper script to make building C-based extensions as loadable modules easy on any supported platform.

```
$ build-jim-ext hello.c extra.c
Building hello.so from hello.c extra.c
Compile: hello.o
Compile: extra.o
Link:    hello.so
Test:    load hello.so
Success!
```

Building a loadable module is easy

The build-jim-ext script uses the configuration-time settings to invoke the compiler and linker as appropriate, including for cross compilation.

This is a "mini-TEA" [5] for Jim Tcl.

[6] This is not intended as a criticism of the Tcl package system, which is very powerful. Rather it explains why Jim Tcl uses a much simplified approach.

[7] The Jim Tcl packaging system is similar to the Tcl Module support introduced in Tcl 8.5 (http://wiki.tcl.tk/12999)

4. REFERENCES, GARBAGE COLLECTION, CLOSURES AND LAMBDAS

Jim Tcl provides two features which are combined to provide garbage collected lambdas and closures. These are static variables and garbage collected references.

Static Variables and Closures

As an extension to Tcl, Jim Tcl allows procedures to define static variables. This is a lifetime and scoping mechanism which is similar to namespace variables in Tcl, but associated with a procedure rather than a namespace.

Static variables come into existence when a procedure is created and live until the procedure is deleted. These static variables are accessible (scoped) only to the procedure. Consider the following example.

```
. proc a {x} {{adder 5}} {
      return [incr x $adder]
  }
. a 3
8
```

An extra parameter is specified in the procedure definition [8] which declares and initialises a static variable, adder.

Since the scope of the static variable is limited to the proc, it is convenient to use this mechanism to avoid name clashes instead of global variables.

Now consider a slight change to the procedure definition which does not initialise the static variable.

```
. set adder 10
. proc a {x} {adder} {
      return [incr x $adder]
  }
. a 3
13
```

In this case, the static variable is not initialised directly, but is implicitly initialised from a variable with the same name in the surrounding scope.

Static variables can be used to implement closures, where a procedure captures a variable from the enclosing scope. Note that the variable captures the *value* rather than a *reference* to the variable from the enclosing scope due to Tcl's value semantics (although see the section on references below). Closures are particularly useful when used with lambdas.

References

Tcl is a language with value semantics and thus there is no notion of an explicit reference type[9]. This simplifies the language in many ways, but it makes certain problems more difficult. Jim Tcl adds support for references primarily as a means to implement garbage collection.

A reference can be thought of as a value which contains (or *refers to*) another value, thus providing a level of indirection. As we will see, this level of indirection allows the contained values to be garbage collected.

References provide three important features:

1. The ability to store (and retrieve) a value
2. A managed namespace providing a unique name every time a reference is created
3. An associated finalizer to invoke when a reference is no longer accessible (garbage collection)

Consider the following example:

```
. set r [ref "One String" test]
<reference.<test___>.00000000000000000000>
. getref $r
One String
. set r2 $r
<reference.<test___>.00000000000000000000>
. setref $r "New String"
New String
. getref $r2
New String
```

The command 'ref' creates a references to the value specified by the first argument. (The second argument is a "type" used for documentation purposes). The returned value is a unique reference with a special string format which allows the contained value to be retrieved, and also allows references to be easily identified.

The command 'getref' is the dereferencing operation which retrieves the value stored in the reference. The companion command 'setref' allows the value stored in the reference to be replaced.

Note that a reference is simply a string, so a copy of the reference ($r2) refers to the same contained value.

In this example, no finalizer is specified. Finalizers provide the mechanism for garbage collection as discussed below.

[8] By adding an extra argument to proc, the syntax is backward compatible with Tcl

[9] Of course Tcl is a very flexible language. References can be emulated through the use of global (or namespace) variables, where the name of the variable is the reference. This approach, however, doesn't allow for garbage collection which is the primary purpose for references in Jim Tcl.

Garbage Collection

Normally, all values in Tcl are passed by value. As such values are copied and released automatically as necessary. With the introduction of references, it is possible to create values whose lifetime transcend their scope.

Consider the following example where a reference is created with a finalizer.

```
. proc f {ref value} {puts "F $ref $value"}
. set r [ref 123 test f]
<reference.<test___>.00000000000
. collect
0
. set r ""
. collect
F <reference.<test___>.00000000000 123
1
```

The finalizer command 'f' is associated with the reference when it is created. (The 'collect' command is available to manually run the garbage collector, and returns the number of objects discarded. Normally the garbage collector runs automatically[10].)

The first time that 'collect' is invoked, a variable 'r' exists which contains the reference. Because the reference is accessible the garbage collector has nothing to do. However the second time 'collect' is invoked, 'r' no longer contains the reference. Therefore, when the garbage collector runs it finds this dangling reference and discards it, first invoking the associated finalizer.

The finalizer is passed two arguments, the reference and the contained value, which it may use to perform any necessary cleanup.

The finalizer for a reference may be examined or changed with the 'finalize' command.

```
. finalize $r
f
. finalize $r newf
newf
```

The garbage collector works similar to the Boehm GC algorithm for C/C++ [6]. Here, the special string format makes it easy to identify strings which may be valid references. During garbage collection, the string representations of all objects are scanned for strings which could be valid references. If a given reference no longer exists in any string, the contained object is unreachable and can be collected.

Lambda

Jim Tcl provides a lambda command which provides support for garbage collected anonymous 'functions' (Tcl procedures)[11] and closures.

Consider the following example.

```
. set adder [lambda a {{x 0}} {incr x $a}]
. $adder 1
1
. $adder 2
3
. set adder ""
```

An anonymous procedure is created and stored in the variable 'adder'. The procedure takes one argument which it adds to the static variable 'x' and returns the result. The procedure name '$adder' may be used anywhere a command name is required.

The anonymous procedure is garbage collected. Once it is no longer accessible (perhaps when the procedure which defined it ends), the garbage collector is free to delete the procedure.

The implementation of the lambda command is remarkably simple.

```
# Creates an anonymous procedure
proc lambda {arglist args} {
    set name [ref {} func lambda.finalizer]
    tailcall proc $name $arglist {*}$args
}

proc lambda.finalizer {name val} {
    rename $name {}
}
```

The lambda command takes the same arguments as 'proc' except the name of the procedure is omitted. A reference is created as a unique, anonymous name for the new command. In this case the ability for the reference to contain a value is not used. The reference finalizer simply deletes the procedure. 'tailcall' is used here simply as an efficiency mechanism to avoid the creation of an additional call frame.

Lambdas can be convenient as sorting functions.

```
. set list {1 50 20 -4 2}
1 50 20 -4 2
. lsort -command [lambda {a b} {expr {$a -
$b}}] $list
-4 1 2 20 50
```

[10] The garbage collector runs synchronously. Whenever a new reference is created, the garbage collector will run if a certain number of references have been created or a certain period of time has passed. This means that if references are not used, garbage collection has no impact on performance.

[11] See http://en.wikipedia.org/wiki/Anonymous_function

Lambda Example

The following example shows how lambdas can be useful. First note that Jim Tcl supports object-oriented I/O commands. That is, in addition to the Tcl-compatible:

```
set f [open temp.txt]
set data [read $f]
set pos [tell $f]
close $f
```

Jim Tcl supports:

```
set f [open temp.txt]
set data [$f read]
set pos [$f tell]
$f close
```

This has the advantage that it is easy to "wrap" a file handle with a procedure.

The "open |..." syntax in Jim Tcl is implemented in pure-Tcl by wrapping a file handle with a lambda.

```
 1: # 'open "|..." ?mode?" will invoke
 2: # this wrapper around exec/pipe
 3: # Note that we return a lambda
 4: # which also provides the 'pid' command
 5: proc popen {cmd {mode r}} {
 6:    lassign [socket pipe] r w
 7:    try {
 8:       if {[string match "w*" $mode]} {
 9:          lappend cmd <@$r &
10:          set pids [exec {*}$cmd]
11:          $r close
12:          set f $w
13:       } else {
14:          lappend cmd >@$w &
15:          set pids [exec {*}$cmd]
16:          $w close
17:          set f $r
18:       }
19:       lambda {cmd args} {f pids} {
20:          if {$cmd eq "pid"} {
21:             return $pids
22:          }
23:          if {$cmd eq "close"} {
24:            $f close
25:            # And wait for the child
26:            # processes to complete
27:            foreach p $pids {os.wait $p}
28:            return
29:          }
30:          tailcall $f $cmd {*}$args
31:       }
32:    } on error {error opts} {
33:       $r close
34:       $w close
35:       error $error
36:    }
37: }
```

At line 19, a lambda is created which wraps the file handle '$f'. Most subcommands are simply passed through to '$f' via the tailcall at line 30, however the new subcommand 'pid' is implemented at line 20 and the subcommand 'close' is extended at line 23.

Jim Tcl OO

The Jim Tcl OO system uses static variables and references to implement a pure-Tcl OO system [7] with multiple inheritance in 58 lines of code.

```
$ jimsh
. package require oo
. class Account {bal 0}
. Account method deposit {x} {incr bal $x}
. Account method see {} {return $bal}
. set a [Account new {bal 100}]
<reference.<Account>.00000000000000000000>
. $a deposit 50
150
. $a deposit 25
175
. $a see
175
```

Using the OO package

The 'tree' package included with Jim Tcl is largely compatible with struct::tree from tcllib and is implemented as an OO class.

5. CONCLUSION

Jim Tcl contains many more unique features than presented here, while remaining faithful to the Dodekalogue. Tcl has seen a number of small additions over time such as {*} list expansion, lassign, and exec redirection improvements which have made a huge difference to usability and usefulness of Tcl. Similarly, the unique features of Jim Tcl enhance its usability and facility while remaining small, fast and modular.

Not only has Jim Tcl provided a modern Tcl implementation for embedded systems, it has proven an effective platform for testing improvements to the Tcl language itself.

It is my hope that future releases of Tcl can benefit from the experience gained from implementing these improvements.

6. REFERENCES

[1] http://jim.berlios.de/

[2] http://wiki.tcl.tk/10259

[3] http://uweb.workware.net.au/

[4] http://tinytcl.sourceforge.net/

[5] http://wiki.tcl.tk/327

[6] http://en.wikipedia.org/wiki/Boehm_garbage_collector

[7] http://jim.berlios.de/documentation/oo/

TyCL: an interpreter/compiler of a typed language implementation of Tcl/Tk

Andres Buss, Otlet Technologies Ltda
aabuss@otlettech.com

Abstract

TyCL (Typed Command Language) is an implementation of the Tcl language written in TyCL itself. The language follows Tcl's syntax, but given that TyCL is meant to be a full compiler that generates machine code, a new set of features, expansions and cuts had to be applied to the Tcl's syntax that TyCL understand in order to help the compiler to produce better results. Included in those modifications are the concept of types (hence the name of the compiler), which are optional but when used makes TyCL behave more as an static language than a dynamic one.

Introduction

Even though the performance of Tcl's virtual machine has been improved since its conception (including the Non-Recursive-Engine[1]) it still runs at few orders of magnitude slower than many other languages at this time. After looking at its source code (written in C) one has to wonder how hard would be to try something in such performance endeavors. There is another path that can be taken (may be a lot more painful and time consuming but... hopefully... more gratifying) which is to develop a new implementation of Tcl's features and syntax using another approach, and may be, a different coding-language (other than C), and in the process of doing it (now that one is willing to take the pain) why not try to include some other nice and interesting features? Here is where TyCL come in to the picture.

The main goals of the TyCL compiler/interpreter is to try to improve Tcl's performance, minimize its memory footprint and provide simple mechanisms to interact with other components within a system by creating a whole new implementation of it from scratch. It could be written in C or C++ or even Objective-C (following the people's frenzy for Apple's products at these days) but it might be thought (as Alan Kay did with Smalltalk [2]) that the best language to code this new implementation would be TyCL itself, so we have to deal with one syntax and one set of idiosyncrasies instead of two, besides that any improvements in the language is directly applied to the compiler. In order to do this one must have the first usable implementation of the language already running (chicken & egg problem) to compile itself, in this case, at the beginning, TyCL's implementation is coded in plain Tcl8.5 in order to obtain the first iteration of the needed bootstrapping[3] process and have TyCL compiled by itself.

As a Tcl compiler, TyCL should produce better results as programs/scripts include more detailed information about the data it has to process (information that is not there right know, given the strong dynamic nature of Tcl), which means: is less-difficult to generate efficient machine-code when the compiler knows exactly what data is manipulating... or in other words: TyCL has to include the concept of inline/static data types in its syntax in order to provide this information.

TyCL's architecture

Like any other compiler[4], TyCL has an architecture composed by stages, from the lexical parser to a machine-code generator (see figure 1), the only possible difference is that one of its intermediate-representations could be interpreted by TyCL's Virtual Machine (VM).

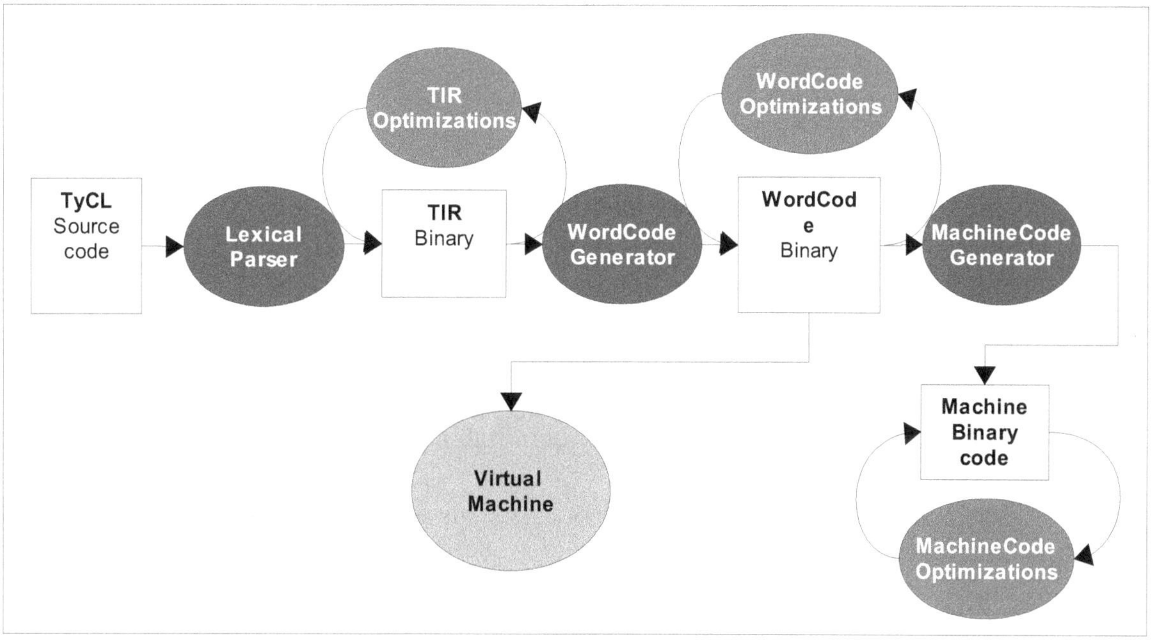

Figure 1. TyCL's block diagram

The program's source code begins its transformation at the lexical parser, which converts the whole text in a kind of Abstract-Syntax-Tree[5] called TIR (TyCL-Intermediate-Representation), by later be synthesized in a WordCode format (WC)[1] by the WC-Generator. At this point, the partial result is composed by a binary block of Word-Codes and a set of data tables (a sort of literals, symbols and references tables) that either could be passed to the TyCL's VM or injected into the machine-code-generator to be transformed in an executable or a system-binary-object (NativeCode).

At the moment, TyCL doesn't implement any form of code optimizations, it runs as a very naive compiler, but they could be integrated into the processing-chain at the TIR, WC and NativeCode sub-products stages as a series sub-processes.

1 The 'WordCode' name was preferred over 'ByteCode' because the granularity of the format is 4-bytes.

The Lexical Parser

As described before, this process converts the source-code from the text representation to a TIR representation using the modified/expanded Tcl's syntax understood by TyCL. Such syntax is very close to Tcl's, except for:

- **The type system**

  The parser tries to imply every value's type by analyzing its value/structure, for example: the text *23.65* is identified as a real number and then its type is *float*, but if the same number is written as: *"23.65"* its type is taken as *string* (which means plain text) because of being quoted. The basic available types are:

  - integer:
    any text composed only by digits from 0 to 9.
    any text in hexadecimal notation (0x##)
  - boolean:
    any of: *t|T|true, f|F|false.*
  - float:
    any number that includes a single decimal separator.
  - char:
    any single character surrounded by quotes or braces.
  - string:
    any text surrounded by quotes or braces. This is the chosen default type if no other could be detected.

  Besides the automatic detection of data types, the program can inform the parser that a certain value should be understood in a particular way by directly declaring its type, a process commonly known as casting, in this particular case: casting from text to the desired type. The way of declaring a casting is:

  TYPE:VALUE

  as an example, the following fragment shows how the types are detected/declared:

```
set a 7                ;# auto-detected integer = 7
set b integer:"456"    ;# integer = 456
set c true             ;# auto-detected boolean = true
set d "false"          ;# auto-detected string = 'false'
set e boolean:45       ;# boolean = true
set f 3.1415           ;# auto-detected float = 3.1415
set g float:3.4        ;# float = 3.4
set h float:{56.8576}  ;# float = 56.8576
set i char:w           ;# char = 'w'
set j char:67          ;# char = 'C'
set k hello            ;# default-detected string = 'hello'
set l "hello world"    ;# auto-detected string = 'hello world'
set m string:6.28      ;# string = '6.28'
```

Each of the created variables in the previous example has then a value with a particular type, but also each one of them can have any other typed-value later on. In order to force a variable to always have values of an specified type, the new command: "*define*" was added to the syntax to complement the traditional assignment command: "*set*", that does exactly the same assignment but also bounds a type with the variable being assigned. So instead of writing:

```
set a float:5.6
```

one would write:

```
define b float:5.6
```

the difference between *a* and *b* is that *b* can only hold values of type *float* and its type can not be changed until it is destroyed and created again.

- **References**

Additionally to these basic types, there is on more basic but almost hidden type of value called: "*reference*" that, as its name suggests, allows a variable to reference another one in a transparent way. It is thought to be almost hidden because values of this type are not directly manipulated as the other basic types (like integers or floats, which can be changed in expressions), instead, they are operated through another new command called: "*let*" , whose only function is to assign and acquire references to and from variables. Its syntax is:

```
let VAR            ;# returns a reference to the variable: VAR
let VAR_1 VAR_2    ;# sets VAR_1 as a reference to VAR_2
```

Only the command "*let*" is allowed to set, get and change reference-values, this means that for the rest of the program, when such a variable is operated, what is actually manipulated is the value of the final variable referenced by the original one, for example:

```
set a 4     ;# variable a = 4
let b a     ;# variable b refers to a
let c b     ;# variable c refers to b
set c 9     ;# setting c = 9 actually sets: a = 9 because:
             # c → b → a
```

As this example shows, references are transparently followed internally. From a strictly Tcl's point of view they don't exist.

- **Structural data types**

  Just as having basic data types to identify values more precisely can help the compiler in its job, structural data types could make its life better yet, allowing the compiler to generate more compact and hopefully efficient code by knowing how the data/values should be organized in memory.

  There are many ways of organizing data but the most generic ones could be:

Name	Length	Internal types	Description
arrays	fixed	multi-typed	A group with a fixed number of values
typed arrays	fixed	single-typed	An array of values of the same type
lists	variable	multi-typed	A group of values that can be expanded/shrunken
typed lists	variable	single-typed	A list of values of the same type
structs	static	static-typed	A group of explicit and ordered set of typed-values
unions	static	mixed-typed	A group of values that shares the same memory space

Table 1. Generic structural data types

Currently, Tcl only implements the *array* (as a hash table) and *list* data types in a very general way, the problem with this implementation is that it isn't very compiler-friendly in the sense that it is very difficult to infer the real structure of the data being put together. For this reason TyCL includes types to strictly declare the structural organization of data, trying not to loose Tcl's general forms also. Included so far are:

  - Arrays
    Implemented as an ordered collection of values with a fixed quantity of items (completely opposed to Tcl's arrays, which are variable in length and internally unordered)

    In order to use arrays, a definition of its characteristics (length and value's type) must exist before it can be manipulated, for example:

```
set a array:4                 ;# array definition of length = 4
                               # composed by values of any type

set b array:{3 integer}       ;# typed-array definition of length = 3
                               # composed by integer values

set c a:{44 "hello" 0 5.8}    ;# array of length = 4

set d b:{1 2 3}               ;# typed-array of integers of length = 3
                               # with values = {1 2 3}
```

- Lists

  In this case, TyCL tries to follow Tcl's way of handling lists of values, the only difference is that the parser doesn't imply/convert lists automatically, they have to be explicitly declared as such, like:

```
set w list:{a b c {1 2 3} d e}      ;# without the explicit cast
                                     # to a list, 'w' would have
                                     # been handled as string
```

- Groups

  Groups are really typed-valued-lists, they can increase or decrease their size dynamically but only can hold values of the same declared type. As typed-arrays, a definition of a *group* must exist before its values can be accessed of modified.

  Following is an example of a group called: '*a*', defined by items of type *float* and another group defined by the group '*a*' composed by the values: *2.1* , *0* , *5.4*

```
set a group:float        ;# group definition composed by
                          # values of type: float

set b a:{2.1 0 5.4}      ;# a group of floats
```

- Structs

  Corresponds to a collection of values with fixed types and order, and that uses an specific amount of memory (just as the C-language define them). Again, an *struct* definition must be present before it can be accessed later on.

  An *struct* definition is composed by a list of item declarations of the form: *TYPE:ITEM_NAME* , where to each item is given a type. So, in order to create an *struct* definition for, say a rectangle, one could write something like:

```
set rectangle struct:{
      float:h            ;# height component, type = float
      float:w            ;# width component, type = float
      integer:color      ;# color, defined as an integer
}

set r1 rectangle:{12.3 9.65 255}    ;# r1 = rectangle struct
```

- Unions

  Unions, also present in the C-language, are basically structs whose values share the same physical space, thus having a footprint defined by the value whose type uses the most amount of memory.

Their syntax is exactly as *struct*, for example:

```
set data union:{
      integer:i
      float:f
      boolean:b
}
```

The variable: *data* can hold values of type *integer*, *float* or *boolean* when its items: *i*, *f* and *b* are accessed.

- **Functions/Procedures**

Besides the previous data and structural types, functions have their own type also and are treated like any other typed-value referenced directly by a name within a variable or indirectly when they are created right on the spot where they are needed (anonymous functions). Regular functions (named functions) are created/declared as in Tcl using the command: *proc* like:

```
proc add {a b} {
      return [expr $a + $b]
}
```

and anonymous functions are created by the same command but without the name, for example:

```
set add [proc {a b} {
      return [expr $a + $b]
}]
```

both declarations actually do the same thing except that for the second one, the variable '*add*' could be changed later in the program while the first one not, the variable is bound to that function and only its body can change.

The function's parameters (including its return value) could be value-typed also by following the same syntax that *structs* and *unions* have for their members, mixed with the current Tcl's way of declaring parameters. Using the previous function *add*, one could write a complete typed function as:

```
proc add {integer:* integer:a integer:b} {
      return [expr $a + $b]
}
```

The special parameter '*' actually refers to the return type of the function. If by any chance a *return* call tries to pass a value with a different expected type, an exception should be thrown. For parameters that have a default value, Tcl's syntax is used, in this case, for our add function, the complete example would be like:

```
proc add {integer:* {integer:a 0} {integer:b 0}} {
      return [expr $a + $b]
}
```

where the value '*0*' is the default value for parameters *a* and *b*.

Finally, in order to allow principally anonymous functions to call themselves (recursion) the special function name: '*self*' was added to the syntax, which refers to the function being executed (named or anonymous).

- **Function arguments**

  Normally, Tcl passes arguments as values (as opposed to by reference) into functions. TyCL continues with this practice but only for the basic types: integer, float, boolean, char and reference, all the rest of types are passed by reference, which means that they can be modified by the function's body when it is executed. The only way to avoid this behavior is to create a copy of the data that is going to be passed by using one of the following commands:

  - copy: creates a new value by copying the first layer of data from the source. As an example:

```
set a list: {1 2 list:{x y z} 3}
set b [copy $a]    ;# b = {1 2 {x y z} 3}
                    # {x y z} refers to the same list for a and b
```

  - clone: creates a new value by copying all data from the source. Again, as an example:

```
set a list: {1 2 list:{x y z} 3}
set b [clone $a]  ;# b = {1 2 {x y z} 3}
                    # {x y z} is a different list from a's
```

- **The object-oriented system**

  TyCL includes a native object-oriented system based on prototypes rather than classes. The base type for this kind of data is the type: *object*, which builds the objects as a collection of named-variables implemented as hash-maps within a hash-table. When a

member is needed, first is searched inside the object's hash-table, if the member is not found then is searched inside its prototype (if the object has a prototype) and so long until there is no prototype to follow. When a new member is added, such member is inserted into the object's hash-table without following its prototype.
Objects are composed by members of two kinds: variables and methods. Variables are declared as:

VARIABLE_NAME VALUE ;# for regular variables
TYPE:VARIABLE_NAME VALUE ;# for typed-variables

and methods are declared as:

~METHOD_NAME PARAMETERS BODY

the character: '~' at the beginning of the method's name indicates that the member is going to be a method instead of a variable, also sets the member as function-typed, which means that only its body can be changed later on but not its general description (parameters and return type). There is another way of declaring methods with the difference that methods described in this way can be changed for anything after its declaration, they even can become variables, such syntax is:

METHOD_NAME [proc PARAMETERS BODY] ;# by using an anonymous function

The syntax for creating/declaring an object is like the following example, where an object: *square* is created with 4 members (3 variables and 1 method/function):

```
set square object:{
      color "red"              ;# a regular variable
      float:width 12           ;# this is a typed-variable
      float:height 9           ;# another typed-variable
      ~area {} {               ;# this is a method
            return [expr $my.width * $my.height]
      }
}
```

After the object is created, new members can be added into the object, variables are added by using the commands: *set* or *define,* and methods are created using the command: *proc*, for example:

```
set square.outline false       ;# a new variable: outline was added

proc square.maxside {} {       ;# new method: maxside
      if {$my.width > $my.height} {
            return $my.width
      }
      return $my.height
}
```

In case that the program would like to modify the square object, it could do so by applying the modifications directly into the square object or by creating a new one and having *square* be its prototype, in this last case, the code could be like:

```
set mysquare object:{
      prototype $square

      ~area {{magnification 1.0}} {
            set a [next]
            return [expr $a * $magnification]
      }
}
```

Now we have a new object: *mysquare* whose prototype is the previous: *square* and its method: *area* has been extended to handle a *magnification* value to be multiplied to the calculated total area, which is actually computed by the *area* method owned by the *square* object (called by using the command: *next*)

- **Scope and accessing variables, fields, function and methods**

  Currently, Tcl has few variable's scopes, there is global (variables defined at the root level in the stack and accessed via the *global* command inside functions), local (accessed directly inside functions and namespaces) and namespace's scopes (accessed directly or by providing its namespace path). TyCL supports the global and local scopes but not namespaces yet, however the syntax to reference such variables is a bit different.

  - Local variables
    In this case TyCL follows exactly what Tcl does, it supports local variables inside any functional block (functions and methods) and they are accessed by the variable's names like Tcl does.

  - Global variables
    These variables, as previously mentioned, are variables created at the root of the calling stack, TyCL has its own way to reference this variables from any part of the program without using the command: *global* (as Tcl does) but by using a different way to write their names at the moment where their data is needed, more exactly: by prefixing the name with a dot (.), thus, any access to a variable that starts with a dot means that TyCL has to search for that particular variable in the global scope, for example:

```
set a 4              ;# global variable

proc foo {x} {
      set .a $x      ;# the global 'a' is accessed
}
```

```
foo 99          ;# actually: 'a' is set to the value: 99
```

- Object's members

  As objects have their own set of members (variables and methods), they can be accessed by joining the object's name and the variable's name with a dot (.) and by following the previous rules if the object is a global object or a local one. If the access to a member is present inside one of its own methods, a new prefix: 'my' must be used to indicate that such member is present inside itself.

  So, as an example, the following code creates an object *'a'* with a method *count* that shows how many times this method have been called:

```
set a object:{
      x 0
      ~count {} {
            incr my.x 1                     ;# access to a.x
            puts "call number: $my.x"       ;# access to a.x
      }
}

a.count     ;# It should print: 'call number: 1'
a.count     ;# It should print: 'call number: 2'
```

- Struct's and union's fields

  Just like objects, the fields of any *struct* or *union* are referenced by following the same previous rules, thus for an *struct,* a short example could be like:

```
set point struct:{
      float:x
      float:y
}

set point.x 88          ;# access to point's field: x
set point.y 314         ;# access to point's field: w
```

- **Indexes and Ranges**

A new syntax was created to handle indexes an ranges for data-types that support them, which account for all except *objects* and *structs.* Their syntax is:

VARIABLE_NAME(INDEX) ;# for indexes
VARIABLE_NAME(INITIAL_INDEX .. FINAL_INDEX) ;# for ranges

their functionality is conditioned by the data-type of the operated variable as:

- Integers: gets or sets particular bits.
- Floats: gets or sets particular bits.
- Boolean: gets or sets bits, but the complete values is stored always as 0 or 1.
- Chars: gets or sets particular bits.
- Strings: gets or sets particular characters.
- Arrays: gets or sets particular values.
- Lists: gets or sets particular values.
- Groups: gets or sets particular values.

Additionally to its general use, indexes can also be used to insert, append or remove items within a variable's content (although not all data-types support this behavior) by using the following syntax:

*set VARIABLE_NAME(*INDEX) VALUE* ;# inserts the value before index
set VARIABLE_NAME(INDEX) VALUE* ;# inserts the value after the index

if the index is -1, it references the las item in the content, thus an append would be written as:

set VARIABLE_NAME(-1) VALUE* ;# this is an append

if the value is the *null* value, the operation is actually a remove operation.

The WordCode-Generator

As previously mentioned, the WC-Generator (WCG) takes the created TIR tree by the lexical-parser and converts it in a series of binary codes composed by chunks 32-bits wide each which contains TyCL's virtual machine opcodes, indexes to the literals table and inline values to name a few. The WordCodes are able to handle 0, 1 or 2 8-16-32-64-bit operands depending on the opcode's needs, thus the minimum size of a WordCode is 4-bytes (0,1 or 2 8-bit operands) and its maximum size is 20-bytes (2 64-bit operands). The format for each WordCode varies between opcodes but a generalization can be made as follows:

FULL OPCODE (32-bit)				**OPERAND** (32-bit)	**OPERAND** (32-bit)	**OPERAND** (32-bit)	**OPERAND** (32-bit)
OPCODE (12-bit)	OSIZE (4-bit)	L-OP (8-bit)	R-OP (8-bit)	optional	optional	optional	optional

Table 2. General description of a WordCode

Basically, a WordCode (WC) is composed of a full-opcode followed by 0, 1, 2, 3 or 4 32-bit operand values, depending on the actual opcode located at the highest 12-bits of the full-opcode and its 4-bit OSIZE field, which is composed by two 2-bit values that indicates each operand's current size like this:

L-OSIZE or R-OSIZE (2-bit)	**Operand's size (L-OSIZE referes to the left operand and R-OSIZE to the right operand)**
0 0	8-bits
0 1	16-bits
1 0	32-bits
1 1	64-bits

Table 3. Operand's size descriptor values

As it would be expected, there are some special WCs intended for jumps (including conditional jumps) that may use the OSIZE in conjunction with L-OP and R-OP to create a single 20-bit value.

The Virtual Machine (VM)

Like any other virtual machine, it walks through the WCs, decoding and executing each instruction and manipulating the variables and values, which at the moment are kept in memory with memory manager and a garbage-collector based on reference-counting[6], using the data structures described in figure 2.

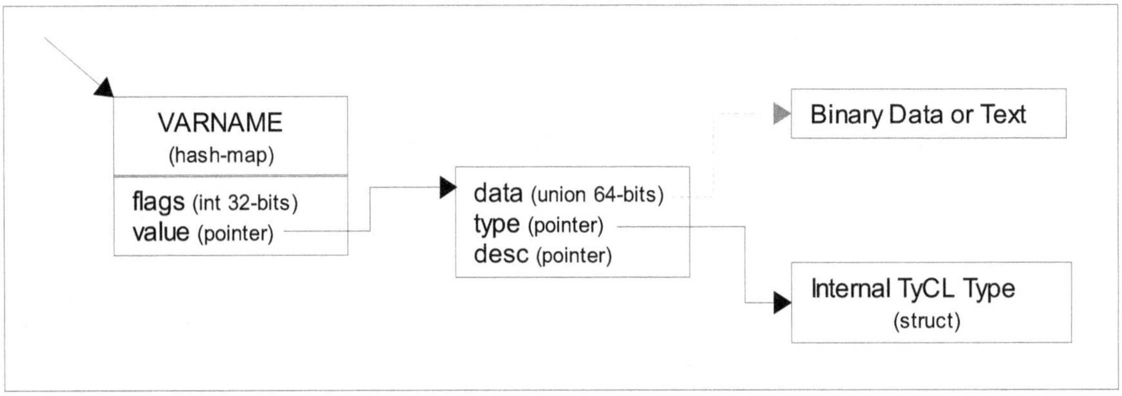

Figure 2. General diagram of the data structures for variables and values.

The Machine-Code-Generator

This stage, at the moment, just translates the WordCodes into machine-codes using a series of previously defined tables, almost like writing in native-code what the VM needs to do in order to process a particular WC. This solution is only temporal and was developed in this way in order to minimize the developing time of the initial iterations of the compiler.

Conclusion

Even though, writing a compiler for a very dynamic language like Tcl is a very difficult and time consuming task, its benefits surely pay for all the pain that one have to suffer in the process. The inclusion of types as first class-citizens into the syntax and the language in general, at the end, not only should help the compiler produce better results but helps the programmer also by providing a way to reduce bugs due to data-type collisions or invalid-values.

By having TyCL written in itself, it minimizes the dependencies on other components (like external compilers or linkers), avoids the need to handle two different languages (one for the coding of the compiler itself and the language that the compiler process) and allows to reuse any improvement made in the compiler on itself and on the applications it builds.

References

[1] Miguel Sofer, "NRE: the non-recursive engine in Tcl8.6", 15th Annual Tcl/Tk Conference, October 16, 2008

[2] Alan Kay, "The Computer Revolution hasn't happend yet", "12th Annual ACM SIGPLAN Conference on Object-Oriented Proramming Systems, Languages and Applications", October 5, 1997

[3] http://en.wikipedia.org/wiki/Bootstrapping_%28compilers%29

[4] Aho A., Lam M., Sethi R., Ullman J., "Compilers Principles, Techniques, & Tools", Pearson, Addison Wesley, 2nd Edition, 1987

[5] Steven Muchnick, "Advanced Compiler Design and Implementation", Morgan Kaufmann Publishers, 1997

[6] http://en.wikipedia.org/wiki/Reference_counting

Tcl 2011
Manassas, VA
October 24-28, 2011

Invited Talk

Tcl at the NSCL: a 30 (15?) year retrospective

Ron Fox and the Staff and Students of the National Superconducting Cyclotron Lab
Michigan State University

Abstract**—**The National Superconducting Cyclotron Laboratory (NSCL) is an NSF funded laboratory that performs basic nuclear physics research on nucleus-nucleus collisions innvolving systems that are far from stability. The operation of the NSCL has been funded by the National Science Foundation since 1980.

The NSCL has developed and used several Tcl based applications and tool. These tools are used by a broad community of researchers and accelerator technologiest This retrospective will examine the impact of presenting the NSCL staff with Tcl based tools and toolkits. A speculative look forward at the role of Tcl within the NSCL as it constructs the DOE funded Facility for Rare Isotope Research (FRIB)

I. Introduction

The National Superconducting Cyclotron Laboratory (NSCL) is an National Science Foundation (NSF) funded laboratory that conducts basic research in Nuclear Physics. Software based on and using Tcl have been used at the NSCL for a number of years. The purpose of this paper is to describe the ways in which Tcl has been and is now used at the NSCL. Tcl application case studies will also be provided where appropriate.

In December 2008, the Department of Energy (DOE) selected Michigan State University and the NSCL as the location of a new laboratory; the Facility for Rare Isotope Research (FRIB). FRIB is scheduled to begin operation around 2018. The potential application areas and barriers to the use of Tcl will be discussed as well.

The remainder of the paper will be organized as follows:

- The NSCL will be described with a layman's introduction to the motivation behind the research this done here.
- A brief overview of the FRIB project, its purpose, schedule and remaining administrative hurdles will be given.
- A historical perspective of the introduction of Tcl to the NSCL will then be described. Some speculative work in progress will be described.
- Taxonomy of the use of Tcl at the NSCL will be presented along with case studies illustrating each of the elements in this taxonomy.
- Conclusions about the use of Tcl in the past will be presented along with a bit of crystal ball gazing regarding the role of Tcl in the future of the NSCL/FRIB.

II. The NSCL and our Research

What is now the NSCL first started producing accelerated nuclei 1961 when it commissioned the K-50 cyclotron. In 1982 the NSF funded the construction of a K500 (500MeV/A) cyclotron, and later (1989) a K800 cyclotron which outperformed its design specifications and was therefore renamed the K1200. An n NSF grant in 2000 supported running a coupling line between the K500 and K1200 to improve primary beam intensity and to build a fragment separator which started the NSCL on its career as a radioactive beam facility.

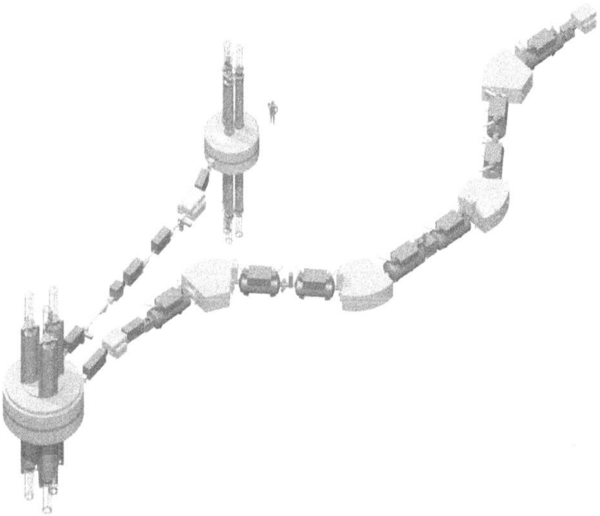

Figure 1 Schematic of the accelerator and separator

Figure 1 above shows a schematic of the beam production facility. An ECR ion source (not shown in the schematic) injects partially stripped ions into the K500 at the top center of the picture (a small grey human figure is provided for scale). Beam extracted from the K500 is transported along a coupling line to the K1200 where it is run through a foil that increases the ionic charge. The more fully stripped ions are injected into the K1200 (lower left). The K1200 beam is then extracted and is transported to a target at the entry of the A1900 fragment separator (running lower left to upper right). The fragment separator selects the desired secondary beam which is then transported to the experimental target.

Figure 2 shows a floor plan of the experimental part of the facility. Each experimental area (to the right of the A1900 fragment separator in the floor plan) has an experimental target as well as detector and electronics packages that are specialized for specific types of experiments and the apparatus in that area.

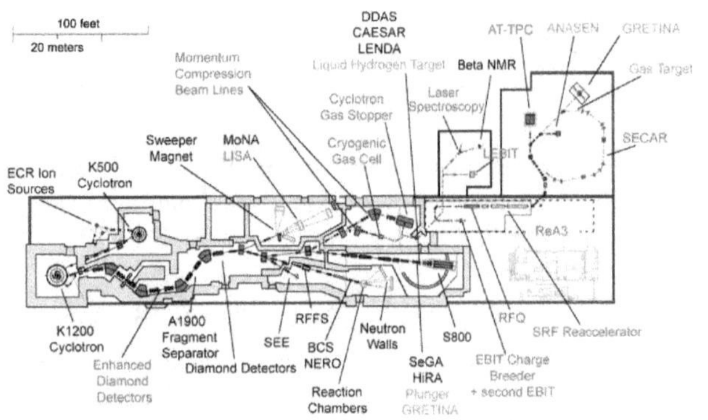

Figure 2 NSCL experimental area floor plan

A. Why do radioactive beam experiments.

In this section we present a brief motivation for the research done at the NSCL.

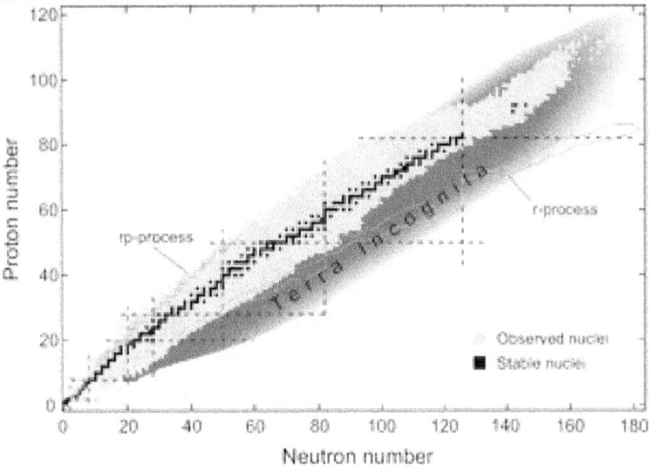

Figure 3 chart of the nuclei

Figure 3 above shows a chart of the nuclei. Each isotope consists of a fixed number of protons (**Z**) (which identify the element) and neutrons. The sum of the neutron and proton count is referred to as **A** which is roughly the nuclear mass. In figure 3 above, stable nuclei are in black. Those which are lighter or darker shades of grey are unstable.

There is a strong belief amongst astrophysicists that most of the heavy elements in the universe have been, and still are being created in nuclear reactions in stars, and that those processes involve decay chains with nuclei far from stability. The nuclei involved in the production of stable heavy elements are shown in Figure3 in the bands labeled *rp-process* and *r-process* as well as a band, not labeled that participate in the *p-process*. An understanding of the rates of these decays and, where several decays are possible, the *branching-ratios* between these decays is critical to an understanding of how the elements we now see were created and what their actual abundances are.

Collisions of heavy ions and unstable neutron rich nuclei create momentary nucleon densities that approach the densities and compositions of supernovae and even neutron stars. The number of nucleons present is already sufficient to help reach an understanding of the liquid-gas phase transition in nuclear matter as it occurs under these stressed conditions.

In short we can imagine the work done at the NSCL as bringing the heavens to earth, allowing us to study what happens in the interiors of stars that are, for now, only observable at a distance.

B. Stopped and Reaccelerated Beams

The technique used at the NSCL to create radioactive isotope beams is called *projectile fragmentation*. This is because we select from the remains of the projectile after it has interacted with the A1900 production target. This has the advantage that the secondary beam will have energies that are essentially those of the primary beam. The secondary beam can therefore be easily transported from the separator exit to the experimental target.

Projectile fragmentation requires beams of sufficient minimum energy. This minimum required energy arises, among other things, from the fact that in order to get two positively charged nuclei to interact, we must jam them close enough together that they overcome the electric repulsive force between them and come within the much shorter range of the nuclear strong force. For example with a primary beam of ^{16}O on a production target of ^{5}Be, a very light projectile on a typical production target, this coulomb barrier is already 20MeV. In practice we use much heavier projectiles and consequently we need higher energies to provide sufficient incident energy to create the desired isotopes. This is because the coulomb barrier goes up like the product of the number of protons in the two nuclei.

While the resulting energetic secondary beams are useful for a broad variety of experiments, there are still a large set of interesting experiments for which we would like to have lower secondary beam energies. The NSCL has developed several methods to stop these high energy beams (the most energetic are moving at about ½ the speed of light)! We have just finished commissioning a reaccelerating LINAC which will allow us to study radioactive isotopes at energies from a few hundreds of KeV to 5MeV.

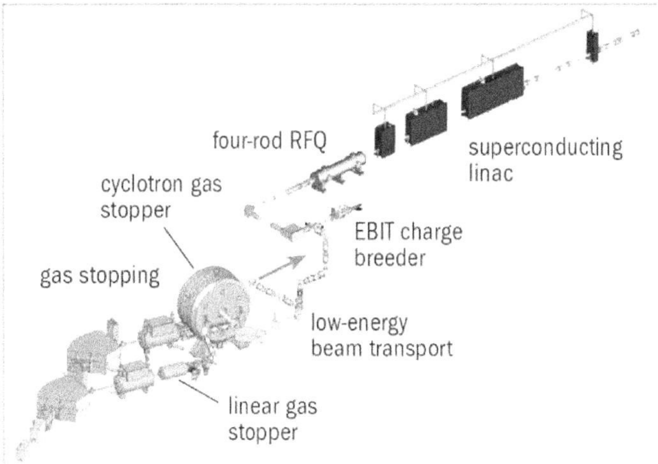

Figure 4 Producing low energy radioactive beams.

The reacceleration line is shown schematically in Figure 4. As most of the stopping techniques allow the ions to recombine with electrons the EBIT charge breeder shown in Figure 4 is required to restore a high charge state to the ions so that the LINAC can efficiently accelerate the resulting stopped beam. Reaccelerated beam experiments are scheduled to start in 2012.

III. Facility for Rare Isotope Beams

Many of the interesting isotopes shown in figure 3 are labeled as "Terra Incognita". This is because they have not been generated at sufficient intensities to allow experiments with them to be performed. This is unfortunate as the *r-process* is believed to take place in this neutron rich realm. The r-process is believed to have produced many of the heavy elements in the collapsing cores of supernovae. In the r-process, as the nuclear matter are compressed, the inner core becomes neutron rich and the nuclei in the less dense outer core can rapidly capture neutrons (r-process is an abbreviation of rapid neutron capture) resulting in very neutron rich, and short lived nuclei. These nuclei decay by sequential β^- decay which converts neutrons to protons, increasing the atomic number (Z) and moving these unstable nuclei step by step closer to the line of stability.

Once more the rates of these reactions, the half lives of these nuclei are important to an understanding of how stars work and how we wound up with the distribution of elements we have today.

To create these neutron rich elements close to the *neutron drip-line* requires higher intensity and higher energies than can be produced by the accelerator systems at the NSCL. To meet that research need, the Nuclear Science Advisory Council (NSAC), in a report presented to the DOE in August 2007, recommended that "DOE and NSF proceed with solicitation of proposals for a FRIB based on the 200MeV, 400kW superconducting heavy-ion driver linac at the earliest opportunity."[1]. In this passage FRIB is an acronym for a "Facility for Rare Isotope Beams" and is pronounced eff-rib.

As a result of a competitive proposal process, the DOE selected Michigan State University and the NSCL to construct this facility in 2008. "The Facility for Rare Isotope Beams (FRIB) will be a new national user facility for nuclear science, funded by the Department of Energy Office of Science (DOE-SC) Office of Nuclear Physics and operated by Michigan State University (MSU). FRIB will cost approximately $600 million to establish and take about a decade for MSU to design and build." [2]

Figure 5 shows the schedule for the construction of this facility. The milestones labeled CD-*n* are *critical decision* reviews. These are making or break reviews of the project progress. The NSCL has successfully passed the CD-1 review and is actively preparing for CD-2 at the time this paper has been written. CD-3 approves the start of the construction and CD-4 is a pre-startup approval.

Michigan State University as further committed funds to support an early start of conventional construction in 2012 approximately one year ahead of schedule.

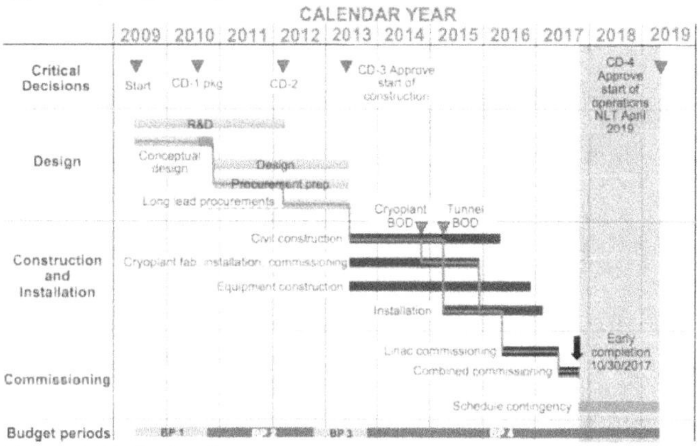

Figure 5 FRIB timeline.

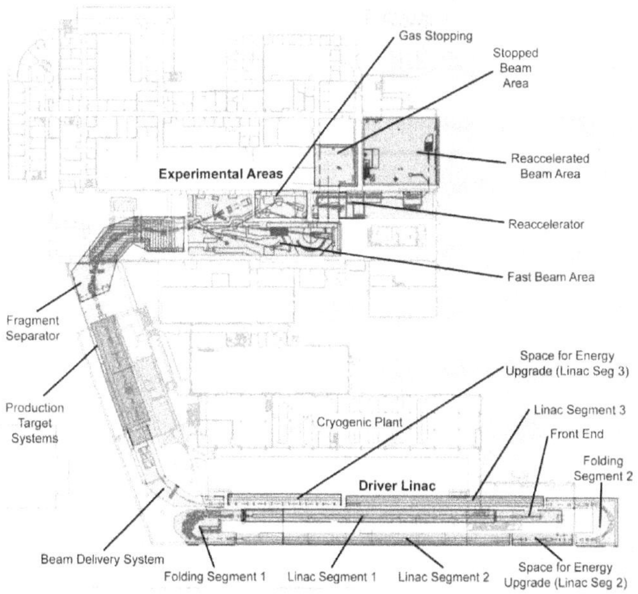

Figure 6 FRIB as planned.

Figure 6 shows the current plan for FRIB. The plan allows for a re-use of the experimental areas and much of the fragment separator, by placing a stacked multistage LINAC driver in a tunnel to the south of the current building. The plan also provides for a later upgrade to the LINAC energiesw by adding space for extensions to two of the planned LINAC segments.

The future looks bright for making the early completion date of late 2017 paving the way for physics runs to start in 2018.

IV. Tcl at the NSCL

A. *History of the First Adoption*

The first use of Tcl/Tk at the NSCL traces back to the commissioning of the S800 spectrograph. The S800 is used by over 50% of the experiments at the NSCL. The spectrograph is shown in figure 7 below:

Figure 7 S800 Spectrograph

For scale, note the three experimenters at the base of the spectrograph.

The S800 is usually run with two detector packages. The white box at the top of the S800 is the focal plane of the spectrograph and contains 2-d position sensitive detectors as well as particle Id detectors, and instrumentation to provide time of flight information through the spectrograph. The experiment target is located at the base of the spectrograph and is often surrounded by an experiment specific detector package.

In 1996 when the S800 was commissioned, the readout systems associated with the detector packages were not powerful enough to handle both packages while maintaining a reasonable dead time. Therefore it was decided to use a readout system for each of the detector packages and to do event building via a reflective memory system that connected the readout nodes.

The readout computers at that time were controlled by RS-232 ports that were connected to terminal servers. We needed a simple method to provide a control interface to users while sending duplicate commands to both systems.

In the previous year, the NSCL had hosted the IEEE 9'Th Biennial conference on Real-time Computer Applications in Nuclear, Particle and Plasma Physics (RT-95). At that conference, Gene Oleynik et al. presented a paper describing the run control system of the FNAL DART data acquisition system, a far more distributed system than required by NSCL experiments.

The DART team chose Tcl as the basis of an implementation of a group communication protocol inspired by the ISIS Distributed Toolkit [3]. They also chose to build user interfaces from Tk. From Oleynik's paper: "We chose TCL because of its extensible interpretive procedures. For graphics, we chose TK…our experience has been that interfaces can be built more quickly with TK than from X…or Motif…The ocp GUI…took on the order of ½-1 hour...We feel this is a big success of the TCL/TK approach."[4] (Capitalization of Tcl and Tk from that paper).

Based on this endorsement of Tcl/Tk and a similarity between the applications (the Readout systems could be thought of as a group containing two members and communication with them implemented as a group communication problem), the S800 run control software was implemented completely in Tcl/Tk. A low level group communication mechanism was built on top of the [socket] command, it was possible to specify an arbitrary number of target system for the group (S800 focal plane only experiments could then use the same software). A simple state machine was built to manage the system state diagram. On top of all of this Tk was used to build a GUI with which the experimenters interacted.

Our experience with using Tcl/Tk for this project was similar to that of the Fermilab group. The entire system came together in a matter of a day or so, including the time required to learn the few bits of the Tcl/Tk language needed to implement the software.

B. *Coupled Cyclotron Facility and adoption of Tcl/Tk.*

Wide-spread use of Tcl/Tk at the NSCL did not occur until the software development group was tasked with creating a new data acquisition and data analysis tools for the coupled cyclotron facility (proposed in 1994 funded in 1996 and commissioned in 2001).

The functional goals of this development project included:

- Breaking the NSCL's dependency on proprietary software (specifically VMS and Tru64).
- Providing better accessibility to the software in the readout computers (which up until now had been embedded computing systems with a very minimal operating system).
- Providing near turnkey online analysis solutions with a high degree of flexibility with a low accessibility threshold to researchers that were not trained computer professionals.
- Provide a high degree of extensibility and customizability for all these systems.

We had as an additional goal to introduce the researchers at the NSCL to modern (at the time) programming techniques.

The data Acquisition system was largely implemented in C++, introducing object oriented techniques to the researchers which, at the time, were largely a FORTRAN speaking community. Each piece of software that required user interaction embedded a Tcl interpreter with an extended set of commands to control the functions of that program. This philosophy is in keeping with Ousterhout's original motivation for developing Tcl as described in the Preface to [5].

A block diagram of the data acquisition system as it is typically used is shown below in figure 8. Components that embed a Tcl interpreter or that are entirely written in Tcl are indicated.

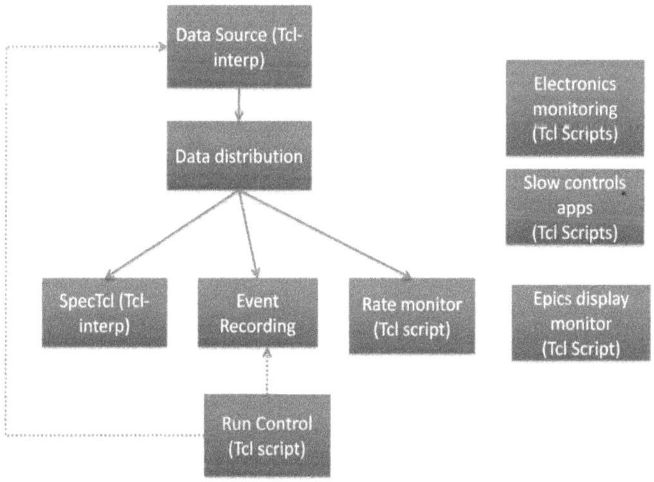

Figure 8 Structure of NSCLDAQ.

The solid arrows represent the flow of event data while the dotted lines represent control flow. Tcl is involved in all but two of the nine boxes in figure 8, and in the case of the boxes to the right of the figure, each box may represent more than one program used by the experiment.

The system was ready for use two years ahead of schedule, in 1999 as evidenced by a description of the data acquisition system and the analysis program SpecTcl in two NSCL 1999 Annual report articles. The gain from using Tcl is best described by a quote from one of those articles: "Components we provide are often used in ways we did not anticipate. This is a good thing. We intend to use the Tcl/Tk scripting language as a base command language for all components of the system. This allows us to support run-time extensions of the functionality of the software and its user interface via Tcl/Tk scripting. It also allows support for compile time extensions of the command set via C++ wrapper classes around the Tcl command registration procedures. Tcl/Tk scripting provides a common basis for automating tasks within the data acquisition system. The Tk component provides powerful GUI creation and modification tools available to all interactive components" [6].

V. How Tcl and Tk are used at the NSCL.

Tcl and Tk are used in the following ways at the NSCL:

- An embedded command language for applications.
- To provide application specific languages and configuration languages.
- To provide enabling components on which pure Tcl/Tk scripts can be built.
- As a scripting language for applications.

The remainder of this section will provide case studies and references to the uses of Tcl/Tk described above.

A. Tcl/Tk as an embedded command language.

Embedding Tcl/Tk and application specific extensions as the command language for an application was the original intent of Tcl. Using Tcl in this way provides several free benefits:

- Common flavor of command language across all applications.
- Ability of application users to automate commonly performed operations as Tcl scripts and [proc]s.
- Ability, via the Tk package facility to provide a GUI front end to the application and for the users of the application to either extend or replace this GUI with one more suited to their use of the application.
- Ability via a well defined internal API and the [package require] command to provide a plug-in architecture that provides for extensions to the application base functionality, and the ability to selectively add these plug-ins at run-time.

The flagship Tcl/Tk application at the NSCL is nsclSpecTcl [8] the online/offline event analysis/histogramming application. Users have extended it in many ways that were not originally foreseen in the design including the replacement of its visualization package with a Tcl/Tk client called SpecTk [9]. Both SpecTcl and SpecTk were described in earlier Tcl conferences.

B. Application specific languages and configuration

Applications that operate in this way use Tcl and extensions to steer the way they operate. The normal pattern of usage is that sometime during the execution of a program, a Tcl interpreter is created and possibly extended. A script is sourced into the interpreter and used to build data structures that define how the program will operate.

The readout software for the focal plane of the A1900 fragment separator uses this technique in its simplest form. A configuration file that consist of a bunch of Tcl [set] commands provide values to Tcl variables that are examined by the C++ level software and used to instantiate readout objects for the various detector packages that can live in the A1900 focal plane.

Taking this to its logical extension, [10] describes using Tcl as a basis for a domain specific language that describes and configures the digitizer devices used in a nuclear physics experiment. The Readout software uses scripts in this language to initialize and configure the described modules and to construct the operations required to read out those modules in response to an event trigger.

The experiment configuration script is also processed NSCLSpecTcl selecting the set of event processors required to process raw events into parameters, and to turn those parameters into an initial set of raw spectra. This technique brings Tcl's high level of abstraction into the domain of defining an experiment leading to what the experimenter believes to be 'programming free' experimental setups.

Figure 9 shows an actual segment of a configuration script used to describe the readout of the Particles And Non-Destructive Analysis (PANDA) detection system used by the Finish nuclear safety organization (STUK)[20]:

```
madc create dsssd1.x -base 0x40000000 -id 4 -ipl 0
madc config dsssd1.x -gatemode common -gategenerator
disabled
madc config dsssd1.x -inputrange 8v
madc config dsssd1.x -timestamp on -timingsource vme \
                     –timingdivisor $madcTimeDivisor
madc config dsssd1.x -thresholds $thresholds(dsssd1.x)
stack create event
stack config event -trigger nim1
stack config event -modules [list fadc
stack config event -delay 40
set     adcChannels(dsssd1.x) $xstrips
lappend adcChannels(dsssd1.x) timestamp
```

Figure 9 Sample Experiment configuration

C. Enabling components and their applications

An enabling component usually takes the form of a Tcl loadable package. The package is normally written by the software development group and provides access to some facility that is not easily accessed by Tcl itself. Researchers use these packages to write pure Tcl scripts to perform operations that they would otherwise find difficult.

While several packages have been written that could be classified as enabling components (including plug-in for nsclSpecTcl), this section will focus on the capabilities and application of two of them, Vme and epics.

1) Vme package

Many hardware components in experiments run at the NSCL are VME cards. VME bus started out as a multi-master computer bus and is now an ANSI/IEEE standard (ANSI/IEEE 1014-1987). As used at the NSCL, however, this bus is largely an instrumentation bus, providing power and data transfer to a host system for experimental electronics.

The Vme package provides access to this backplane from Tcl scripts. The package itself was described in [11]. It provides a mechanism for declaring interest in address windows within the VME and performing simple pokes and peek operations within those windows.

Researchers typically use this package to build graphical user interfaces to control devices that are not in the primary event data flow. Figure 10 below is a screen shot from one of these applications, the discriminator control program for the CAEsium iodide Detector Array (CAESAR) [12]:

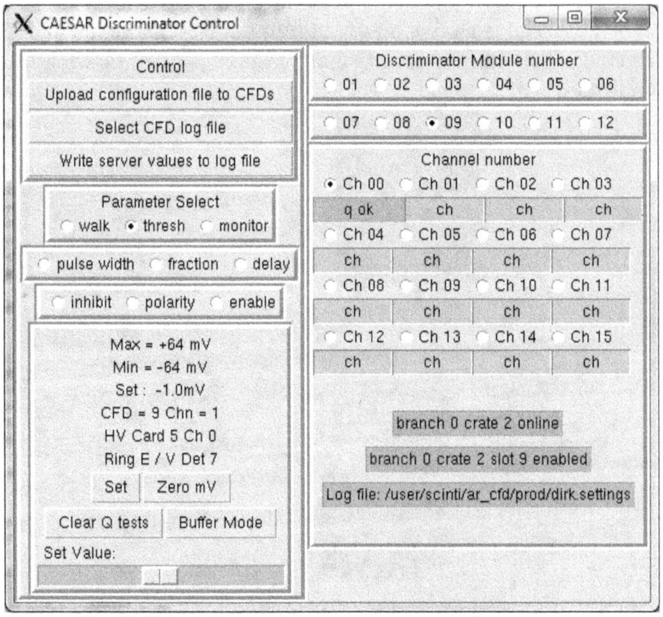

Figure 10 CAESAR discriminator control panel.

This application was written by Andrew Ratkiewicz and NSCL nuclear physics graduate student.

2) Epics Tcl package

The Experimental Physics and Industrial Control System [13] (EPICS) is a control system in common use at accelerator labs. EPICS is used to control accelerators and also to provide control over some experimental devices. For example, the S800 magnets are all controlled via EPICS.

For some experiments it is critical to be able to know the state of the beam line leading up to the experiment or the state of the experimental devices themselves. Furthermore, accelerators tend to be one-of-a-kind devices and when commissioning them it is not always clear what human operator interface is actually required. The Epics Tcl package was built to address these needs. It enables physicists accelerator physicists and operators to rapidly build monitor and control interfaces via Tcl/Tk as well as via snit epics specialized mega widgets that are provided with the package.

The package itself was presented at Tcl 2007[14]. It provides mechanisms to access EPICS channels (called Process Variables in EPICS nomenclature), to bind them to variables and to bind traces to them. A feature of the EPICS package that supports programming in the large is the ability for a one-to-many binding of process variable to Tcl variables, along with application wide process variable coalescence. This allows the programmer to specify an Epics channel, and link variables to it without being concerned about whether the execution trace of the program has already linked to the same process variable elsewhere. Changes in the underlying process variable update all linked variables. Changes in any one linked variable set the corresponding Epics process variable eventually triggering and update of all process variables.

The Epics package played a key role in the debugging and commissioning of the ReA3 re-accelerator. Two accelerator operators build the entire control and monitoring console for ReA3 as a set of Tk applications build on the Epics package.

Figure 11 below shows a screen shot the ReA3 beam line monitor application.

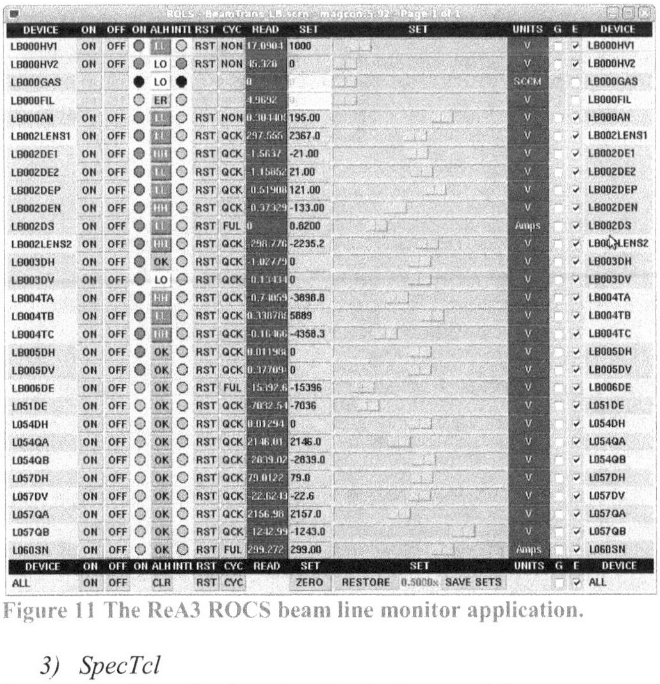

Figure 11 The ReA3 ROCS beam line monitor application.

3) SpecTcl

SpecTcl itself can be thought of as both an enabling technology and an application. Daniel Bazin has implemented a commonly used graphical user interface front end on top of SpecTcl. This front end is shown below in Figure 12:

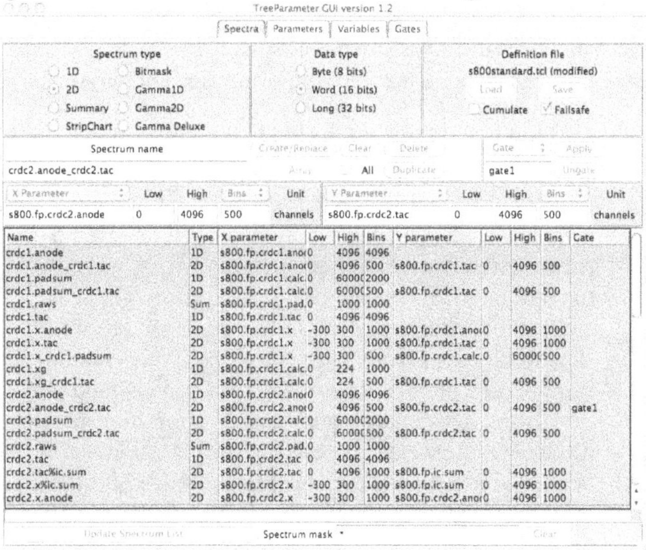

Figure 12 SpecTcl GUI front end

Many other experimental groups have leveraged SpecTcl, and Tk to produce control panels of their own that select data sources or steer the analysis performed by their experiment dependent code.

D. Pure Tcl uses

Tcl and especially Tk are also used as a language to write complete applications. One very successful application is an access controlled 'TclServer'. This is simply a Tcl script that accepts connections from a well defined set of client and accepts Tcl commands over a socket from them. The server is often used in conjunction with a Tcl script that manages a pool of server ports and serves as a directory for those ports enabling clients to discover the ports on which various applications are listening for connections.

VI. Conclusions and a Look Forward

To date, it is safe to say that Tcl/Tk have removed a great deal of the programming load from the software development group at the NSCL. That load has been transferred to end user community by a mixture of tool and application building. An educational program to teach the basics of Tcl to the first generation of graduate students was also useful as knowledge tends to be passed down from one generation of graduate students to the next.

The transfer of programming load from a software development group to the user community is only possible in a community that has a relatively high technical level. The NSCL research staff fit that profile. In our community the end users were actually grateful for the empowerment that Tcl/Tk and the tools we wrote provided. It allowed them to quickly iterate between versions of user interfaces to see what worked best for their application needs. If we had been involved in each iteration of every application, I can only imagine the frustration that would set in. In the end it is likely that model f development would have led to a willingness to settle for sub-optimal solutions.

This empowerment has some cost as well:

- Bad code can be written in any language and physicists are renowned for their ability to demonstrate this fact. This has led to a number of Tcl applications that are essentially un-maintainable even by the group that wrote it. This also results from the rapid cycling of generations of graduate students who are often tasked to develop support code for research groups.
- In addition to knowledge being passed from graduate student to graduate student, folklore is passed as well. This folklore is usually based on a poorly understood solution to a problem that was not well understood in the first place. It can take a great deal of effort to dispel the folklore and associated rituals that spring up around it.
- While the users generally develop user interfaces that meet their needs, they do so by learning the minimum needed to do this. This means that:
    - Interfaces might benefit from the use of widgets the users are not familiar with.
    - There are no user interface standards between or even within groups. That results in having to learn each application from scratch rather than being able to start with knowledge gained from the use of other applications.

The use of Tcl in the nuclear physics community has been largely driven by the widespread adoption of NSCLSpecTcl by the NSCL user community. As such it is appropriate to look in to the future to try to understand what the data acquisition and analysis environment might be at FRIB.

As users have become more comfortable with object oriented techniques, they have also adopted object oriented tools.

- Root[15], developed by R. Brun at al. at CERN for LHC experiments is gaining increasing popularity for late stage data analysis amongst all users in the nuclear physics community.
- Python [16] is also gaining in importance as a scripting language in the community.
- Finally with the advent of good Java implementations of the Abstract Interfaces for Data Analysis (AIDA) [17], physicists are also increasingly turning to Java and its large (though sometimes cumbersome) set of libraries.

If Tcl/Tk is to compete it must meet several challenges:

- One or more OO toolkits must be sold effectively to break the impression that Tcl is only an imperative language.
- Software groups that support nuclear physicists must be encouraged to forge interfaces between Tcl and existing software such as Root and AIDA based applications such as the Java Analysis Studio (JAS) [18], or the Python based Hippo Draw [19]. Jacl and Swank may be of some use in the AIDA front and a set of effective Tcl bindings to Root would help there.
- The benefits of the simplicity of the Tcl language and the speed with which that simplicity enables development must be actively sold.
- The fact that Tcl is an 'old' language needs to be placed in context. C is still a highly used language, however it dates from 1969-1973 while Tcl originally emerged in 1988.

In conclusion, I believe that Tcl has provided a great deal of benefit to the nuclear physics community. If, however it is to continue to be of use to that community there are several significant challenges and hurdles that must be overcome.

VII. References

[1] **Report to the NSAC of the Rare-Isotope Beam Task Force** August 20, 2007 available online at http://science.energy.gov/~/media/np/nsac/pdf/docs/nsacrib_finalreport082007_dj.pdf

[2] http://frib.msu.edu

[3] Reliable Distributed Computing with the ISIS Toolkit Birman, VanRenesse Wiley 1994 ISBN: 978-0-8186-5342-1

[4] **Fermilab DART Run Control** G. Oleynik et al. *IEEE Trans Nucl. Sci* NS43 No. 1 February 1996 pp 20-24.

[5] Tcl and the Tk Toolkit J. Ousterhout Addison-Wesley 1994 ISBN 0-201-63337-X pg xvii

[6] *Development status and deployment of the next generation NSCL Data Acquisition System* R. Fox, E. Kasten NSCL 1999 Annual report available online at http://groups.nscl.msu.edu/nscl_library/pub/annual_reports/1999/fox_deployment.pdf

[7] *Status of the SpecTcl Data Analysis Package* R. Fox, C. Bolen, J. Rickard NSCL 1999 Annual report available online at http://groups.nscl.msu.edu/nscl_library/pub/annual_reports/1999/fox_spectcl.pdf

[8] *NSCLSpecTcl Meeting the Needs of Preliminary Nuclear Physics Data Analysis* R. Fox, C. Bolen, K. Orji, J. Venema Presented at Tcl 2004 available online at : http://www.tcl.tk/community/tcl2004/Papers/RonFox/fox.pdf

[9] *SpecTk: a displayer for SpecTcl – or how even a physicist can build a high level application with Tcl/Tk* D. Bazin Presented at Tcl 2005 available online at: http://www.tcl.tk/community/tcl2005/abstracts/scienceandTech/SpecTk.pdf

[10] *A Domain Specific Language for defining Nuclear Physics Experiments* Ron Fox 15'Th Annual Tcl Association Conference Proceedings October 2008 pp105-111

[11] *The Vme Package at the NSCL; Large leverage from a Small Extension* R. Fox presented at Tcl 2007 and available online at http://www.tcl.tk/community/tcl2007/papers/Ron_Fox/vmepackage.pdf

[12] *CAESAR – A high-efficiency CsI(Na) scintillator array for in-beam γ-ray spectroscopy with fast rare-isotope beams* D Weisshaar, A Gade, T Glasmacher, G F Grinyer, D Bazin, P Adrich, T Baugher, J M Cook, C A Diget, S McDaniel, A Ratkiewicz, K P Siwek, K A Walsh **Nuclear Instruments and Methods in Physics Research Section A: Accelerators, Spectrometers, Detectors and Associated Equipment** (2010) Volume: 624, Issue: 3, Pages: 615-623

[13]*Experimental Physics and Industrial Control System* ANL introduction at http://www.aps.anl.gov/epics/about.php

[14] *Tcl/Tk Tools for EPICS Control Systems* R. Fox presented at Tcl 2007 available on line at:
http://www.tcl.tk/community/tcl2007/proceedings/Gui/epics.pdf
[15] http://root.cern.ch
[16] http://www.python.org
[17] http://aida.freehep.org
[18] http://jas.freehep.org/jas3
[19] http://www.slac.stanford.edu/grp/ek/hippodraw/index.html
[20]PANDA – A novel instrument for non-destructive sample analysis J. Turunen, K. Parajarvi, R. Pollanen, H. Toivonen
Nuclear Instruments and Methods in Physics Research Section A: Accelerators, Spectrometers, Detectors and Associated Equipment
V 613, No. 1, 21 January 2010, Pages 177-183

Tcl 2011
Manassas, VA
October 24-28, 2011

Applications I

A CMake-Based Cross Platform Build System for Tcl/Tk

Clifford Yapp
Quantum Research International Inc.
Prepared under contract W911QX-06-F-0057 for the U.S. Army Research Laboratory*

October 6, 2011

Abstract

Defining build logic for a large software package in multiple software development environments entails a large up-front implementation cost and an ongoing maintenance burden. CMake is an open source cross–platform build tool that allows developers to define relatively abstract build logic that is automatically translated into a variety of build system formats, reducing the burden of supporting multiple development environments. BRL-CAD's integration of Tcl/Tk as a sub-build motivated the development of Tcl/Tk build logic compatible with BRL-CAD's new CMake logic. This paper presents a new CMake based build system for Tcl/Tk and a number of popular Tcl/Tk extensions.

Introduction

Large scale software projects require the development and maintenance of *build logic* governing the compilation, packaging, and installation source code. This logic is the interface between compilation tools (compilers, documentation processors, etc.) that actually translate code into usable form and the code itself. As such, it is the build logic that must identify any idiosyncrasies present in the system's compilation tools and libraries. Once identification is complete, the build system must also generate instructions the compiler can use to compensate for these differences. Over the years, each major software development platform has created systems to manage this process. Microsoft Windows has Visual Studio, Mac OS X has XCode, and most Unix/Linux style platforms have some form of Make, often augmented by GNU Autotools. Each of these tools manages this process for different versions of their specific platform, but generally support *only* that specific platform. This presents a challenge for cross–platform projects such as Tcl/Tk, which must build in *all* of these environments to achieve their goals.

The responsibilities of the build logic include (but are not limited to) listing source files, identifying compilation tools and options needed for files, identifying target libraries and executables, and sometimes expressing the logic for generating user-installable packages of the finished package. While specific compilation instructions are typically unique to each operating system and tool, the actual *task* to be accomplished is often the same. For example, when building a C library, many if not all of the C files themselves are common to all platforms. Despite this commonality, the addition of a single new C file requires altering not one but n build files where n is the number of build systems that need to be defined in order to support all targeted development platforms.

CMake[3] is a *metabuild* system designed to alleviate much of this problem by abstracting build logic one level above makefiles, XCode projects, and Visual Studio projects. Given portable source code, the build logic is expressed in a CMakeLists.txt file that gets translated by CMake into platform native logic using *generators*. The developer then uses the standard system tools to complete the build, and logic common to all platforms is expressed (and need only be updated) in a single set of build files.

Tcl/Tk faces precisely this cross-platform development problem, making the project a good conceptual match for CMake. However, until now Tcl/Tk's

*Approved for public release; distribution is unlimited.

existing build systems have proved adequate for most real-world production use. The marginal benefits of CMake were insufficient to justify both the effort of re-implementing Tcl/Tk's build system and the disruption of existing work-flows. Given these constraints, it is understandable that a cross–platform CMake build had not already been implemented for Tcl/Tk.[1]

Motivation and Requirements

BRL-CAD[1] is an open source Computer Aided Design software package developed by the Ballistic Research Laboratory (now the U.S. Army Research Laboratory.) BRL-CAD has made extensive use of Tcl/Tk since the earliest days of its development. Because so many of BRL-CAD's core abilities depend on Tcl/Tk, availability of Tcl/Tk on a targeted platform is a core requirement for deploying BRL-CAD on that platform. BRL-CAD has a long-standing policy: if system versions of required libraries are either absent or insufficiently modern at configuration time, the BRL-CAD build will utilize local copies of those libraries. As part of comprehensive configuration control, testing and dependency management, BRL-CAD bundles pre–configured copies of all external dependencies. In addition, it has occasionally been necessary to modify such libraries (Tcl among them) to support BRL-CAD's needs or fix bugs encountered. Modifications are contributed back upstream to the primary development teams when possible. It is much simpler to use upstream sources than to maintain a separate version of the source code. However, BRL-CAD deployment cannot wait on those fixes propagating through both the upstream acceptance and customer system upgrade processes. Moreover, the BRL-CAD developers need to be able to verify and validate BRL-CAD functionality for a given configuration that is independent of any platform environment. Consequently, BRL-CAD *must* be able to compile its own local copy of Tcl/Tk at need.

Tcl/Tk has supported multiple platforms for many years, but it currently uses the Tcl Extension Architecture (TEA) autoconf macro system on platforms using Make and either NMake or Visual Studio (MSVC) project files for native[2] Windows compilation. This presented a difficulty for the BRL-CAD project in that neither of these systems integrated well with BRL-CAD's own build systems. As a workaround, BRL-CAD used custom Microsoft Visual Studio files on Windows. On other platforms Tcl/Tk's own build system was usable with a Makefile.am wrapper. This approach worked but represented an undesirable ongoing maintenance overhead.

In the summer of 2010, the decision was made to unify BRL-CAD's build system infrastructure into a single CMake–based system in order to reduce long term maintenance costs and simplify building Windows releases. As most of BRL-CAD's core developers do not use Windows on a day–to–day basis for development, a single cross platform build system would mean build logic written or updated on non-Windows platforms would stand a good chance of working without extensive effort. However, to achieve the desired result the new system would have to build not just BRL-CAD but *all* of its bundled dependencies – including Tcl/Tk.

The initial attempt to integrate Tcl/Tk into a CMake-based BRL-CAD build made use of CMake's ExternalProject_Add functionality for triggering external build systems as sub-builds. Had this worked smoothly on all platforms, it would have been the simplest solution. With Make–based systems, the attempt was reasonably successful despite the drawback of *requiring* installation of the sub-build libraries before the CMake build itself could proceed. MSVC proved to be a considerably greater challenge – between difficulties integrating Visual Studio project files and the problems involved with running NMake build scripts from within Visual Studio, the initial attempts to integrate Tcl/Tk's own Windows build files were not successful. Rather than continue to struggle with the complexity of triggering multiple external build systems on multiple platforms, focus shifted to the integrated approach – implementing enough CMake logic to build the parts of Tcl/Tk needed for BRL-CAD. Implementing CMake build logic for Tcl/Tk would reduce the maintenance burden to a single system for all platforms and integrate well with BRL-CAD's new build logic.

A CMake-based build system for Tcl/Tk needs to satisfy the following requirements:

1. Build Tcl/Tk successfully on Windows (using MSVC), Linux, FreeBSD, Solaris, and Mac OS X from a single set of CMake build files.

2. Implement enough of the Tcl/Tk–specific compilation macro logic in CMake to support build-

[1] Twylite's Coffee project uses CMake to build Tcl, but is primarily focused on Windows: see http://dev.crypt.co.za/coffee

[2] "Native" in this case being defined as building without the use of Unix compatibility environments such as Cygwin.

ing Tcl/Tk on BRL-CAD's target platforms – the goal was to avoid significantly altering the Tcl/Tk source code itself.

3. Run tclsh and wish from within the build directory, without requiring installation. This is a necessity for BRL-CAD, which makes use of Tcl in its own build logic and must run tclsh prior to the installation step.

4. Support compilation of Tcl/Tk extensions, either in conjunction with BRL-CAD's own copy of Tcl/Tk or using a system Tcl/Tk. BRL-CAD sometimes needs to compile Tcl/Tk extensions even if a system Tcl/Tk satisfies the feature and version requirements, hence build logic for those extensions needs to support both cases.

Building Tcl/Tk – What It Takes

CMake provides very general mechanisms for expressing build logic, but still requires that any project-specific compiler options be included by the developer. It also requires that specific functionality tests for libraries, header checks, function checks, etc. be set up in the CMakeLists.txt file(s) according to the needs of the particular software in question. Hence, the first step in writing new build logic for Tcl/Tk was to examine the existing build logic to determine what functionality it provides.

Tcl Extension Architecture – Strong TEA

The venerable TEA system[4] implements a large number of tests designed to identify platform specific issues and quirks that may affect Tcl when trying to build. It also defines standard layouts, platform specific compiler flags, and a wide variety of other settings evolved over many years. It utilizes autoconf from the GNU Autotools suite.

There are two versions of this logic – one in Tcl/Tk proper whose macros use a SC_ prefix (SC standing for Scriptics) and an extended version using the TEA_ prefix used with extensions. Both files are named tcl.m4, and a comparison of the two reveals a great deal of shared code, but the tcl.m4 with TEA prefixes is regarded as the "official" TEA. System functionality tests (such as missing POSIX headers) required for compilation were of primary interest to a CMake effort. Detection of installed Tcl/Tk configurations is the responsibility of the FindTCL.cmake macro – that being the case, it was not necessary to translate TEA macros pertaining to Tcl/Tk configuration detection into the primary CMake build logic.

Because platforms such as HPUX, IRIX, and SCO Unix are no longer supported by BRL-CAD, logic specific to supporting them was not needed in the first–cut implementation of CMake logic. Hence, the decision was made to only implement as much of TEA's functionality as was needed for BRL-CAD's target platforms rather than attempting a full TEA implementation in CMake from the get–go.

Visual Studio, NMake, and MSYS/MinGW

Microsoft Windows–based software compilation is accomplished using a wide variety of development environments, some of which bear little resemblance to the standard Unix tools. One of the most common tools for building software on Windows is Visual Studio's Integrated Development Environment. Visual Studio also provides a command line utility called "nmake" which is similar in spirit to the Unix style Make. The open source community has produced compilation environments for Windows, notably GNU gcc within the Cygwin Unix emulation environment and the MinGW environment (often used with MSYS) which can produce native Windows binaries. Tcl's README indicates that the Cygwin environment is *not* supported – MinGW/MSYS and Visual C++ 6.0 + nmake.exe are the standard tools.

Visual C++ compiler flags have little in common with those supported by most open source C/C++ compilers, and there is not really a direct MSVC analog to the Autotools *configure* step. Feature detection on Windows is generally restricted to Unix-style emulation environments such as Cygwin. The introduction of CMake allowed for many new possibilities in that respect when building on Windows.

The Structure of Tcl/Tk – Separate But Intertwined

The first survey of the Tcl/Tk building system prompted the question "why not just generate a tcl_config.h header file to hold all of these options, instead of building up definitions on the command line?" A small trial quickly demonstrated that there is indeed a reason for the current Tcl/Tk approach. Tk makes use of "internal" Tcl headers. In order to build Tk, it is necessary to specify the location of a Tcl source archive. These internal Tcl headers in turn need proper definitions from the configuration logic. However, when building Tk, a hypothetical *Tcl* generated tcl_config.h header is not guaranteed to be present. If the Tk and Tcl builds are treated as separate systems, Tk would have to re-generate the *Tcl* configuration header in addition to its own and sort out how Tk headers might pull in *either* or *both* tcl_config.h and tk_config.h. Under the circumstances, it is simpler just to supply any needed definitions via command line arguments to the compiler – these are passed through to all headers as needed.

Unfortunately, this use of "internal" headers is also a fact of life in several common third party Tcl/Tk packages. Tcl/Tk 8.6 is introducing a new pkgs directory to help address this problem, but that only avoids the issue by allowing sub-build logic to assume a fixed parent location for source files. Another approach, used by the Visualization ToolKit (VTK), is to include local copies of various versions of the Tcl/Tk internal headers with the package source itself. Regardless of the approach used, it complicates the building (and build logic) of Tcl/Tk extensions.

Beyond straight C compilation, Tcl/Tk extensions also require pkgIndex.tcl files that instruct Tcl/Tk how to load that particular extension. This is of particular concern to BRL-CAD, because experience has shown it is all too easy to create confusing and dysfunctional situations when multiple Tcl/Tk installations are present. If Tcl's *auto_path* variable happens to be set in such a way that a local Tcl/Tk finds packages in a system Tcl/Tk installation, the results can be "almost working" runs of Tcl scripts that fail in cryptic and mysterious ways.

The CMake Build System

A full introduction to CMake is beyond the scope of this paper – for a more complete overview see Martin and Hoffman[2]. The focus here will be on differences between the TEA build system and CMake, as well as CMake solutions to particularly tricky compilation and installation issues.

Running CMake

Building Tcl/Tk with CMake is similar to the TEA build cycle, but the command line syntax and configuration options are somewhat different – see Table 1 for a mapping between TEA options and CMake.[3]

CMake itself can be run one of three ways – either as a straight command line program (cmake), with a curses based interface (ccmake), or with a graphical interfaces based on the Qt toolkit (cmake-gui). To specify settings on the command line, the prefix "-D" is used – e.g. -DCMAKE_INSTALL_PREFIX="prefix" instead of –prefix="prefix". All three front ends support the same basic abilities, although the Qt graphical interface in particular supports some nice extra features that help a new developer discover the system. When using the graphical or curses–based interfaces instead of the command line, *configuration* (detecting system characteristics) and *generation* (actual writing of the build files) are separate operations. The command line cmake binary combines both of these steps into one operation.

Layout

The basic source code layout of Tcl/Tk has not been altered, but the location of the CMake files relative to the source files *is* different than the corresponding TEA/win32 files. While the unix subdirectory contains the bulk of the TEA logic and the win subdirectory contains Windows specific build files, the primary CMakeLists.txt file that specifies sources for all platforms lives in the top level directory. The library and doc subdirectories have their own CMakeLists.txt files due to the specialized nature of the logic they require (more on this later,) but all C source code is handled by the top-level CMakeLists.txt file.

Macros defining CMake logic specific to Tcl/Tk are in a new top-level directory called CMake, in keeping with standard CMake conventions. Among the files present here is tcl.cmake, which is the closest match in the CMake logic to the original SC prefix tcl.m4 file.

For convenience, the current Tcl/Tk 8.6b2 CMake logic is organized with one higher top-level directory above Tcl/Tk and other extensions for which CMake build logic has been implemented. A small CMakeLists.txt file in this directory suffices to unify all of the subdirectories (tcl, tk and any extensions) into a single build. Among other benefits, this combines all configure stages for all of the packages into a single configure step – once a particular test is run for a particular subdirectory, CMake does not need to repeat

[3]With CMake, it is generally much better practice to run the configuration and building routines in a working directory *other* than the top-level source directory – either a subdirectory in the source tree or a directory entirely outside the source tree. For examples in this paper, a subdirectory named "build" located in the top-level source directory will be assumed.

Table 1: Configuration Options – TEA vs. CMake

Feature	TEA	CMake
Run configuration	../configure	cmake ..
Specify location of sources	–srcdir="DIR"	"DIR"
Installation prefix	–prefix=	CMAKE_INSTALL_PREFIX
Executable prefix	–exec-prefix="EPREFIX"	Not Implemented
Symlinks for manpages	–enable-man-symlinks	Not Implemented
Compress manpages	–enable-man-compression	Not Implemented
Add suffix to manpages	–enable-man-suffix=STRING	Not Implemented
Enable Threads	–enable-threads (off)	TCL_THREADS (AUTO)
Build Shared Libraries	–enable-shared (on)	BUILD_SHARED_LIBRARIES (ON)
Enable 64 Bit support	–enable-64bit (off)	TCL_ENABLE_64BIT (AUTO)
Disable rpath support	–disable-rpath (on)	N/A
Use CoreFoundation (OSX)	–enable-corefoundation (on)	TCL_ENABLE_COREFOUNDATION (ON)
Allow dynamic loading	–enable-load (on)	TCL_ENABLE_LOAD (ON)
Debugging Symbols	–enable-symbols (off)	Several CMake options
Use nl_langinfo	–enable-langinfo	TCL_ENABLE_LANGINFO (ON)
Enable "unload" command	–enable-dll-unloading	TCL_ENABLE_DLL_UNLOADING (ON)
Enable DTrace support	–enable-dtrace (off)	Not Implemented
Package as frameworks (OSX)	–enable-framework (off)	Not Implemented
Specify encoding	–with-encoding (iso8859-1)	TCL_CFGVAL_ENCODING (Defaults to cp1252 on Windows, else iso8859-1)
Install timezone data	–with-tzdata (autodetect)	TCL_TIMEZONE_DATA (AUTO)
Use Aqua windowingsystem (OSX)	–enable-aqua (no)	TK_ENABLE_AQUA (AUTO)
Use XScreenSaver	–enable-xss (on)	TK_ENABLE_XSS (AUTO)
Use freetype/fontconfig/xft	–enable-xft (on)	TK_ENABLE_XFT (AUTO)
Specify tcl source directory	–with-tcl=	TCL_SRC_PREFIX TCL_BIN_PREFIX
Use X11	–with-x	(auto)

it for the next. This painless integration of sub–builds is an important feature for BRL-CAD, and will hopefully prove a useful convenience for other developers.

Running from the Build Directory

One convenience offered by CMake is sophisticated control over the handling of run–time search paths (RPATH). With the correct options set, CMake's generated build files will set RPATH values to the correct values for build directory execution when compiling executables, and then automatically adjust them to the correct *installation* values when "make install" is run. This means developers do not even have to set LD_LIBRARY_PATH to run from the build directory, and using built-but-not-installed software within the build process itself becomes simpler.

Tcl/Tk has an additional complication beyond standard RPATH issues – pkgIndex.tcl files have to be correct for build paths in the build directory and install paths in the installation directory. The CMake solution implemented for this problem is to generate *two* pkgIndex.tcl files – one in the correct place relative to the build path locations of Tcl/Tk's files, and the other in a non-functional (within the build directory) location with the instructions to install *that* version when the time comes for installation. See Figure 1 for an example of the CMake code that achieves this for the Tk package.

Man Pages

Tcl and Tk use a shell script named installManPage to generate a large number of manual pages from a base set that are present in the Tcl/Tk doc subdirectory. This poses something of a problem in that CMake does not know ahead of time what files this script will generate, and thus cannot incorporate those generated files into its own install commands. One option would be to list explicitly every file generated by the installManPage script in the CMake logic, but this would be both extremely verbose and a maintenance burden. The solution currently in place runs the installManPage script during the configure stage and has CMake itself identify all the files generated. CMake is then aware of the full file list and can generate proper installation commands. The most significant drawback of this approach is that man page changes impacting the list of generated files require re-running CMake instead of simply re-running the build logic, but that appears to be the price that must be paid in order to allow CMake to perform installa-

```
# pkgIndex.tcl - installation location
get_target_property(TK_LIBLOCATION tk LOCATION_${CMAKE_BUILD_TYPE})
get_filename_component(TK_LIBNAME ${TK_LIBLOCATION} NAME)
file(WRITE ${CMAKE_CURRENT_BINARY_DIR}/pkgIndex.tcl
    "package ifneeded Tk ${TK_PATCH_LEVEL}
        [list load [file join $dir .. .. ${LIB_DIR} ${TK_LIBNAME}] Tk]")
install(FILES ${CMAKE_CURRENT_BINARY_DIR}/pkgIndex.tcl DESTINATION lib/tk${TK_PATCH_LEVEL})

# pkgIndex.tcl - build directory location
FILE(WRITE ${CMAKE_LIBRARY_OUTPUT_DIRECTORY}/tk${TK_PATCH_LEVEL}/pkgIndex.tcl
    "package ifneeded Tk ${TK_PATCH_LEVEL}
        [list load [file join $dir ${CMAKE_LIBRARY_OUTPUT_DIRECTORY} ${TK_LIBNAME}] Tk]")
```

Figure 1: Example CMake pkgIndex.tcl generation logic

tion of the manual pages. BRL-CAD needs CMake to manage these generated files to ensure they are incorporated in binary packages, and the current approach meets that requirement. The routines only generate the pages if sh and sed are present, so the MSVC build does not use them.

Package Installation

Tcl includes a number of scripts that are installed in lib/tcl8, with subdirectories and file names based on the scripts themselves – for example, http/http.tcl is installed to lib/tcl8/8.4/http-2.7.5.tm in Tcl 8.5 and lib/tcl8/8.6/http-2.8.2.tm in Tcl 8.6. This location and naming appears to be based on the package version number and required Tcl/Tk version in the script itself. Initially the destination for each file was hard–coded in the library CMakeLists.txt file, but this proved problematic moving from Tcl 8.5 to Tcl 8.6. Current logic uses CMake's regular expression facilities and parses the required information from the tcl scripts themselves. This macro places all tcl8 script files correctly based on their own contents.

SC / TEA Macros

Most of the time spent in converting Tcl/Tk's build logic to CMake involved studying the macros in tcl.m4 and determining how to express their logic in CMake. After a few false starts a systematic approach proved necessary – a tcl.cmake file was organized along the same lines as tcl.m4, and whenever a test from tcl.m4 proved necessary the corresponding functionality was implemented in tcl.cmake. As of the time of this writing all SC tcl.m4 macros have not been implemented (see Table 2) but enough of them exist to successfully build on BRL-CAD's target platforms and more will be implemented if needed. Some of the TEA functionality (in particular, identifying Tcl configurations) has been expressed elsewhere in the new CMake build.

Dependent Options

Another feature available in CMake is a type of option that is displayed or not displayed based on values assigned to other options - a *dependent* option. Tk's CMake build logic makes use of this feature for features requiring the presence of X11 - the CMake GUI will not list those options for the user if the current windowing system is Win32 or Aqua. The Xft option is actually conditional on multiple variables - the Tk windowing system must be X11 and both xft and Freetype need to be found for TK_ENABLE_XFT to be displayed as an option. The code that achieves this is displayed in Figure 2.

Tcl/Tk Extensions

CMake uses pre–package routines, typically in files named according to the FindPKG.cmake template, and the *find_package* command to locate system installations of packages and libraries. CMake includes a FindTCL.cmake, but it proved insufficient for BRL-CAD. This necessitated the implementation of a new version, which has been submitted for upstream inclusion in CMake. Its distinct features include:

1. Detection of the windowing system in use by the found Tcl/Tk version (Aqua, X11, etc.). This is particularly important on Mac OS X.

2. Successful detection of a second system installation of Tcl/Tk if the first fails to satisfy specified criteria – for example, if X11 is required on OS X, the system Tcl/Tk framework will fail but an X11 version (if installed) will be found instead.

```
include(CMakeDependentOption)
CMAKE_DEPENDENT_OPTION(TK_ENABLE_XFT "Use freetype/fontconfig/xft" ON
                       "TK_SYSTEM_GRAPHICS STREQUAL x11;FREETYPE_FOUND;${X11_Xft_FOUND}" OFF)
```

Figure 2: Dependent Xft option definition in Tk.

3. Finer control of what is needed from a Tcl/Tk installation – for example, if Tcl without Tk is sufficient for a particular project, an option can be defined to indicate that to FindTCL.

BRL-CAD requires not just Tcl/Tk but a host of Tcl/Tk extensions and all of those extensions needed CMake logic of their own. For the most part routines already defined for Tcl/Tk in combination with the new FindTCL.cmake proved sufficient for both local and system Tcl/Tk extension compilation scenarios, but there were a few significant exceptions.

The use of internal Tcl headers remains a significant complication for compilation of Tcl/Tk extensions, and a system installation of Tcl/Tk is not sufficient in such cases – the Tcl source code must be available, just as in the case of Tk. In the case of BRL-CAD this situation is usually workable due to the Tcl source code being guaranteed to be available in BRL-CAD's own source tree. Currently BRL-CAD requires Tcl/Tk 8.5, but in order to support more general cases (such as using an 8.6 system Tcl/Tk) extensions need more than the Tcl/Tk 8.5 headers. Rather than accept that limitation, experiments are underway using a solution from the VTK codebase. Local copies of various versions of the internal headers are included in the extension's own source tree. The new FindTCL.cmake identifies the system Tcl/Tk version numbers and the correct internal headers are included from the extension's own source tree. This avoids requiring the developer to locate and download source trees that match the installed Tcl/Tk. Use of such local copies runs the risk of crashes if the system Tcl/Tk should happen to have modifications not compatible with the standard headers, but the same problem exists when downloading the Tcl/Tk sources themselves. The only sure solution is to build a local copy of Tcl/Tk as well, which defeats the purpose of using a system Tcl/Tk installation. Including the internal headers does increase the size of the extension source trees somewhat (approximately 2.4 megabytes, uncompressed,) but it is a relatively clean solution to an otherwise thorny configuration management problem.

Longer term, it would be ideal if extensions were no longer required to use non-public APIs to extend Tcl/Tk (or were rewritten to not use them if they don't really *need* to.) Working with the situation as it exists today header inclusion appears to be the most flexible and functional option available.

Extensions currently built with CMake in BRL-CAD include tkhtml, tktable, togl, incrTcl, iwidgets, and tkpng.

Results

Except for the lengthening of Tcl's configure step due to the inclusion of installManPage processing in the CMake configuration, the time needed for configuration and compilation is within ten percent when comparing a TEA based build and a CMake based build. The performance numbers below were generated on a Gentoo Linux machine with an AMD Athlon II X2 245 Processor. All builds are single core (e.g. make with no -j flag).

Operation	TEA (sec)	CMake (sec)
Tcl Configure	6.3	8.4
Tcl Build	48.2	50.5
Tk Configure	2.8	4.0
Tk Build	35.8	38.7
Total Time	93.1	101.6

In addition to matching TEA's compilation performance, CMake has successfully generated working Tcl/Tk build logic on Windows (MSVC), Mac OS X, FreeBSD, Linux, and Solaris (using gcc.) Generators used successfully so far include Visual Studio 8, Visual Studio 10, Unix Makefiles and XCode. There are a number of other possible generators to test, include Eclipse, KDevelop3, NMake Makefiles and MinGW Makefile. Clean integration with BRL-CAD's own logic simplifies cross–platform BRL-CAD development, and the new system has already replaced BRL-CAD's earlier Windows compilation logic in production use.

It is difficult to compare the size and complexity of build systems – the following table reports the line counts for Tcl's autoconf[4], Windows[5] and CMake[6] build systems. This is a raw number (without attempting to filter comments) and it should be noted again that the CMake build does not claim to implement all features of the TEA system.

Autoconf	Windows	CMake
7111	5746	4342

The initial implementation of a working Tcl/Tk build with CMake consumed about 12 man-weeks of effort, although the work was actually performed part-time over the course of one year. Initial efforts used the modified Tcl/Tk 8.5.9 codebase present in BRL-CAD's source tree. Subsequent work has focused on the latest 8.6 beta release. The initial 8.5 to 8.6 conversion of the CMake build system involved a few hours for the initial effort, and a couple of days for subsequent clean-up work in preparation for this paper.

Conclusions and Future Work

The Tcl/Tk CMake build is already the production method of BRL-CAD's Tcl/Tk compilation on Windows, and is being phased in on all other supported platforms. Based on experience accumulated thus far, building Tcl/Tk with CMake represents a fast, effective, low maintenance, and cross–platform solution. It is expected that the new system will reduce BRL-CAD's long term maintenance costs, particularly when it comes to supporting seamless portability to Windows.

The largest remaining task is to finish surveying the TEA build options and identify any tests or settings in the current CMake logic that are inconsistent with Tcl/Tk's Autotools build system. Other remaining items include general clean-up and addition of CPack logic to generate source tarballs, Linux RPM, Mac OS X pkg and Windows NSIS installers. Currently the build does not support running from the build directory when multiple configurations such as those used in MSVC and XCode (Debug, Release, etc.) are present – it may be desirable to generalize existing routines to support such configurations.

The BRL-CAD project will be maintaining and enhancing this new build system as part of its ongoing development, and invites other Tcl/Tk users and developers to build on what has been accomplished to date.

References

[1] BRL-CAD Development Team, BRL-CAD – an Open Source Solid Modeling System, http://brlcad.org

[2] Martin, K. and B. Hoffman, Mastering CMake: A Cross-Platform Build System , Kitware Inc., 2003

[3] Kitware, Inc., CMake - Cross Platform Makefile Generator, http://www.cmake.org

[4] Welch, B. and M. Thomas, "The Tcl Extension Architecture" *7th USENIX Tcl/Tk Conference*, Austin, TX, Feb. 14-18 2000.

[4] In the unix subdirectory – .in files and .m4 files

[5] In the win subdirectory: buildall.vc.bat makefile.bc makefile.vc rules.vc tcl.dsp tcl.dsw Makefile.in configure.in aclocal.m4

[6] Contents of CMake + CMakelists.txt files + FindTCL.cmake

Table 2: Mapping of TEA macros to CMake

SC Macros	TEA Macros	CMake Macros
SC_PATH_TCLCONFIG	TEA_PATH_TCLCONFIG	
SC_PATH_TKCONFIG	TEA_PATH_TKCONFIG	
SC_LOAD_TCLCONFIG	TEA_LOAD_TCLCONFIG	(part of FindTCL.cmake)
SC_LOAD_TKCONFIG	TEA_LOAD_TKCONFIG	(part of FindTCL.cmake)
SC_PROG_TCLSH	TEA_PROG_TCLSH	(part of FindTCL.cmake)
SC_BUILD_TCLSH	TEA_PROG_WISH	(part of FindTCL.cmake)
SC_ENABLE_SHARED	TEA_ENABLE_SHARED	
SC_ENABLE_FRAMEWORK		
SC_ENABLE_THREADS	TEA_ENABLE_THREADS	SC_ENABLE_THREADS
SC_ENABLE_SYMBOLS	TEA_ENABLE_SYMBOLS	
SC_ENABLE_LANGINFO	TEA_ENABLE_LANGINFO	SC_ENABLE_LANGINFO
SC_CONFIG_MANPAGES		
SC_CONFIG_SYSTEM	TEA_CONFIG_SYSTEM	
SC_CONFIG_CFLAGS	TEA_CONFIG_CFLAGS	
SC_SERIAL_PORT	TEA_SERIAL_PORT	SC_SERIAL_PORT
SC_MISSING_POSIX_HEADERS	TEA_MISSING_POSIX_HEADERS	SC_MISSING_POSIX_HEADERS
SC_PATH_X	TEA_PATH_X	(use FindX11.cmake)
	TEA_PATH_UNIX_X	(use FindX11.cmake)
SC_BLOCKING_STYLE	TEA_BLOCKING_STYLE	
SC_TIME_HANDLER	TEA_TIME_HANDLER	SC_TIME_HANDLER
SC_BUGGY_STRTOD	TEA_BUGGY_STRTOD	
SC_TCL_LINK_LIBS	TEA_TCL_LINK_LIBS	SC_TCL_LINK_LIBS
SC_TCL_EARLY_FLAG	TEA_TCL_EARLY_FLAG	
SC_TCL_EARLY_FLAGS	TEA_TCL_EARLY_FLAGS	
SC_TCL_64BIT_FLAGS	TEA_TCL_64BIT_FLAGS	SC_TCL_64BIT_FLAGS
SC_TCL_CFG_ENCODING		SC_TCL_CFG_ENCODING
SC_TCL_CHECK_BROKEN_FUNC		SC_TCL_CHECK_BROKEN_FUNC
SC_TCL_GETHOSTBYADDR_R		SC_TCL_GETHOSTBYADDR_R
SC_TCL_GETHOSTBYNAME_R		SC_TCL_GETHOSTBYNAME_R
SC_TCL_GETPWUID_R		SC_TCL_GETPWUID_R
SC_TCL_GETPWNAM_R		SC_TCL_GETPWNAM_R
SC_TCL_GETGRGID_R		SC_TCL_GETGRGID_R
SC_TCL_GETGRNAM_R		SC_TCL_GETGRNAM_R
SC_TCL_IPV6		SC_TCL_IPV6
	TEA_PREFIX	
	TEA_SETUP_COMPILER_CC	
	TEA_SETUP_COMPILER	
	TEA_MAKE_LIB	
	TEA_LIB_SPEC	
	TEA_PRIVATE_TCL_HEADERS	
	TEA_PUBLIC_TCL_HEADERS	
	TEA_PRIVATE_TK_HEADERS	
	TEA_PUBLIC_TK_HEADERS	
	TEA_PATH_CONFIG	
	TEA_LOAD_CONFIG	
	TEA_LOAD_CONFIG_LIB	
	TEA_EXPORT_CONFIG	
	TEA_PATH_CELIB	
	TEA_INIT	
	TEA_ADD_SOURCES	
	TEA_ADD_STUB_SOURCES	
	TEA_ADD_TCL_SOURCES	
	TEA_ADD_HEADERS	
	TEA_ADD_INCLUDES	
	TEA_ADD_LIBS	
	TEA_ADD_CFLAGS	
	TEA_ADD_CLEANFILES	

WyattERP: A Non-Sissy ERP Application Development Platform

Authors: Kyle Bateman Bret Barney

Development History

Original flat-file, command-line C programs

My partner and I started Action Target in 1986. The only computer I had access to at the time was a Wicat Systems 68000 with an operating system that was kind of a cross between VMS and Unix. It had a decent C compiler and supported any number of ASCII terminals. Having learned C pretty well in college, I was comfortable building any kind of simple application I needed. So as the business grew, I began tracking things like inventory and production runs in simple flat files with command-line driven programs to manipulate the data.

My idea of a database at the time was the Unix password file. However, I didn't really care for the colon as a field delimiter so I started using a pipe character since it didn't ever occur in my data. Eventually I had a whole suite of programs for dealing with various aspects of the business. I could track my customers, my employees and my vendors. I could also write A/P checks and payroll checks, and I had an accurate bank account balance and a pretty elegant purchasing system.

By about 1993, I was running into trouble with my hardware. Wicat had gone out of business and I literally had a shed full of their old computers to keep my systems running. But I could see that it wouldn't last forever and so I was looking for a more permanent platform I could migrate to. I was not at all impressed with the Microsoft platform and it was clear that a port to DOS would be a lot more work than a port to Unix. So I was getting ready to bite the bullet and buy SCO Unix when I first heard about Linux. I knew instantly it was for me and set forth to get my first system up and running.

I think it only took me a couple of weeks to get my whole system ported over to my first slackware box running a pre-1.0 kernel. My old command-line utilities worked very well on Linux. And with the help of a terminal server, my old Wicat computers became dumb terminals. And as they had problems or as I needed to scale, I could buy new Wyse terminals to keep me going.

Life was pretty good until I hit my next scaling hurdle. In about 1998, it was becoming clear that the business was growing out of my system. I had multiple salesman who wantied to be able to access customer files at the same time. My file locking prevented them from overwriting each other, but it also prevented simultaneous access of various parts of the data. In addition, there was increasing pressure to expand the system to include better accounting and more elaborate tracking of various processes in the business. People were also becoming more accustomed to graphical environments and it was getting harder and harder to get people to be productive with the command-line interfaces. I knew it was time to change again.

Up until that time, I had been of the opinion that "Any program worth anything could and should be written in C." My experience with interpreted languages was limited to Basic and Forth which I considered to be toys--certainly not for use in serious projects. I had heard of databases but didn't really know much about them. I had seen and used graphical programs, but it seemed like an unimaginably complex job to write one so I wasn't sure where to start.

My research on databases lead me to Postgresql. It seemed like the best choice for several reasons: It had early support for triggers, stored procedures and transactional integrity, and it had a good developer community and was working toward compliance with published standards. So I set forth to learn SQL and database architecture.

At the same time, I wanted to learn how to make GUI applications. My research on this lead me to Tcl/Tk. At that time, I didn't find much to compete with Tk for a graphical toolkit. Since it seemed to be inseparably linked to Tcl, I set forth to learn how to use this new (and strange) programming language.

I remember reading for several hours trying to figure out what in the heck a "widget" was. But eventually, it started coming together. And before long I had a simple customer database running with a Tcl/Tk front end and a Postgresql backend.

First pass

I eventually came to call this first attempt my "pass one" version. My Tcl (and SQL) programming was somewhat awkward at that point. For me, Tcl was just the language I had to use in order to get Tk--which is what I really needed to put my graphical widgets on the screen. But an interesting thing began to happen: The more I used Tcl, the more I began to understand the genius of its simplicity. Over time it became the language of choice for many type of tasks.

Specifically, I came to understand the benefits of an interpreted language. Previously I had put a lot of stock in the processing speed of a compiled C program. After all, isn't it better to have a program execute in 100 us, rather than 100 ms? Well, eventually I determined that it isn't always that important. Really, if the difficulty of the program development cycle gets reduced to the point that the application can come into existence at all, I don't really care how fast it executes as long as it is fast enough to keep my employees productive. I could buy faster computers. But I could only code so fast. And I had begun to see how much more I could do and how much faster I could turn it out in Tcl/Tk than I had been able to do in C. I recognized that it wasn't always pretty and not always something I could have readily sold to others. But it was doing the job for my company and we were beginning to see productivity benefits from the new programs.

Also a part of pass one was figuring out how to deal with the objects I was creating in the backend. In Postgres, it wasn't always easy to modify the database (at least for a beginner). And besides that, I just felt uneasy about the idea of issuing create commands and then later issuing alter commands to modify things in place. I didn't really trust the idea of the newly altered version of my database existing only inside the black box of Postgres. I had come from the world of C programming where there was source code, and there was object code. Source code was the authoritative description of the program. Object code was just an instantiation of the real program for this or that target machine. But the object code could be deleted at any time and re-created as needed from the authoritative source document.

Issuing alter commands to the database felt kind of like using a binary editor to change your compiled object code. What would be the point of that? The next time the program would be compiled, the changes would be lost. Dumping the altered schema from the database felt to me more like running a dis-assembler--reverse engineering at best. I wanted a way to author my schema outside of Postgres in an authoritative source document. And then I wanted to be able to instantiate that schema inside the database any time (and as many times as) I wanted.

That was the beginnings of what would eventually be called Wyseman (WyattERP Schema Manager). At that point, it was a collection of text files and shell scripts. The main concept was simple though: I created chunks of SQL code capable of creating (and destroying) each of the objects (tables, views, functions, etc.) I wanted in the database. Then, I recorded which objects were dependent upon which other objects. Using my scripts, I could then remove any object from the database, and rebuild it fresh from my source documents. If the object had other dependent objects, those objects could be included in the process as well. If the object list contained tables, the data from those tables would first be saved out to files. Then, once the fresh schema components had been created, the data would be imported back in.

Second pass

By the time I had a bare cores of modules running for the business, I had began to become disgusted with my own programming style. I had started to figure out how to make Tcl more modular and object oriented by using namespaces more effectively and by structuring my code better. I had begun to understand the concept of building up more complex GUI components (mega-widgets). And I was getting better with hiding complexity in libraries so my main program could become simpler and cleaner.

Pass two was my next step to implement these changes. Unfortunately, the new structure was totally incompatible with my pass one programs. But as I began to port each application to the new structure, most of my reusable code got tucked into a main library. And my applications got much shorter and cleaner. Often a fairly complex application like a customer contact manager could be expressed in about 150 lines of code. All the rest was now in a library--available for use by other applications.

I began to standardize the way my widgets and mega-widgets would operate. This was modeled after the way basic widgets behave in Tk itself. Each widget was implemented in its own namespace. Each one had a constructor. And when a new widget was instantiated using that constructor, it would always create a widget command for the new instance (a global command with the same name as the widget instance itself) which could be used to access all the functionality in the widget. Each new widget module had "class variables" and "instance variables" much like you would expect in a C++ object. But these were not managed by an OOP language--just by discipline and convention in the coding style.

Tk widgets allowed a suite of command line parameters and switches which could optionally be abbreviated. So I adopted this same structure in my widgets. I added a further extension of this concept which I called "Dynamic Lists." A dynamic list looks just like a set of command line arguments such as: "-switch1 value1 -switch2 value2 -switch3 value3" except in certain instances, some of the switches can be omitted from commonly used parameters such as: "value1 value2 value3" This way, common parameters could be given in a pre-determined order as shown above. Or all values could be prefixed with a named switch and then given in any order. Additionally, switches could be spacified more than once on the command line. For items that can only hold a single value, the last occurring switch on the line would take presidence. For some items, the system could collect and use all specified values.

Also using dynamic lists, my megawidgets could strip the values out of the command line that they wanted to use. All other switches could remain in argv and simply be passed down to subordinate widgets. So for example if I had a mega version of an entry widget that also included a label widget, my megawidget could strip off the command line information about how to build the label. But things like -background and -length (native to an entry) could just get passed down to the entry widget itself. This made the megawidget appear to inherit all the characteristics of the component widgets it used internally.

Another important part of pass two was the introduction of Wyseman. I had wrestled with the way I was managing my schema objects using text files and shell scripts. I liked the concept of maintaining an external and authoritative source document for the creation of the database schema. I dabbled with the idea of a completely GUI front-end for creating database objects, but it seemed like that had already been done in a number of different ways. I experimented with Filemaker for a time, but I found it very limiting. After all, I wasn't trying to make database design accessible for less experienced users. I was trying to bring better organization and management to potentially very complex schemas. I determined that an abstraction layer between me and the database would only limit the functionality I would be able to access in the abstraction layer. I needed something that would allow me to continue to access every obscure feature Postgresql was able to offer. And while helping with keeping my database objects documented and organized, I also wanted a way to hide the complexity of some of my more elaborate objects such as a macro processor.

Finally, I needed a data dictionary for my objects. In pass one, things like column titles and pop-up context helps were all over the place. I wanted to be able to create and document the objects one time and in one place and then relieve the application of the burden of supplying that information.

I really tried to not do Wyseman in Tcl. After all, I was starting to like Tcl--a lot. I was worried that I had just substituted one dogmatic approach (all programs should be written in C) for another new one (all programs should be written in Tcl). Having previously written a full-on macro language entirely in m4, I experimented with that. I re-considered doing it in C. I tried XML. I tried creating a database schema and storing my sql chunks inside tables in the database (cool from a purist point of view, but introduced a nasty bootstrap dilemma).

In the end, I came back home to Tcl. I determined that my dynamic list format was probably the best and cleanest structure for storing my schema data. The Tcl syntax turned out to be pretty good for storing SQL chunks. Once inside a set of literal quotes ({}) I could express pretty much anything SQL needed, without having to further quoting or escaping. I wrote a fairly simple macro scanner to look inside quoted SQL for escapes back into the TCL interpretor and viola! I had macro capacity.

The fact that I was writing in native Tcl and storing chunks of native SQL meant that I had preserved the full power of both languages. Instead of being limited to what I could express just in SQL, I could also write Tcl procedures capable of churning out etremely complex SQL objects (like views with long lists of columns and/or rules). I could hide the complexity and messyness of repetitive tasks (like implementing insert and update rules on views).

I did a one-time port of all my object descriptions into the new format, rebuilt the database from my new objects, and reimported my old data. It worked pretty much flawlessly. And I never turned back or regretted the decision to implement Wyseman in Tcl.

Third pass - Wylib

My borderline ADD never seemed to allow me to fully port all of my applications from one pass to the next. By the time I had finished porting about 80% of my applications to pass two, it was becoming obvious what I needed to do next. And I was more anxious to get onto it than to sit around porting really obsolete code to newly obsoleted code. I was ready for pass three.

I was starting to feel like my stuff might be good enough for other people to start using it. Grateful for what open source had done for me, I determined to release something under an open source license. I had already come up with the idea for the name WyattERP but then I found out that some AS400 people were already using it. But it looked like their project was slowing dying, so I kept the name and registered the domains myself.

I began by taking all my shared code from pass two and pulling out the parts that were specific to the ATI implementation. That core of the code became the central library, Wylib (WyattERP Library). Wylib includes wrappers for all the standard Tk widgets. It also includes all the standard mega widgets and support functions for making a WyattERP database application.

As I stripped out site dependent code, it had to go somewhere. So I came up with the idea of a site library. You can name your site library anything you want--just tell Wylib about it by setting the environment variable WYLIB_SITELIB and it will automatically get loaded if it exists. The site library can include any number of customizations to each of the standard modules in wylib. It can also include any other modules that the site designer needs that are specific to his implementation.

As I continued this porting process, it became obvious that there were some modules that didn't really fit into either Wylib or the site library. For example, we developed interfaces to the FedEx web site and to the asterisk phone server. While these were too application specific to really fit into Wylib, still they could be applicable to multiple sites. And so Waplib (WyattERP Application Library) was born.

I dutifully posted early versions of Wylib on the WyattERP website complete with some sample applications. But the demands of the business did not leave me with much time to maintain the distribution. There were many things about the ATI implementation that were proprietary to the business model and so could not really be open sourced without compromising ATI's competitive edge in its market. So I found that I really had to concentrate on keeping the ATI implementation moving forward and I wasn't able to keep the open source project and its sample applications current and useable. Because there wasn't much in the way of a useable schema design with the project, I think people couldn't really get the hang of it just by downloading the project. So although I left the project site up, I resigned myself to the fact that I would have to just concentrate on keeping our in-house code moving forward rather than devoting time to the open source project.

The next few years were very challenging for me at ATI. It was time to implement a fully GAAP compliant accounting model in the ERP. This took even more time and so any hope of devoting time to the open source project was delayed even further. But with effort, we were able to complete a fully functioning general ledger with most of the data coming from the standard operations modules.

Next, it became necessary to move the business into a new larger facility. I redesigned the way material management would work and implemented a full inventory control system using WyattERP. That took another year or two to get that fully up and running.

Fourth pass - In Process

As always, the ADD started kicking in again around the time pass three was getting close to completion (but never done). Again, it was time to implement lessons learned from past efforts. In pass three, I had wanted to make WyattERP move useable to other sites. Wylib was a good stab at this for the front-end. Wyseman was also fully functional for multiple sites. The main weakness, however had always been in the schema itself. Although I had released a run-time library for the front end, and a tool for managing the schema, my schema itself had always remained closed and proprietary.

By this time, my job duties at ATI were starting to taper off a little. I had also gradually diversified my holdings to include several other businesses to include a farm and a private loan company. Through the development of the accounting functions for ATI, I had learned a good deal of accounting. A lot of the lessons learned were after the fact, so there were a number of things I would have done differently. But I had not yet had the energy to create ERP's for these new businesses. And they were simple enough that I could track them pretty effectively in Gnucash.

But as time has gone by and they are getting more and more complex, I have been feeling more need to get them set up on a real ERP.

So one goal of pass four is to create an actual open source schema to go with Wylib and Wyseman. This is now called Wyselib (WyattERP Schema Library). It turns our that Wyseman is pretty good at selectively pulling multiple bits of SQL together from any number of sources. So the idea is to create a set of independent schema modules. Then the site author can pick which modules he can use "out of the box." And which ones he wants to do custom. In some cases, he might be able to use the standard modules and just add a few custom columns.

Ideally, Wyselib would evolve into a basic functioning schema to include all the basic functions of a simple business. For example: employee tracking, payroll, customer tracking, orders, material management, inventory, vendor tracking, purchase orders, and so forth.

My goal is to create a schema which I can use to run my current businesses--each one as a different site, but sharing all the code possible in both the front end and the back end. Ideally, I would like to incorporate all the lessons learned from the creation of the ATI schema (although many of the implementation details of ATI's business model will still remain proprietary).

Underlying Philosophy

As WyattERP evolved through its various stages of development, several philosophies slowly evolved. Some of these were based on my own beliefs about how to best run a business. Others had more to do with leveraging the strengths of Tcl, SQL and Linux. In many cases, the lessons were learned by first doing it the wrong way and then improving things in later iterations.

Small Main/Configuration File

In the early days of software development, it was not uncommon to distribute source code to the end user. Likely this was a necessity because no developer would be able to perfectly anticipate the varying needs of every end user. Inevitably, users would need to customize their software somehow to better server the unique needs of their business or institution.

But commercial developers didn't really like distributing their source code because it was too hard to maintain a competitive edge when you are showing everyone exactly how you do things in your code. So in order to facilitate closed source development and still maintain the ability to do a certain amount of customization, it became necessary to invent the "configuration file." In this context, I use the term "configuration file" to mean any sort of data or procedural code, modifyable by the end user, that an application might read at startup or while running to tell it how to behave with respect to the end-user's specific needs.

Often site configurations are maintained in a setup file. And the existence of a setup file implies the need for a specified syntax or language in which to express the setup. The existence of a language for the setup file implies the need for a parser to read and interpret the setup file. And the parser as well as the language itself needs to be thoughtfully constructed so that it gives the end user sufficient access to all the complexities of the application necessary to customize the application well enough for each diverse end user's needs.

Experienced programmers will recognize the fact that they often end up in the parser business in order to configure their applications. In fact, Tcl was invented for the very purpose of creating a standardized syntax for configuring applications. The idea was to create a small, portable parser which could be included inside any larger application. This way, the application could be configured with this Toolkit Configuration Language (TCL) and programmers could then concentrate on writing the rest of the application without having to invent a new syntax and parser each time.

The interesting thing is, in order to make a toolkit configuration language that could be used by any application for any purpose, it would certainly need to be powerful. Specifically, it would need to be "Turing Complete" or include conditionals, branching, internal variables and the like.

Essentially, it would need to be a complete programming language--which Tcl turned out to be.

Then, the programmer is faced with an interesting dilemma. Now that the configuration language is a complete programming language, and the end user can express arbitrarily complex procedural and/or data structures in the configuration code, where does the application end and the configuration begin. In essence, the application becomes a library of specialized functions that perform tasks specific to its area of expertise. But it is the site-specific configuration code which, in the end, can control that application telling it how to behave in the end users' environment.

So why is the library the top-level object calling the site-specific code. Shouldn't it be the other way around? At least with open source development, it is easy to do this by turning the configuration paradigm up-side-down.

In this structure the main program, implemented in Tcl, becomes the application. Endowed with a powerful lower level set of library functions, it can call upon those functions in a very high level way to define the operating parameters of the program. If there are two or more applications which operate similarly but on different data or in a different way, ideally the main would contain only that data and those procedures which differ between the two functions. All commonalities would be expressed in shared code and data contained in the shared libraries.

In the ideal case, this makes the main program relatively small and concise (just like an ideal configuration file). All the real work is being done in the shared code. The site specific code (now in the main loop) can access all the richness of the shared libraries, but it is not limited to a pre-conceived set of configuration options. Rather, it also enjoys the full power of the underlying programming language itself. So the programmer can go to any depth necessary in producing application specific code.

Module Pyramid

With this code structure, we end up with a pyramid-shaped set of modules or components.

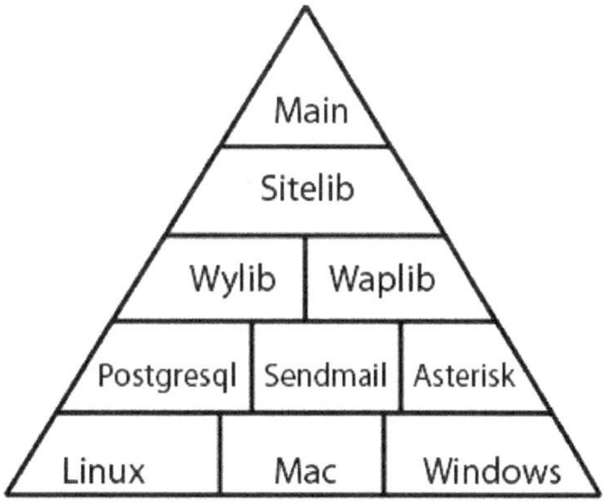

Any time features are needed or added, it is peferrable to add them at the lowest level where they may appropriately belong. That way, code can be shared by as many different processes as possible.

The front-end code structure above is fairly well organized in pass three and beyond. One purpose for pass four is to apply these principles to the way the back end is constructed. A similar pyramidal diagram can be constructed for the database schema construction:

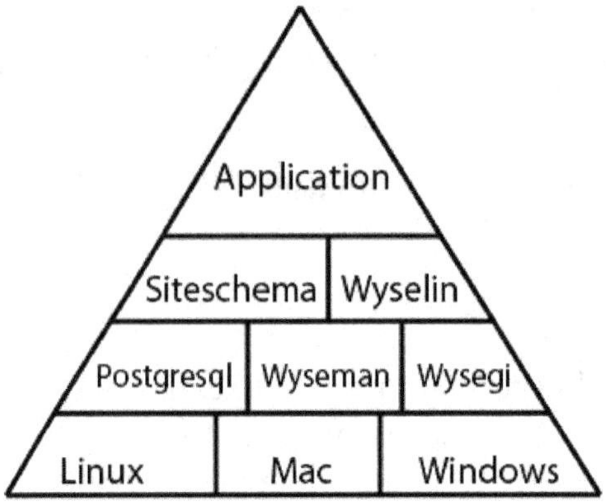

Exposed Model GUI

Immediately upon using a Wylib-based application, you will notice a very different GUI presentation. This is intentional. Most applications start with the premise that screen real estate is going to be limited. You typically have a single menu bar of some kind across the top, and then a series of virtual screens or pages you can access by pushing the right navigation buttons. Web sites tend to follow this paradigm. You can only view one page at a time so you have to navigate from one page to the next to get your job done.

While there is nothing inherently wrong with this approach, Wylib lends itself better to an approach that might be called a "dashboard" or "control panel" view. The goal here is to get as much data as possible to present on the screen at once and to minimize the amount of navigating that will be necessary in order to do the job. While this approach tends to have a steeper learning curve, my experience is that in an enterprise people can eventually become more productive when the number of mouse clicks can be reduced.

The other important principle is what I call "exposed model." Relational databases are very powerful. The foreign key relationships established in the database tie records together in a way that explains how they are related to each other. For example, we may have one table containing a list of customers. Another table might contain a list of orders.

In the exposed view paradigm, we would try to make it relatively easy to show both the list of customers and the list of orders on the screen simultaneously (not requiring you to navigate between them one at a time). Then if you select a given customer for editing, the list of orders should automatically update to show the orders associated with that customer. In this way, the user will begin to understand the foreign key relationships intuitively--even if they don't know what a foreign key is.

So WyattERP applications will typically have a single menu bar at the top like traditional applications. However it will also contain multiple panes, each of which may have its own menu bar. And it will be possible to launch other top-level windows for simultaneous display, each of which will have its own menu bar and containing its own panes and their associated menu bars.

In most cases, these new top-level windows express a class of sorts which can be instantiated on the screen any number of times. So in our example, we could have multiple lists of customers showing at once and each one could have its own relational list of orders as well.

Model, View, Controller

Model-view-controller (MVC) is a software architectural method which lends itself well to application development in WyattERP. MVC was not, in the strict sense, in my mind through the early development of the ATI ERP. However, I was very mindful of the need for multiple, simultaneous views accessing a common core of data.

As I studied MVC and attempted to use it in later architecture, I was convinced that it could be helpful in future design phases of WyattERP and Wylib applications. Rather than going into depth in this paper about how MVC works, I would refer the reader to Wikipedia or some other good resource for a detailed explanation. But the basic concept is simple:

The model represents the state of the project or enterprise. It contains all data that expresses how things have progressed so far. And as more progress is made, the model records the new state of the data (and optionally, a record of the changes along the way). So for a business, we will keep a list of our customers and another list of our employees. Each time a customer or employee is added, the data will change and the model will keep track of this state along the way.

It is the job of the model designer to evaluate the real world problem (the enterprise) and determine a way to represent the salient quantities in that reality in tables, rows and columns. Anyone who has designed a relational database before knows that this task can seem deceptively simple until you start trying to pack actual real-world data into your model. So the goal is to find a model sufficiently complex that it can represent the bulk of your real-world cases while being sufficiently simple that your users can effectively interact with it.

The controller portion in the MVC method contains rules about how data changes in the model. In Postgresql and similar products, triggers and rules can certainly constitute a part of the controller layer. For example when we push a button in our GUI to issue a payroll check to one of our employees, there will typically be a set of procedural functions that will have to be performed before allowing the data to be recorded. We might first check to see that valid work time has been recorded by the employee. We might check to see if overtime needs to be paid or if withholdings need to be made. These are all examples of rules or restrictions on how and when the model is allowed to change.

Since WyattERP is based on the client-server model of Postgresql, a lot of our controller code is bound to be running on the back end. However, it is usually awkward to have all control logic happening in the back end. For example, when adding a new employee record, it is usually a good idea to make sure the user has included a birthdate and a valid taxpayer ID number. Ideally, we would disallow the record addition until these are specified.

While this type of a data check can (and should) be performed in the back end, it should probably also be screened in the front end as well where we are more likely to be able to issue a more user-friendly and specific error message. So in WyattERP, the controller layer is expected to be as much as possible in the back end, but understood to also occupy some space in the front end.

The view consists of the widgets shown on the screen and the buttons or links the user might click in order to accomplish the desired tasks. Ideally, any number of views can exist at one time. And when the user performs an action on the database, he should access the same set of control code regardless of which view he is in. And he should operate consistently and transactionally on the same set of data in the model regardless of which view he is using. Furthermore, when the data changes in the model, all applicable views should ideally update to reflect the change.

Permission Model

When WyattERP is used in a multiple user environment, there will typically need to be some kind of restrictions on which data can be viewed and modified by which users. For example, in a business environment you might want one person to deposit the checks and a totally different person to apply the income to invoices. One person might enter new employees in the database while a different person might issue payroll checks. In this way, there are greater controls on the data and less chance for someone to do something they shouldn't.

WyattERP starts by creating a basic permission model using Wyseman. When schema components are created, you can specify modules (essentially groups or roles) that will be able to access those objects in various ways. Each module permission is created with three different levels: limit, user, and super. So if I create a table and tell it that the "entim" (entity information manager) module will be accessing it, Wyseman will create three roles: entim_limit, entim_user, and entim_super. Additionally, you define which types of accesses each of the three levels will get to the object. For example entim_limit might have select only permission to the table. We might give entim_user the ability to insert and update. But we might only give entim_super delete permissions.

Wyseman allows for a fairly compact syntax to represent which modules and levels get what access to which objects in the database. If your schema includes a user table, you can use Waplib functions to add and revoke permissions to the modules you have defined.

Additionaly, there is support for role groups (like "finance" or "sales" for example, each of which can contain module permissions of various levels. This will allow you to grant a set of module permissions to a user based on their job description.

In addition to granting select, insert, update and delete to database tables, it is sometimes desirable to limit a user's access to certain columns within a table. While Postgresql has support for column-level permissions, WyattERP lends itself well to simply creating a custom view for each module. When defining the view, you can specify separately which fields can be selected, inserted, and updated. Wyselib contains helpful macro functions to help you manage this without creating a large code footprint.

Other fine grained permission controls might include such things as limiting access to a table based on a location or the time of day. These can easily be handled by rules and triggers within the database.

Main Components

Wlib - WyattERP Library

Wylib contains Tcl and Tk functions which are considered to be site independent and also generic enough that they would be likely to be shared by a wide variety of applications. Wylib is designed to be used with or without Tk. So support and maintenance scripts can require it as well as GUI applications. If you don't want the GUI components, just don't invoke them.

Some of the more common GUI components will be introduced here:

Dbp (Database Preview):

This widget can display all or some of the records from a single table in the database. It looks somwhat like a spreadsheet, showing rows and columns of data. Controls are fairly standard to a multi-column listbox you might see in another application.

This widget is built upon a similar but lower-level widget called an MLB (multi-listbox) which does most of the same things, but is not associated with a database. Rather, it can contain any abitrary data.

Typically, you would use the standard LoadBy button in the menu bar of the Dbp to select a certain class of records you are interested in. Then you would double click on one of the records to "execute" (do something interesting with) it. The Dbp can be operated in a mode where multiple records can be executed at once if wanted.

It is very common to link a Dbp to a Dbe widget (see below). In this case, executing a record will load it into the Dbe.

A Dbp will largely configure itself from the data dictionary created by Wyseman. However, you can specify additional configuration parameters such as the default order in which fields will appear and what action functions will appear.

```
top::add [eval dbp::dbp $w.p -ewidget $w.e {-m clr -m def -m rld -m all -m prv -m sel
-m nxt -m lby -m see -m aex}] entp
pack $w.p -side top -fill both -expand yes
```

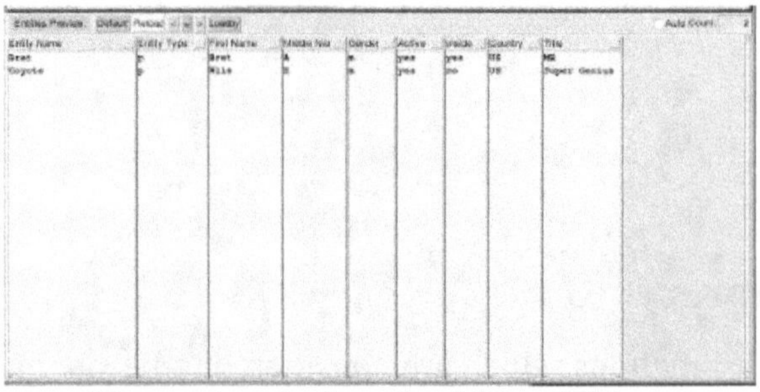

Illustration 1: Standard Dbp Widget

Dbe (Database Edit):

This widget can contain a single record from a single table at one time. Typically, it gets loaded up with a record somehow (often from an associated Dbp). This will allow you to view and edit the contents of the record. Then when you are ready, you can commit your changes back to the database.

A Dbe typically requires a bit more configuration than a Dbp. For example, we need to define where the various fields will appear in the editing pane. While this could probably be done automatically, a human-crafted layout will usually yield a more pleasing result.

Data Editors:

Wylib contains a wide array of editor widgets for a variety of data values. For example, there is a widget just for selecting dates. Another one is good at selecting the time of day. One displays a listbox with a number of values to choose from. Another will prompt for the input of a number, but displays a calculator for use in coming up with your answer.

These data selection widgets can be specified as data-entry helpers in a Dbe, or as part of a pop-up dialog (or anywhere else for that matter).

```
top::add [eval dbe::dbe $w.e -pwidget $w.p p -table ent_v {-m clr -m
adr -m upr -m dlr -m prv -m rld -m nxt -m {ldr -s Ld} -m sep} -bg blue -
bd 3] ente

pack $w.e -side top -fill both
```

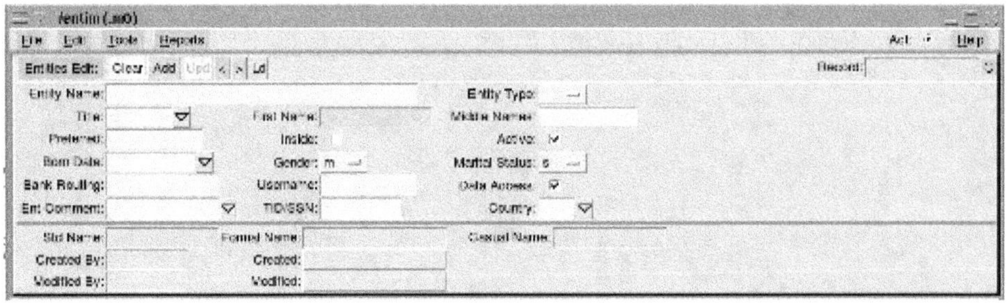

Standard Widget Wrappers

There are a handful of features that I really wished were built into the standard Tk widgets. Absent these, I opted to create a standard wrapper around each one. So Wylib contains classes such as "wentry" which is the Wylib wrapper for an entry. This includes support for a pop-up context help feature, and a way to store the various values that have been used in the entry (a history stack).

Similarly, there is a wrapper around each of the standard Tk widgets. The wrapper gets renamed over the global native widget. So later invocations of a standard "entry" will actually call the wrapped widget, getting the enhanced Wylib entry features.

Utility Tcl Code

Wylib also contains a handful of support functions such as the interface to the Postgresql API. Other examples include support for printing from standard widgets, parsing command line parameters, and interfacing with internet sockets.

Test Suit

While admittedly short on documentation, there is a test folder containing a variety of example scripts to test the various widgets and features. These were typically used during development of the widgets, but can serve as an additional source of useage examples.

Waplib - WyattERP Application Library

In the early development, Wylib contained everything that was considered "sharable code." But over time, it began to get cluttered with lots of fairly esoteric code that didn't get uesd very often. Waplib became the new home of such code. With the new development of reusable schema components in Wyselib, Waplib also holds the standard front-end support functions to interface to these standardized back-end objects.

Examples of estoteric but sharable code includes a module for interfacing to the Federal Express web site, an a module for creating Nacha (direct deposit) payroll files. It also includes a module for generating paper checks and a graphing module for creating gantt charts (in development).

Wyseman

Wyseman is actually a package that includes a command line tool (wyseman), a graphical interface (wysegi) for examining and changing data in the database, and a run-time library for accessing the data dictionary. When invoked, wysegi will show a list of tables and views in the database.

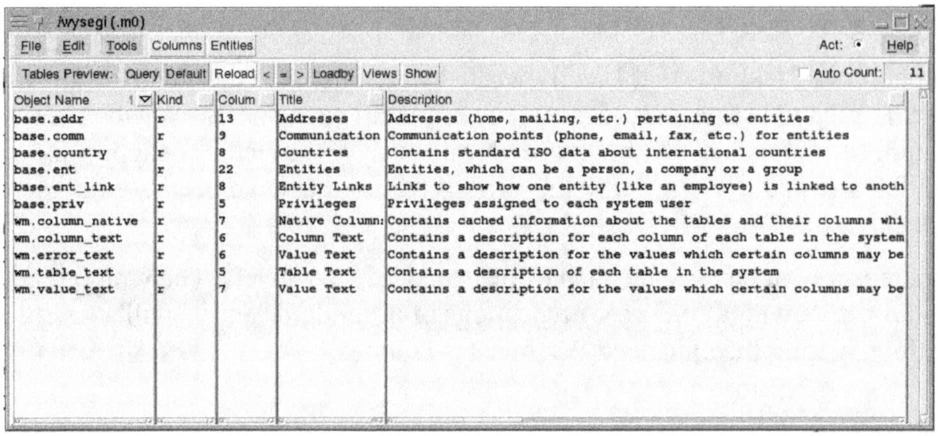

These database objects are displayed in a standard Wylib preview widget (Dbp) so you have access to all the standard features it offers (such as Loadby, ordering and so forth). If you double click on an object, wysegi will attempt to open a standard Wylib editing widget (Dbe) which will allow you to edit the selected record. These widgets are all automatically generated solely from data available in the data dictionary, so the layout of fields is not as optimized as you might see in a human generated layout.

Most of the time, the database designer should not have to access the data dictionary directly. Rather, the standard Wylib widgets will access it for you in order to display column titles, context helps and so forth. However, it us useful to know what it contains--especially when coding your Wyseman files.

To see the data dictionary, look at the tables contained (using wysegi) in the "wm" schema. For example, you will see a table that holds a titles and helps for each table in the system. Another table holds similar descriptions for table columns. A third table holds values for certain enumerated-value columns you will create.

As you create your own database design, you will author files (described below) that will define the database objects, will populate the data dictionary, and will define how various object data will be displayed on the screen.

At the heart of Wyseman is the wyseman command line utility itself. It will parse your schema description files. And according to how you invoke it, it can build some or all of your schema (your collection of database objects). Or it can destroy (and optionally rebuild) specified portions of it as well.

The Wyseman parser (just the Tcl interpretor itself) understands the following new commands which mirror their SQL counterparts:

- table
- view
- sequence
- index
- function

* rule
* schema

Each of these objects can be created by invoking the command, followed by a Wylib dynamic list of parameters which include:

* Name <object name>
* create <create script>
* drop <drop script>
* grant <module permissions>
* version <object version>
* text <title description>

With the first 5 of these able to be expressed with their switches omitted as long as they are in this exact order. So, for example, we might create a table with the following code:

```
table base.ent_link {base.ent} {
        org_id     int4   references base.ent (ent_id) on update cascade
        , mem_id    int4   references base.ent (ent_id) on update cascade on delete
cascade
        , primary key (org_id, mem_id)
        , role       varchar
        , supr_path   int[]
        subst($glob::stamps)
}
```

Note that we do not have to insert the words "create table <name>" in the create script. We can just start enumerating the column creation portion of the syntax. Wyseman will fill in the blanks if it thinks it needs to .But if it see the words "create table" at the beginning of your script, it will know not to try.

Likewise, there is no drop script specified. Unless there is something fancy involved in dropping this object, just let Wyseman create that part for you. For a table it is just "drop table <name>" so it can figure that out just fine.

Most SQL objects behave this way, you can take certain shortcuts as long as you fill in the parts that can't be figured out. For example, if you create a trigger that calls a function, Wyseman will include the function name in the object dependency list for you (if you haven't done it already).

The dependency list should just be a list of all the object names in the database that must exist before you can create this object. So if you create a view that is based on a table and a function, you should list that table name and function name in the dependency list as shown in the example:

```
view base.ent_link_v {base.ent_link base.ent_v} {
        select eval(fld_list $base::ent_link_se el)
    , oe.name               as org_name
    , me.name               as mem_name
    , el. oid as _oid
        from        base.ent_link   el
        join        base.ent_v      oe on oe.ent_id = el.org_id
        join        base.ent_v      me on me.ent_id = el.mem_id;

eval(rule_insert base.ent_link_v base.ent_link $base::ent_link_v_in {} $glob::stampin)
eval(rule_update base.ent_link_v base.ent_link $base::ent_link_v_up
$base::ent_link_pk {} $glob::stampup)
eval(rule_delete base.ent_link_v base.ent_link $base::ent_link_pk)
} -grant {
   {entim     s {i u d}}
}
```

The grant parameter simply specifies a list including a module permission and a sub-list showing the (possibly abbreviated) permissions to allow to users of levels limit, user and super within that permission. Wyseman will create all the necessary roles if they do not already exist in the database. Remember that in Postgresql, objects like tables and views exist only within a specified database However roles, exist across all databases within your current instance. This could cause you some headaches if you are trying to create multiple Wyseman databases within a single instance.

The object name consists of the exact name of the object as you would refer to it in SQL. For functions, this includes the parenthesis and the full parameter list. This is necessary because Postgresql allows you to overload function names (more than one function with the same name). The Postgresql parser does not care if you put spaces between function parameters, but if you put those spaces in the name of your object in Wyseman it will remove them to create the object name. So when you refer to the object as a dependency of another object, you had better specify it with no spaces in the parameter list (see the example below):

```
function {base.priv_role(name,varchar,varchar)}
```

The procedural language plpgsql also allows alias names for parameters in the declaration. These will be stripped out as well when forming the official object name. So make you do so when referring to the object as a dependency.

```
function {equip_logdep(ei int4, se int4, td date)} {equip_items_v equip_dep
equip_caldep(varchar,numeric,numeric,int4,int4)} {            returns boolean
language plpgsql as $$
```

In addition to the standard SQL objects outlined above, there is one "catch-all" object creator called "other." This is just like "table," "view," or any of the other object creators. Except you need to specify a full SQL create and drop script. Not much can be assumed by Wyseman in this case. This command might be used to create a custom type, aggregate, or operator as shown here:

```
function neqnocase(text,text) {} {
```

```
        returns boolean language plpgsql immutable as $$
        begin return upper($1) != upper($2); end;
$$;}
        other neqnocase_o neqnocase(text,text) {
                create operator !=* (leftarg = text,rightarg = text,procedure =
neqnocase, negator = =*);
        } {drop operator !=* (text,text);}
```

There is a command called "tabtext" which is used for defining titles and context helps for tables, columns, and values. For example, to create the text information for the table defined in the example above, we would include the following:

```
tabtext base.ent_link {Entity Links} {Links to show how one entity (like an employee)
is linked to another (like his company)} {
   {org_id          {Organization ID}      {The ID of the organization entity that the
member entity belongs to}}
   {mem_id          {Member ID}            {The ID of the entity that is a member of
the organization}}
   {role            {Member Role}          {The function or job description of the
member within the organization}}
   {supr_path       {Super Chain}          {An ordered list of superiors from the top
down for this member in this organization}}
} -errors {
   {NBP             {Illegal Entity Org}   {A personal entity can not be an organization
(and have member entities)}}
   {PBC             {Illegal Entity Member} {Only personal entities can belong to
company entities}}
}
```

Note that this same chunk of text can optionally be specified as a parameter to the table or view command itself (using the -text switch).

Another command called "tabdef" is used to define the default way in which columns and values will be displayed in the Wylib GUI. This is not really the same kind of data dictionary information provided by the tabtext command in that this is a little more specific to the point that we are using Tk as a front-end. Realistically, the data expressed inside the tabdef command could be parsed by other front-end generating code. But at the moment all Wyseman does with it is it creates a Tcl library which will be required by Wylib (assuming you make it and put in the right place). It will include properly Tcl-formatted argument lists for attachment to the Dbe (and in some cases, Dbp) widgets. I have given some thought to also moving some of this data to the back end, but at the moment that is not being done. A typical tabdef command looks like this:

```
tabdef base.ent_link -focus org_id -fields {
   {org_id          ent    6     {1 1}         -just r}
   {mem_id          ent    6     {1 2}         -just r}
   {role            ent    30    {1 3}         -spf exs}
}
```

When this dynamic list is parsed, it is simply re-formatted as follows:

```
package provide wmd_acme 1.0
namespace eval wmd_acme {
  namespace export base.ent_link
  proc base.ent_link {{tag {_}}} {
    switch $tag {
      {} {return {-focus org_id}}
      org_id         {return {-style ent -size 6 -sub {1 1} -just r}}
      mem_id         {return {-style ent -size 6 -sub {1 2} -just r}}
      role           {return {-style ent -size 30 -sub {1 3} -spf exs}}
      {_} {return {org_id mem_id role}}
    }
  }
}
```

This code can be referenced directly by Wylib to display the column widgets on the screen the way the user wants.

Note that there are some fairly esoteric switches that can be specified in the tabdef columns. Because each widget at each level just strips off the argument that it wants or needs, you should be able to specify any kind of switch here, all the way down to the background color of an entry in the Dbe.

To discover all the various switches that can be specified, one must understand that a Dbe (database editor widget) consists of an Mdew (Multi data editing widget). An Mdew consists of multiple Dew's (Data Editing Widgets). Dew's consist of a data field (an entry, a text box, a checkbox, a menu button, etc.) and a prefixing label. If you study the available options to each of these classes and understand that the capabilities are essentially inherited as you move up to the megawidget, you can quickly discover what options will be available to you. Until then, to get started, just follow some of the examples provided for the various types of data fields.

Finally, the "define" command is included as a macro facility. Remember that you are in native tcl all the while in your schema description file. So you can use all the power of Tcl including set, for, while and so forth. But on occasion, it is nice to have a small macro processor as well.

So you can define a macro using define as follows:

```
define Tquant {case when a = %1 then b else 0 end}
```

This would then be invoked as simply:

```
Tquant(z)
```

Which would expand to:

```
case when a = z then b else 0 end
```

A macro can have any number of parameters which you would refer to in your definition as %1, %2, %3. Or it can have no parameters. However, if it has no parameters, you must still invoke it with empty parenthesis as follows:

```
define myDef()    1234
```

```
field    int    not null default myDef(),
```

In the sample schema provided, normal database objects are defined in a file with a ".wms" extension. All the tabtext stuff is in a file with a ".wmt" extension. And all the tabdef items are in a file with a ".wmd" extension.

While this is not a strict requirement of Wyseman, it does make it easier to specify which objects you want when it comes to build time. Wyseman command line commands can get pretty complex so I usually use a Makefile to do most of the work. For more complex database designs, there can be a lot of different files to pull object definitions out of. When I start including Wyselib schema components, it can get even more complex.

So I now create a little Tcl script called "modules" in the build directory. This command will produce a list of schema definition files. And optionally, it can find ones that match one or more specified extensions. So for examples, I can specify:

```
./modules wms wmt
```

And it will give me the names of all the *.wms and *.wmt files I need for my schema. I can then call `$(./modules)` from inside my makefile to avoid long lists of files and/or directories where I might be pulling from.

Wyselib - WyattERP Schema Library

The last component is Wyselib. When I first developed the ATI schema, it was all closed and proprietary. Only Wylib, Waplib, Wyseman and so forth were open sourced. I did create a couple of small sample schemas for people to play with to get the idea. But I quickly found that I didn't have the time nor the desire to maintain those sample schema.

So in pass four, I am now moving certain core functions into the new Wyselib. The idea is to build up the operating schema for a couple of my other businesses strictly on Wyselib with a very small corpus of site specific code if necessary. Since this stuff can all be open source, it will be something (hopefully) other people can use. And it will be something I have an incentive to maintain.

If it turns out to be good enough, I may want to go back to the ATI schema and back-port sections of the schema to the Wyselib stuff.

So far, wyselib has a set of payroll withholding functions (actually these are being used in the ATI schema now). It has an experimental base module which consists of a common core for tracking users (entities), their addresses and communication points, and what permissions they have. I also have a module for tracking employees which uses a new nifty kind of pseudo table that actually overlays the entity table. This is very experimental, but it looks like it will have some very cool benefits when fully implemented.

Customers and vendors are planned to be implemented similarly to employees. And I am including some basic accounting and asset management structures as well.

Conclusion

As I reflect on the history of WyattERP, I am happy that it has done such good things for Action Target. We have been able to build a very successful company on a home-grown ERP, and grown through all the stages of our development so far. We are able to maintain GAAP accounting, and track millions of dollars of material flow and other transactions, reconciled in a precise and accountable way.

I had grand plans to see WyattERP used more in the open source community. But it has been largely a one-man show. And I have always had my hands full just meeting ATI's needs. So far, it has been difficult to give the support necessary to maintain the package in a way the open source community could benefit from. However, I continue to be open to the idea. I just think it would require a few other parties who were interested in using the system for their own needs and who would be willing to collaborate on the project to fill in the parts that are missing (like documentation, and other refinements).

I have several other hopes for the future as well. WyattERP has never really been configured for web-wide deployment. At the moment, it has to run on a Linux front-end because of a number of dependencies hastily written into the code. In recent years, I have begun to install the hooks which would allow true multi-platform deployment. But some effort would still be required in order to get there.

In order to use WyattERP for my farm, it will be necessary to achieve this in some degree. For example, one use will require a laptop (probably windows) connected via wireless ethernet to track cattle as they are processed in the field. I would like to be able to just use any old laptop, just hit a web page, and be able to download whatever I need in order to get the application started.

Some people have talked about writing a php or flash front-end for WyattERP. But to tell the truth, the thing that is so cool about it is that it is written in Tcl/Tk. The dashboard design paradigm would be quite a lot of work to re-create inside a browser as well.

So of late, I have become convinced that a well designed starkit might be the best answer. I would like to be able to click a link on a web page and have that download a basic starkit. That application would allow me to connect to the Postgresql database and log in with my credentials. Once the system knew who I was and what module permissions I had, it could then determine what applications I needed. I think these applications could then be downloaded right into my starkit by way of starsync or a similar mechanism.

Once the system had all the latest code for the application(s) I needed, I could have a simple dialog pop up to ask what app to run and the user would be ready to go.

This approach would enjoy several benefits. First, the front-end code could run more or less as-is without needing to be ported to another language or platform. All views would look and act the same regardless of whether they were running over the web or in the main office. The deployment model would benefit from all the advantages of a self-updating starkit. The database author could simply worry about deploying the latest code to a central repository and all his users would automatically get the latest stuff each time they connected to the database.

There are quite a few things I would like to do differently and better when it comes to accounting. There has historically been quite a divide between operations software and accounting software. My experiences of recent years have taught me a lot about what accountants, auditors and banks are looking for in a reporting system. My experiences building several successful businesses have taught me a lot about what operations folks need in order to make their businesses work.

All too often businesses are satisfied to let the operations people shop for their own solution and let the accounting people do a different solution. IT is often successful in creating a more-or-less automated export from the operations system to the accounting system. But it is quite rare that the bridge works in both directions. And it is very rare that the data remains completely consistent between the two sides.

I still don't believe that a successful business can just buy its software off the shelf. Most of the innovators I have seen became successful by developing something in-house that allowed their vision for their own business logic to flourish. After all, if you run your business on someone else's ERP, you are really trusting them to write your business logic. And your competitors can replicate your business quite completely simply by buying the same software you bought.

But when innovators find a new way to do things that is more effective than the competition, they need a way to implement that novel logic in their ERP. They need a way to cook up a system that will capitalize on what they have done that is novel and better. WyattERP provides a platform that can allow that rapid development without the distractions from writing all the GUI and database support code from scratch.

Fluid Dynamics experiments with Tcl

Ron Fox[1], Vaibhav Khane[2]

Abstract—**Computer Automated Radioactive Tracking (CARPT) has emerged as a powerful Technique for mapping fluid flow under a variety of conditions. This paper describes the adaptation of a general purpose nuclear physics event-based data acquisition system to the needs of the CARPT apparatus at Missouri University of Science and Technology. The resulting software is a C++ multithreaded framework which communicates via events with a thread running a Tcl interpreter. The Tcl scripts run by the interpreter provide Experimental control, online-data analysis and data storage for later offline analysis.**

I. Introduction

Understanding how fluids flow through chemical reactor vessels is an important piece in the puzzle of optimizing many industrial processes. Ab-initio fluid dynamic calculations and even simulations are not able to provide solutions for realistic reactors. Furthermore since larger reactors, as well as those which several material phases (e.g. solids, liquids and gasses in the same vessel) are optically opaque, experiments to track fluid flow in these reactors are not trivial..

As one often quoted author in the field says: "Multiphase reactors are widely used in petroleum, chemical, petrochemical, pharmaceutical and metallurgical industries as well as in materials processing and pollution abatement….the physical phenomena that affect the fluid dynamics of such systems are not yet entirely understood. This makes a priori predictions of important process parameters… very difficult."[1] Figure 1 at right is a schematic of a Circulating Fluidized Bed (CFB) reactor that gives an idea of the scale of these devices. An understanding of the flow of fluids through reactors like this and others is essential to the optimization of a large variety of industrial processes.

The remainder of this paper is organized as follows:

- The CARPT method is introduced and described.
- The computer problem being solved is described.
- We describe how the base NSCL VM-USB readout framework was modified to meet the needs of this system.

II. Tracing fluid flow with radioactive sources

1. National Superconducting Cyclotron Laboratory Michigan State University.
2. Missouri University of Science and Technology Very High Temperature Reactor (VHTR) consortium.

In recent years, introducing radioactive tracers into the flow of fluidized reactors has been a fruitful way to perform experimental studies of the fluid dynamics of these devices. One such method, called Computer Automated Radioactive Particle Tracking involves injecting a radioactive source that has neutral buoyancy into the fluid being studied.

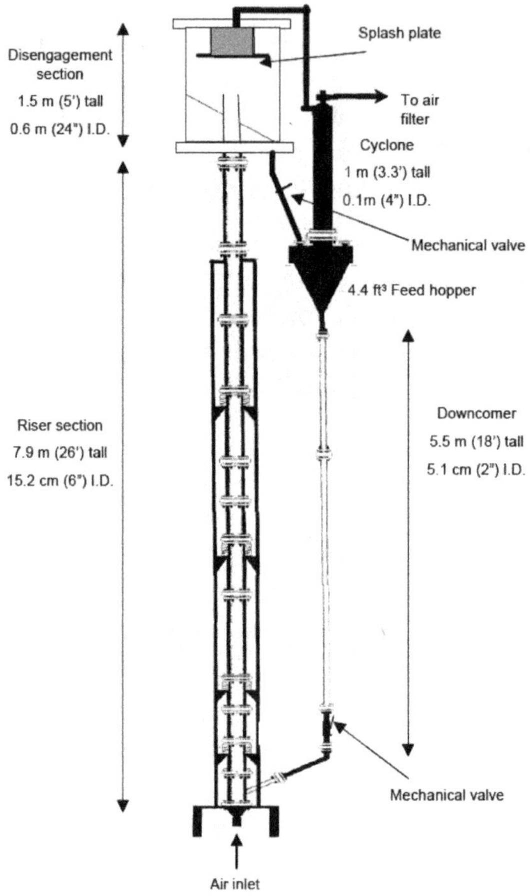

Figure 1 CFB reactor prototype [2]

Detectors placed around the reactor vessel track the position and velocity of the source as a function of time. Normally sources composed of ^{46}Sc are used. ^{46}Sc decays emitting a β^- and a γ-ray with characteristic energies of 900KeV, 1.0 and 1.3 MeV. NaI, detectors sensitive to the long ranged γ are used to track the particle. This is shown schematically in Figure 2.

The position of the source is determined by measuring the count rates in the detectors as a function of time. Position/intensity maps obtained during calibration runs are then used to derive the time evolution of the position and vector velocity of the particle. This simple sounding procedure is actually quite complex because:

- A good knowledge of detector efficiencies is required t o understand what a specific detector rate means.
- Detector acceptance depends on angle of incidence.
- Pile-up either due to a highly active source or the recovery time of the detectors need to be factored in (While the signal rise times of NaI crystal is quite fast, the fall time can be several 10s of microseconds).
- The rector contents can absorb gamma rays resulting in a position dependent attenuation of the rawintensity.

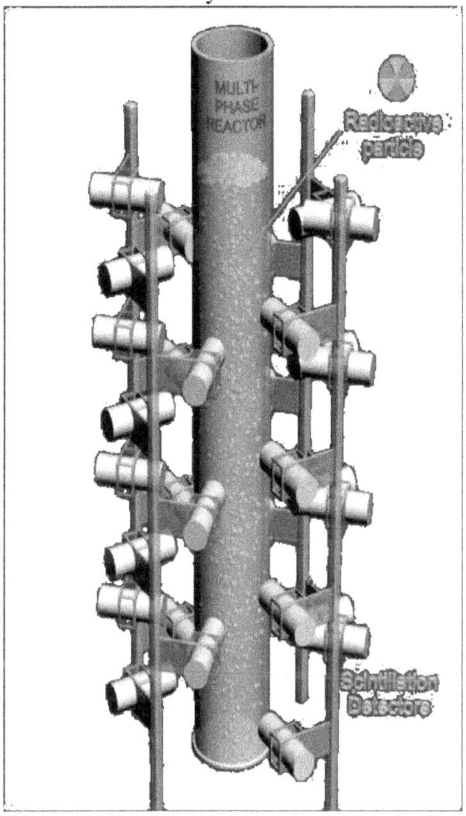

Figure 2 Schematic of a CARPT system.

The flow of data analysis is shown in Figure 3.

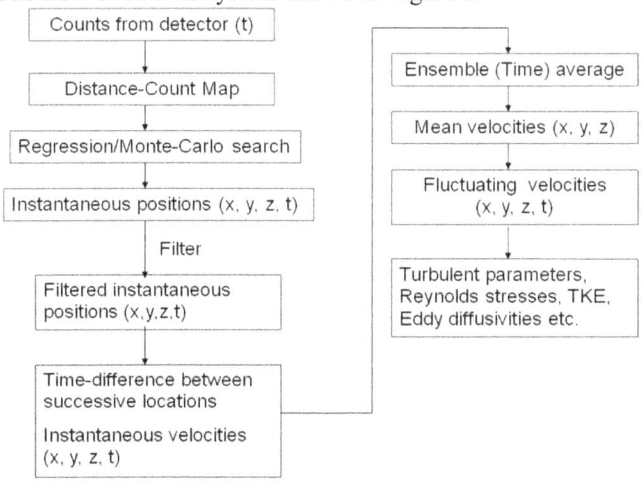

Figure 3 Flow of CARPT data analysis

III. Hardware Problem and Solution

The Chemical & Biological Engineering Dept. at Missouri University of Science and Technology Rolla (MST) performs CARPT studies of several types of reactors. In early 2010 they contacted the first author of this paper about upgrading their system. Figure 4 shows a block diagram of their system at that time:

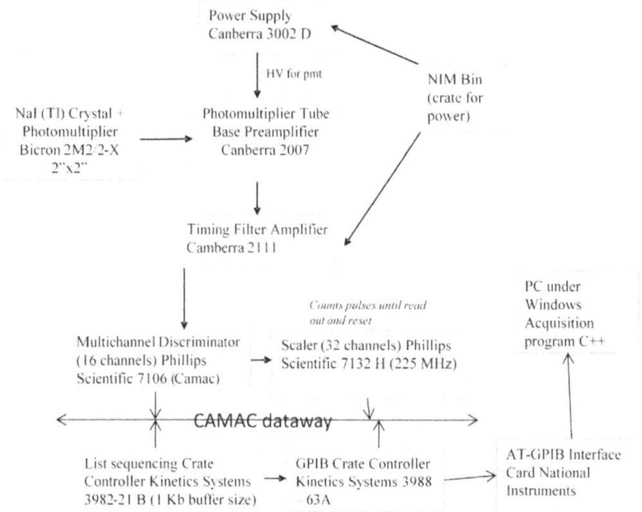

Figure 4 Original system block diagram.

Of concern to the MST group were the bottom three elements of Figure 4. Those devices are no longer manufactured. Additionally, the software on the Windows PC was not sufficiently flexible, nor reliable.

CAMAC [3] (Computer Automated Measurement and Control) is a very old instrumentation bus. It was first used in the Automotive industry adopted by the nuclear physics community about that time, and standardized for use in nuclear physics data acquisition systems in 1972 (ESONE/EUR 4100). The IEEE standardized the system, bus controllers and host interfaces and software APIs for FORTRAN Programs in 1982 (IEEE standards 585,683, 596, 595, 726, 675, 758 inter alia).

The goal of the project was to replace and modernize the CAMAC readout system/host interface and computers while retaining the existing analog electronics and CAMAC instrumentation. While it would have been nice to update the computer interfaces from CAMAC to something more recent, that was beyond the budgetary scope and capabilities of this project.

Many smaller nuclear physics labs have a significant investment in CAMAC electronics and are "trapped" in this technology either because they are insufficiently funded to replace their electronics or they don't have sufficient on-site expertise to convert their software once they do replace their hardware. To meet the needs of those laboratories, Weiner Plein & Baus Elektronik markets a USB CAMAC crate controller the CC-USB. Thanks to modern gate array technology, this module provides much of the functionality of the three CAMAC interface modules used in the original system in a single simply laid out module.

A block diagram of the CC-USB is shown in Figure 5. This is taken from the module's manuals. The block referred to as "Stacks" in the figure allows operation lists to be downloaded and triggered by various conditions.

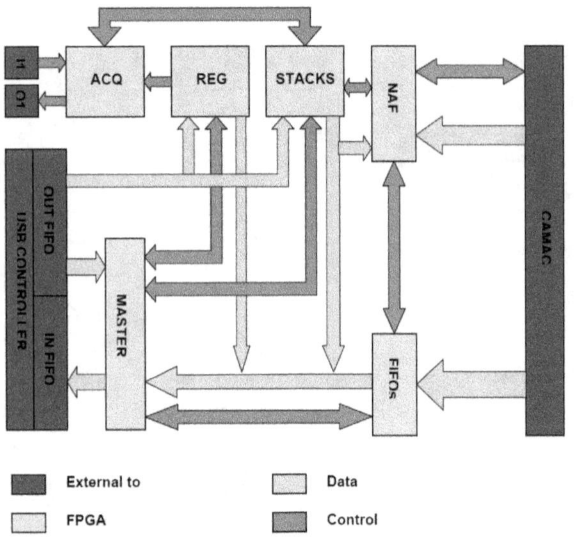

Figure 5 Block diagram of CC-USB

The specifications require that scaler readouts be triggered at relatively stable timed intervals. The CC-USB contains onboard resources that allow a periodic pulse to be generated on one of its outputs. The stability of this timing signal is on the order of one part in 12.5ns which is far superior to the required timing. The periodic output pulse is then cabled to the input that triggers execution of the CC-USB primary event readout list.

The CC-USB connects to a host computer via a USB A to B cable, such as that used to connect many USB printers.

IV. Software

This section is subdivided as follows:

- First an overview of the requirements of the software is presented.
- Second a description of the NSCL DAQ CC-USB readout software is given.
- The modifications performed on the base software are described along with some of the operational characteristics of the resulting software.

A. Software requirements

In order to understand the software requirements and data acquisition modes it is important toknow a bit about the electronics. Each gamma ray interacts with the NaI in the detector to produce light. This light is collected, amplified turned into an electrical pulse by means of a photo multiplier tube. The resulting electrical pulse is then electronically amplified. If the pulse rises above a threshold, it is counted by a channel in the scaler module. The number of counts in a scaler channel per unit time represents the intensity of the source as seen by each detector. The algorithms in Figure 3 can map those intensities to positions given position./intensity map.

In production data runs, the source is moving, this leads to the common mode of data taking. The scalers are allowed to count for some dwell time, and then read and cleared. The output from a production run is a file that consists of a record of the scaler counts for each dwell period and the length of the dwell period. The precision to which the positions and velocities of the source can be reconstructed therefore depends on the dwell time as well as other factors.

In addition to production runs there are two other modes of data taking:

- Threshold hunt mode.
- Position calibration mode.

NaI detectors are sensitive to gamma-rays as well as cosmic background and the gamma rays emitted by background sources. It is the leading edge discriminator (LED) that determines which pulses are counted and which are not. The threshold hunt mode provides information to the experimenters to help them set the LED thresholds. In this mode, a source is placed where all detectors can see it. After each dwell time the discriminator threshold is incremented. Differentiating the counts with respect to the dwell time produces a crude spectrum with discriminator settings as the channel number. The position of the peak(s) due to the source provides the discriminator settings.

The original system required that the output file from threshold hunt data taking be fed into software that then did the peak location. The requirements for the new system were to produce the same output file but also provide support for visualizing spectra constructed from these data so that the results of the peak finding software could be double checked.

Position calibration mode is required to produce intensity to position maps. In this mode of data taking, a source is placed at a known position in the system with the detectors mounted in their production data taking positions. After each dwell time the source is moved to a different position. The output f this mode is a file that contains a map of counts as a function of position. These data are used to reconstruct positions from production runs. Having a correct setting for the LED is a precondition for this sort of run.

B. NSCL DAQ CC-USB base software

In [4] I reported on a software system that provides a domain specific language to describe nuclear physics experiments to data acquisition software. The system described in [4] interfaced to digitizers resident in a VME [5] backplane via a USB-VME controller. What was not mentioned in that paper was that a similar system was also written that interfaces to

CAMAC via the CC-USB. This CAMAC system was used as the starting point for the CARPT data acquisition system.

This section focuses on the structure of the Readout software, shown in Figure 6.

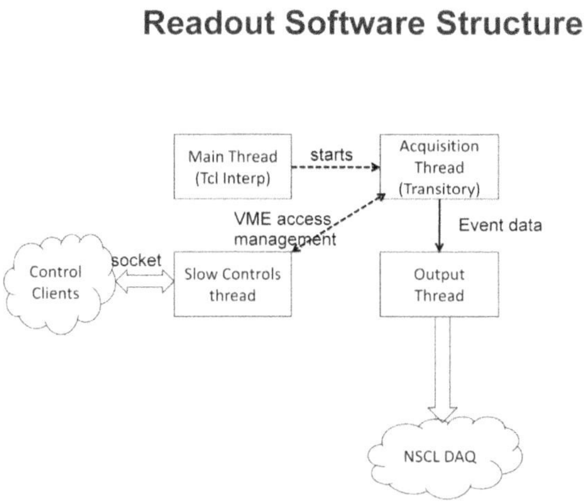

Figure 6 Structure of original CCUSB readout

The main thread embeds a Tcl interpreter with a few additional commands to control data taking. If the user requests that a data taking run start, the acquisition thread is started. The acquisition thread processes the configuration file through an extended captive Tcl interpreter, sets up the CC-USB, downloads readout lists and starts taking data.

Data from the CC-USB come in 8Kbyte buffers. As each buffer is received from the CC-USB it is passed to the output thread. The output thread normally does some light weight reformatting so that the resulting buffer is correctly structured for the NSCL data acquisition system. The reformatted buffer is sent to the NSCL DAQ data distribution server which makes it available to interested clients.

The slow controls thread runs an additional Tcl interpreter. It accepts TCP/IP connections and performs CAMAC operations on behalf of the client. If acquisition is active the slow controls thread requests a pause in data taking, performs the requested operation then resumes data taking.

This Slow controls thread is required because on Linux, USB programming via libusb allows only one process to access each USB device. Furthermore, single shot CAMAC operations cannot be executed on the CC-USB when data taking is in progress.

C. Modifications to the base software.

Figure 7 shows the modified structure of the Readout program.

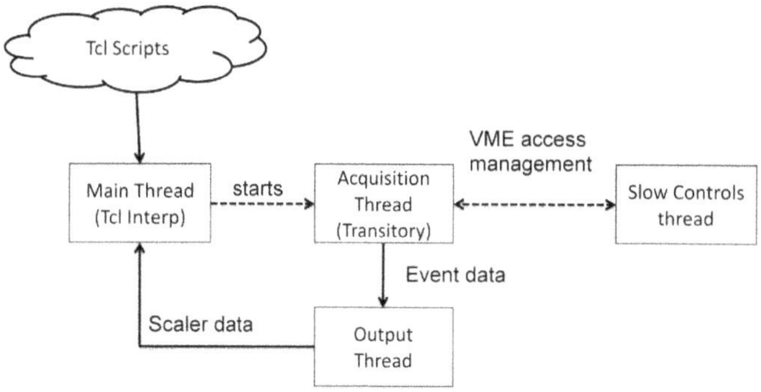

Figure 7 Structure of modified software.

The major difference between Fig. 6 and Fig 7 is that in Fig 7, the output thread has been rewritten to queue Tcl events back to the main thread's interpreter. The Tcl_Event struct used has been extended to hold the raw scaler data.

When the interpreter in the main thread dispatches the event, the event handler reformats the raw scaler data into a list of Tcl lists. Each inner list is the set of scaler values. Each outer list one dwell time worth of data (several scaler dwell times fit in a single VM-USB buffer). The resulting list is passed to the Tcl proc **onEvent** which performs mode dependent processing of the data.

This architecture:

1. Removes the need to run the NSCL data acquisition system, which is serious overkill for this application.
2. Allows the online processing of scaler data to be done in Tcl scripts.

The Tcl scripts sourced into the main thread's interpreter interact with the slow controls thread to set discriminator thresholds and output widths. These scripts provide GUI's that intrat with the slow controls thread over a Tcp/IP socket allowing that part of the architecture to remain unchanged (normally a separate GUI process interacts with the slow controls thread).

Tcl scripts were then written for each of the three modes of data taking. A 'master' Tcl script allows the user to select which operating mode they want to run. In the case of the discriminator hunt mode, Plotchart [6] was used to display the spectrum and a cursor position indicator was provided to allow the users to read the discriminator threshold setting directly from the resulting spectrum.

Figure 8 below shows a spectrum from the threshold scan mode when a ^{137}Cs and a ^{60}Co source were both counted by the detectors. Note that ^{60}Co emits γ-rays at both 1.3 an 1.7MeV providing a pair of peaks close together in the energy spectrum.

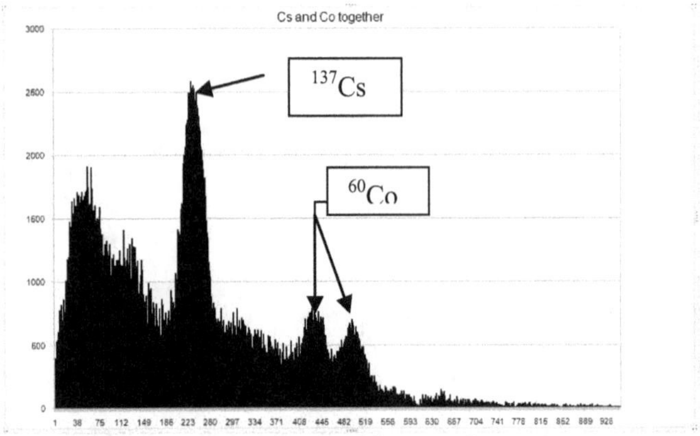

Figure 8 Spectrum from threshold hunt mode.

V. Conclusions

Tcl provided an ideal platform on which to develop the software for this project. Since the data rates are quite low (typical dwell times are a few seconds, each data point delivering 32 x 32 bits of data), Tcl scripts were more than equal to the task of handling these data, even in the more challenging threshold scan run where data were actually analyzed online.

The original structure of the readout software made the modifications required to handle the data at the script level relatively easy. Once those modifications were written, development went at the speed of Tcl. Thanks to Arjen Markus's Plotchart package, providing the spectra of the threshold hunt mode could be easily displayed and trivial mouse motion event handlers written to allow the user to pick off the correct LED thresholds from the plots.

VI. References

[1] *Opaque Multiphase Reactors: Experimentation, Modeling and Troubleshooting"* M.P. Dudukovich Oil & Gas Science and Technology Rev. IFP V 55 (2000) #2 pp 135-158.
[2] Final Report: Flow mapping in a Gas-Solid Riser via Computer Automated Radioactive Particle Tracking (CARPT) M. Al-Dahan et al. Washington University
[3] ANSI/IEEE IEEE Standard Modular Instrumentation and Digital Interface System (CAMAC) 585 1982 IEEE
[4] *A Domain Specific Language for defining Nuclear Physics Experiments* Ron Fox Proceedings of the 15'th Annual Tcl/Tk Conference Tcl Association Press. ISBN 978-0-578-00296-5.
[5] VME IEEE 1014-1987 (note more common is VME 64 which is specified by ANSI/VITA 1-1994).
[6] Plotchart Arjen Markus http://wiki.tcl.tk/11265

Tcl 2011

Manassas, VA

October 24-28, 2011

Tcl Techniques

因循

Agent Based Modeling with Coroutines

Presented at the 18th Annual Tcl/Tk Conference (Tcl'2011)
Manassas, VA

Sean Deely Woods
Senior Developer
Test and Evaluation Solutions, LLC
400 Holiday Court
Suite 204
Warrenton, VA 22185
Email: yoda@etoyoc.com
Website: http://www.etoyoc.com

Abstract:

Coroutines have been introduced into the Tcl/Tk core with version 8.6. And many developers ask "what on Earth would I do with them?" This paper describes how coroutines are used to model human actors following complex, interdependent procedures. During the paper, we will develop a coroutine based general use architecture for task management. We will also describe some of the common edge cases to look out for.

This paper is based on my experience developing the Integrated Recovery Model for T&E Solutions.

Introduction to Coroutines

What are Coroutines?

I was looking for a definition for coroutines, and I found a Chinese expression, 因循 *[yīn xûn]* which translates[1] to:

- to continue the same old routine
- to carry on just as before
- to procrastinate

They are a form of cooperative multitasking. Depending on your application, they could replace threads. (de Maura, 2004)

Coroutines were introduced with TIP #328, and have been available in the Tcl core since Tcl/Tk 8.6a2. (Sofer, 2008)

This paper will focus on the application of coroutines for discrete time simulations. More specifically modeling human agents in naval casualty scenarios within T&E Solutions Integrated Recovery Model (IRM).

A Simple Example

Let's write a very simple task. Imagine we have a toy train. We want it to stop when it reaches a destination. Our environment provides a few functions:

- **close_enough** - Returns true if the agent is close enough to the target to be considered "there".
- **location** - Returns the current position of the agent.
- **motor_direction** - A procedure that calculates which direction is the target, Ahead (+1), Behind (-1), or Stop (0)
- **move_train** - Move the agent for one time step
- **place_train** - Manually set the position of the agent to an absolute location
- **speed** - Applies power to the agent's wheels: Forward (+1), Reverse (-1), or Stop (0)

Our microcontroller runs a Tcl-like interpreter, so the script for our task looks something like this:

```
proc move_to B {
 puts "Starting towards $B"
 set x [location]
 while {![close_enough $x $B]} {
  set x [location]
  puts "I am at $x"
  speed [motor_direction $x $B]
  move_train
 }
 speed 0.0
 puts "Arrived at $B"
}
place_train 0.0
move_to 100.0
puts "(Toot Toot)"
```

Run the script and we'll see:

```
Starting towards 100.0
I am at 0.0
I am at 1.0
I am at 2.0
...
I am at 98.0
I am at 99.0
I am at 100.0
Arrived at 100.0
(Toot Toot)
```

Of course, if this were running in a real microcontroller we wouldn't have a **move_train** routine. The laws of physics would take care of movement, and our task would simply be a monitor. We'll get to that later.

But bear with me, as I'm going to take this same logic and make it into a coroutine:

[1] Translation according to: http://www.websaru.com/因循.html

```
proc move_to B {
 puts "Starting towards $B"
 set x [location]
 while {![close_enough $x $B]} {
  set x [location]
  puts "I am at $x"
  speed [motor_direction $x $B]
  yield 1
 }
 speed 0.0
 puts "Arrived at $B"
 return 0
}
place_train 0.0
coroutine travel_to move_to 100.0
while {[travel_to]} {
 move_train
}
puts "(Toot Toot)"
```

Let's go ahead and run our example, I'll explain the notation in a second:

```
Starting towards 100.0
I am at 0.0
I am at 1.0
I am at 2.0
...
I am at 98.0
I am at 99.0
I am at 100.0
Arrived at 100.0
(Toot Toot)
```

Our output is the same, even though the proc **move_to** no longer calls **move_train**.

We use the *coroutine* command to create **travel_to**. **travel_to**, in turn, calls our **move_to** proc. The caller of **travel_to** sees whatever value is yielded or returned by **move_to**. And this arrangement we use to drive the *while* loop, which actually moves the train.

Try **move_to** on it's own and you'll see:

```
place_train 0.0
move_to 100.0
ERROR:
yield can only be called in a coroutine
```

The error is pretty self-explanatory. The yield command only makes sense to the Tcl interpreter within the confines of a coroutine.

Note that the "Starting towards" and "Arrived at" strings print only once, even though we call **travel_to** 100 times. That is because our coroutine picks up on the next call where it left off, at the **yield**.

yield can take an argument. That value is returned to the caller, as though it were given in a **return**.

Once a coroutine calls **return** it dies. If we to call **travel_to** after our *while* loop terminates we would would see:

```
travel_to
ERROR:
invalid command name "travel_to"
```

Let's tweak our example. Say we would like our train to return to the place it left from.

```
proc travel_circuit {A B} {
  move_to $B
  puts "(Toot Toot)"
  move_to $A
  puts "(Toot Toot)"
  return 0
}
place_train 0.0
coroutine travel travel_circuit 0 100
while {[travel]} {
 move_train
}
puts "(Done)"
```

Our coroutine now calls a proc **travel_circuit** which calls our earlier proc

move_to. But it calls it twice with two different destinations.

```
Starting towards 100.0
I am at 0.0
I am at 0.0
I am at 1.0
I am at 2.0
...
I am at 98.0
I am at 99.0
I am at 100.0
Arrived at 100.0
(Toot Toot)
Starting towards 0.0
I am at 100.0
...
I am at 1.0
I am at 0.0
Arrived at 0.0
(Toot Toot)
```

The bot moves from A to B, reverses direction, and moves from B to A. The coroutine picks up wherever the **yield** left it. Even if the **yield** is inside of another procedure!

```
while ->
  travel ->
    travel_circuit ->
      move_to ->
        while ->
          yield
```

Coroutines and TclOO

Now, the next question you surely have. Can I use coroutines with TclOO? Yes!

Let's rebuild our example in object oriented code. The rest of the class is defined elsewhere. There's only one method that is interesting at the moment:

```
oo::define train {
 method move_to {B} {
  set x [my location]
  puts "[self] Starting towards $B"
  while {![close_enough $x $B]} {
   set x [my location]
   puts "[self] I am at $x"
   my speed [motor_direction $x $B]
   yield 1
  }
  puts "[self] Arrived at $B"
  my speed 0.0
  return 0
 }
}
proc travel_circuit {train A B} {
  $train move_to $B
  puts "(Toot Toot)"
  $train move_to $A
  puts "(Toot Toot)"
  return 0
}
train create zephyr
zephyr place_train 0.0
coroutine travel \
  travel_circuit zephyr 0.0 100.0
while {[travel]} {
 zephyr move_train
}
puts "(Done)"
```

Instead of running as a procedure, **move_to** is now a method in a TclOO object *zephyr*, of class *train*. **travel_circuit** is still a procedure, but we pass it the name of the object, and it calls the object's methods.

And we find that despite all of these changes, our example still works:

```
::zephyr Starting towards 100.0
::zephyr I am at 0.0
::zephyr I am at 0.0
::zephyr I am at 1.0
...
::zephyr I am at 98.0
::zephyr I am at 99.0
::zephyr I am at 100.0
::zephyr Arrived at 100.0
(Toot Toot)
::zephyr Starting towards 0.0
::zephyr I am at 100.0
::zephyr I am at 99.0
::zephyr I am at 98.0
...
::zephyr I am at 1.0
::zephyr I am at 0.0
::zephyr Arrived at 0.0
(Toot Toot)
(Done)
```

The coroutine has no problems descending into an object and exercising its methods. In fact, we could call out to multiple objects within a coroutine, and the coroutine would properly react as the specific object. Conversely, multiple coroutines could also call this same method.

Just to show this is an ordinary object, if we call that method outside of a coroutine, I still get the same error as our earlier **move_to** procedure:

```
zephyr move_to 100.0
ERROR:
yield can only be called in a coroutine
```

Coroutines as Objects

A useful property of coroutines is that they maintain their own internal state. If I define a variable, the value of that variable is preserved in between calls.

Let's suppose we are a lazy high schooler, and we want to solve the classic Two Trains Problem[2].

> Train A, traveling 70 miles per hour (mph), leaves Westford heading toward Eastford, 260 miles away. At the same time Train B, traveling 60 mph, leaves Eastford heading toward Westford. When do the two trains meet? How far from each city do they meet?

Instead of using algebra, we will brute force the solution with Tcl code. We begin by modeling each train with a coroutine. That coroutine calculates an updated position for the train every time step, and yields the current position:

```
proc advance {start end speed} {
  set x $start
  if { $start < $end } {
    set dX [expr $speed*$::dt]
  } else {
    set dX [expr -1.0 * $speed \
       * $::dt]
  }
  while 1 {
    set x [expr {$x + $dX}]
    yield $x
  }
  return $x
}
```

Our simulator is no longer looking for when the train reaches the destination. Instead, we are interested in when the position of **train_a** crosses **train_b**. Since the position of A is counting up, and B is counting down, we'll be at our solution point the iteration where A surpasses B in value:

[2] Text of the problem copied from: http://mathforum.org/dr.math/faq/faq.two.trains.html

```
set ::dt [expr {1/60.0}]
coroutine move_a advance 0 260 70
coroutine move_b advance 260 0 60
while {1} {
  set a [move_a]
  set b [move_b]
  if {$a > $b} break
}
puts "They Met at..."
puts "$a From Westford"
puts "[expr 260-$b] From Eastford"
puts "(Done)"
```

Run our simulation to get our answer:

```
They Met at...
140.0000000000001 From Westford
120.0 From Eastford
(Done)
```

Notice that we are running two copies of the same procedure at the same time. The fact they ran inside of two different coroutines meant that each had a different set of parameters, and each maintained a different recollection of X for every time step.

Discrete Time Agents

The simulations I work with play very much like board game. The scenario is broken into "steps". The steps are broken into phases, so that each actor gets a chance to affect the simulation equally.

However, some physical phenomena don't tend to happen in neat 1 second intervals. Up until now, we have taken for granted that our agents move at a constant speed. Most simulations must account for momentum.

Before I'm accused of having a one track mind, let us transition away from examples with trains, and into problems I deal with in the real world. Well, real, virtual world.

Crew Movement

The major application thus far for coroutines within the IRM is modeling crew behavior.

Now you may be wondering, why did I start with so many examples of moving in one dimension? Crew can move in 2 dimensions, with a limited ability to move in the third dimension via stairways and ladders.

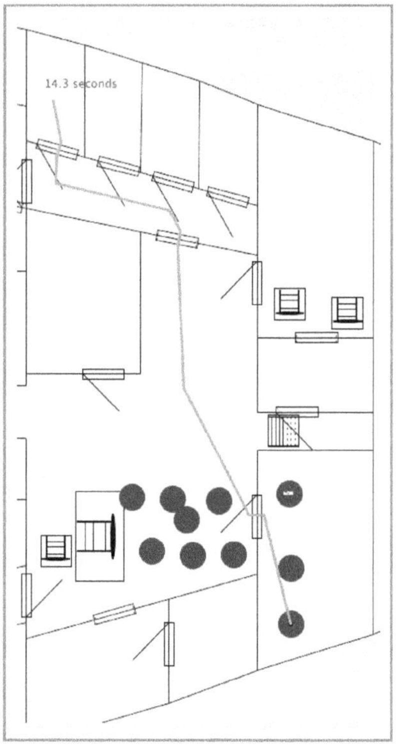

Well, it turns out that once the crew member has selected a route, he or she breaks the path into segments. Each of those segments is a line or spline, and we can consider the movement along it to be the very same one dimensional "Am I there yet?" problem that I opened this paper with.

Exception Handling

However, we have a few other rules that come into play.

Because we are calculating a route in a ship that can include spaces that are on fire, flooded, or both, it's a very real possibility that no route exists between two points. In that case we must fail our task.

An agent may find him or herself in a hazardous situation, or discover that a compartment he/she was intending to route through is inaccessible. If that is the case, he/she should withdraw to a safe location and compute a new route.

We also have to account for the fact that this task may be interrupted. And when we get control back, the agent may be in a different location than where we had intended to be.

```
method movement location {
  set here [my location]
  if {[my isNearby $destination]} {
    return 0
  }
  set route [crewroute find $here \
     $destination]
  if {[llength $route]==0} {return -1}
  my route $route
  while 1 {
    if {[my goal] != $destination} {
      return 2
    }
    if {[my hazard_detect]} {
      my withdraw
      return 2
    }
    if {[my isNearby $destination]} {
     return 0
    }
    yield 1
  }
}
```

In agent based modeling there are a different grades of exceptions. I imagine there are canonical terms for them, but I classify them as blocks, conflicts, and punts.

A **block** exception is when something external temporarily impedes the progress of our agent. The task simply bides it's time until the blockage has cleared.

A **conflict** exception is when two tasks require the same resource for mutually exclusive goals. A higher power sorts out which task gets priority. But the loser of that battle will have to restart from square one the next time it's called.

A **punt** exception is one which terminates the task because the conditions that justify the task's existence are no longer valid.

Standardize Yield and Return Codes

> *Fighting with a large army under your command is nowise different from fighting with a small one: it is merely a question of instituting signs and signals.*
> *--Sun Tsu, The Art of War, Chapter V*

One trouble with coroutines is that once they return a value, they cease to exist. Calling a completed coroutine will cause an error.

In my systems, I use the code returned to tell us the fate of the coroutine. An active coroutine yields a 1. Any other value indicates that the coroutine terminated, and will need to be restarted.

Code	Meaning
-1	Exception
0	Normal Exit
1	Running
2	Waiting
3	Blocked

The caller can interpret these codes, and react accordingly.

Task Nesting

It's very useful to break large goals into smaller goals that can be reused. We often have a crew member go out to a device, operate it, and come home.

But our toplevel task may want to respond to exceptions in it's own way.

I've found it useful to employ a bit of syntactic sugar in the form of the **subtask** command.

```
method attend {objective} {
  set location [objective location \
    $objective]
  # Go to the device
  while 1 [subtask movement $location]
  # Operate the device
  while 1 [subtask mitl $objective]
  # Return home
  set home [my home]
  while 1 [subtask movement $home]
  return 0
}
```

With **subtask**, we assume that a positive value (even if non-one) will not allow the program to continue. A zero indicates success, and allows the program to continue. A negative value represents an exception that should be punted.

Without **subtask**, the method above would look like:

```
method attend {objective} {
  set location [objective \
    location $objective]
  # Go to the device
  while 1 {
   set result [movement \
     $location]
   if { $result < 0 } {
     return -1
   } elseif { $result > 0 } {
     yield 1
   } else {
     break
   }
  # Operate the device
  while 1 {
    ....
```

(And continue on to fill the entire column on the right.)

The implementation for **subtask** is as follows:

```
proc subtask {cmd args} {
 set positive {yield 1}
 set negative {return $result}
 set zero {return 0}
 foreach {f v} $args {set $f $v}
 foreach f {
   positive negative zero cmd
 } {
  lappend replace %${f}% [set $f]
 }
 return [string map $replace {
  set result [{*}%cmd%]
  if { $result < 0 } {%negative%} \
  elseif { $result > 0 } {%positive%} \
  else {%zero%}
 }
}
```

Note, **subtask** doesn't run code, it builds code. That block of code becomes the body of the while loop.

subtask can take options (positive, negative, and zero) which allow the developer to control the agent's reactions to the sub-task's return code.

High Level Tasks

Agents often have to deal with competing goals. Because we've gone through the trouble of standardizing our return and yield codes, it's easy to detect when one goal is running, and could potentially block another task from running.

Let's refactor our methods so that we have three top level goals. One is to "attend". If the agent is assigned a device, he/she will walk to and operate the device. How the agent receives the assignment can vary. It is quite possible that after completing the first assignment the agent could have received a communication to do a second or a third. So it wouldn't be very efficient to walk home after each time.

The next goal is to return home, but only if we have nothing to do.

Preempting either goals is the **safety_check**. **safety_check** is a reflex that will cause the agent to flee a space if he or she detects danger.

We also include a method "task" which will kick off a coroutine if it isn't operating yet, or evaluate one iteration of a coroutine that does exist.

You can see all of this put together in an example on the right.

Multitasking

All of this is work as built up to a system for multitasking that, while powerful, turns out to be simple and relatively uninteresting. Because coroutines are engaged in cooperative multitasking the loop for running an entire simulation with a few hundred agents can be as simple as:

```
proc simulation_step {} {
  physics_step
  foreach agent [agent::list] {
    $agent behavior
  }
}
```

In the IRM I have a routine no more complex than this that runs 40 odd crew members, 30 automated devices (which also behave as agents), and still operates in real time[3].

```
method attend {} {
 set objective [my get_assignment]
 if { $objective eq {} } {return 0}
 set location [objective \
    location $objective]
  # Go to the device
  while 1 [subtask \
    {movement $location} negative {
      record_failure $objective
      cancel_assignment $objective
      return 0
    }]
  # Operate the device
  while 1 [subtask mitl $objective]
  cancel_assignment $objective
  return 0
}

method go_home {} {
  set home [my home]
  while 1 [subtask movement $home]
  return 0
}

method safety_check {} {
  if {![my hazard_check]} {return 0}
  set dest [my escape_route]
  my route [route $dest]
  while 1 {
    if {![my hazard_check]} {return 0}
    yield 1
  }
  return 1
}

method task name {
 set coro [self]/coro_$name
 if {[info command $coro] == {} } {
  return [coroutine $coro [self] $name]
 } else {
  return [$coro]
 }
}

method behavior {} {
  my variable task_status
  set task_status {}
  foreach task {
    safety_check
    attend
    go_home
  } {
    set status [my task $task]
    dict set task_status $status
    if {$status > 1} break
  }
  return $task
}
```

3 Granted with a lot of the heavy calculations optimized in C.

Conclusions

Coroutines, while not new as a concept, are new to Tcl. In this paper I have have demonstrated that coroutines can be used to run complex discrete time simulations. And not just run, but run simply.

Coroutines are particularly well suited for simulations:

- That require multitasking across multiple agents
- Operate in discrete time
- Are amenable to cooperative multitasking.

Bibiliography

de Moura, Ana Lu ́cia and Ierusalimschy, Roberto, 2004, Revisiting Coroutines, (PUC-RioInf.MCC15/04 June, 2004), http://www.inf.puc-rio.br/~roberto/docs/MCC15-04.pdf, (October, 8 2011)

Sofer, Miguel and Madden, Neil, Coroutines, (Tip #328, Revision: 1.6), http://www.tcl.tk/cgi-bin/tct/tip/328.html, (October 9, 2011)

An Overview of the Next Scripting Toolkit

Gustaf Neumann and Stefan Sobernig

{firstname.lastname}@wu.ac.at

Tcl/Tk 2011 Conference, October 2011

Abstract

This paper introduces the Next Scripting Framework (NSF) and the Next Scripting Language (NX). The paper presents features such as the definition of object systems, parametric objects, initialization and interfacing to object states, creating object behavior, and designing object interfaces and interactions. Along the way, we review some syntactic additions and developer support tools for developing NSF/NX programs. Our goal is to provide a comprehensive overview of the NSF/NX features, including hands-on code examples, by comparing NX to its next relative XOTcl.

A Toolkit for Developing A Family of OO Languages

The Next Scripting Framework (NSF) and the object system NX have been developed between 2008 and 2011 at the Institute for Information Systems and New Media of the Vienna University of Business and Economics. These systems continue a research line and a development effort, starting in the late 90s, to develop better language support for adopting OO Design Patterns, for managing program variability by first-class abstractions (e.g., aspect and feature modularization), and for creating different object-oriented languages in Tcl, as well as special-purpose application languages; e.g., embedded, textual DSLs [15]. As the first code artifact, XOTcl was presented in 2000 [4] and introduced novel language constructs: filters, as well as per-object, per-class, and transitive mixin classes [7]. XOTcl heavily influenced the design of TclOO [5], which is in many respects a simplified and streamlined descendant of XOTcl.

The Next Scripting Framework (NSF) generalizes many ideas of XOTcl. NSF allows for fully scripted definitions of object systems, while preserving (and even improving) the performance properties of C-based implementations. For example, the scripted NSF implementation of XOTcl 2.0 is significantly faster than the C-based XOTcl 1.6 implementation [3].

NSF lets the Tcl programmer create several object systems in a single interpreter. Object systems are initially created without any predefined behavior (methods), granting the object system designer (Tcl developer) the full freedom of defining and naming method interfaces. With scriptable object systems and new composition techniques (e.g., method aliasing), NSF adds to Tcl's support for language-oriented programming [8].

While XOTcl 2.0 is designed for backward compatibility with XOTcl 1.* scripts, the Next Scripting Language (NX) is the result of an extensive re-design and perfective refactoring of XOTcl. This further development builds on the experience of several large-scale development projects (i.e., several hundred thousand lines of Tcl/XOTcl code, 10+ developers, etc.). The NX language is designed to ease language learning by novices (e.g., by using "mainstream" terminology, higher orthogonality of method interfaces, smaller core interfaces), to improve maintainability (e.g., preventing common errors) and to encourage developers to create better structured programs. Providing different types of interface abstraction, code evolution and collaborative development between several developers are facilitated.

The remainder of this paper expands on key features of the NSF/NX programming toolkit. In this feature presentation, we want to stress the advancements achieved since our Tcl'09 paper [3]. First, we introduce some basics of the object system model (in particular, entity and relationship types) underlying any NSF-based language. In a subsequent step, we guide through the major contributions: Concrete syntax enhancements (scripted init-blocks, prefixes for instance variables and methods), new language abstractions (method ensembles, method aliases, properties), and added language expressiveness (object parametrization, parameter types). We also sketch out the developer support provided by the NSF/NX toolkit, including DTrace integration and a memory debugging facility, generator support for developing Tcl/C APIs and extension libraries, a functional testing environment (nx::test), and a documentation generator (nxdoc). We conclude by reporting performance data collected for the NSF/NX language runtime.

Scripted Definition of Object Systems

NSF offers a low-level API providing a small set of primitive commands to define the behavior of tailored object systems. An object system is formed from a subset of the (extensible) base features with free naming support. The notion of object systems stresses objects as the first-class entities. Objects can be related differently, including meta-class/class, class/instance, mixin, and composition relations [4]. For managing object states, APIs of different expressiveness and complexity (primitive setter/getter commands, accessor/mutator methods, slots) can be adopted. For defining object behavior, methods can be defined for various scopes (e.g., object, class, mixin) and advanced forms of implementation reuse (e.g., method aliasing of Tcl procs and Tcl/C commands) are available in addition to forwarders. Method properties such as redefinition and call protection can be specified. Parametric objects and methods can be realized using a unified parametrization infrastructure, equipped with non-positional and positional parameters and parameter type annotations.

Once defined, multiple object systems can coexist in a single Tcl interpreter, the object systems can be used interleaved in a script. For example, NX is provided as a purely scripted Tcl package (loadable via "package require") in the same way as the backward-compatible XOTcl 2.0 object system.

The Next Scripting Framework (NSF) provides a set of about 30 language-programming primitives in the `nsf` namespace. The primitive `nsf::objectsystem::create` allows for declaring a pair of root objects for an NSF object system: a root class (first argument) and a root meta-class (second argument).

Listing 1: A minimal NSF Object System

```
# Create an object system with the base classes named "myObject" and
# "myClass"
nsf::objectsystem::create myObject myClass

# Bind a pre-existing method for creating objects from the methods
# pool in "nsf::methods" as "+" to "myClass". After this method is
# registered, every class/meta-class of this object system can use "+"
# to create objects or classes.
nsf::method::alias myClass + nsf::methods::class::create

# Bind a pre-existing method for deleting objects from the methods
# pool in "nsf::methods" as "-" to "myObject". Once this method is
# defined, every object of this object system can be deleted using
# "-".
nsf::method::alias myObject - nsf::methods::object::destroy

# Create an application class using the method "+":
myClass + C

# Create an instance of the application class:
C + c1

# Delete the instance using the method "-":
c1 -
```

As can be seen from Listing 1, the names of the base classes (`myObject` and `myClass`) are provided to the command `nsf::objectsystem::create` as the first two arguments. The root objects determine elementary relationship types between the objects living in a given object system and describe common behavior for all objects. The creation command for the object system covers several tasks: To begin with, the memory stores for the root objects are created. Once allocated and registered as Tcl commands, the root objects are put into elementary relations to each other (e.g., instance-of and superclass/subclass relations; see below). Finally, the essentially behavior-less root objects (i.e., their empty method records) can be populated with behavior by the language designer.

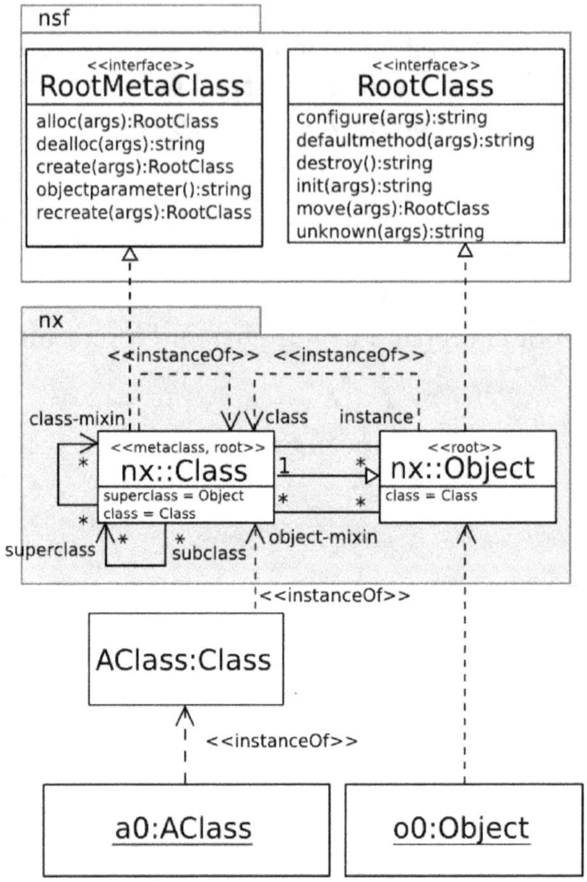

Figure 2. The NX Object System

While the bare root objects do not carry any predefined or built-in methods accessible at the script level, the NSF engine requires the root objects to support basic lifecycle operations (e.g., object creation, deletion, recreation etc.). These methods might not only be called in the script, but also from within the NSF engine. For these cases, one can optionally bind methods to the system callbacks during the definition of the object system (not shown above). In this sense, the root objects implement interfaces required by the NSF engine (see `RootMetaClass` and `RootClass` in Figure 2).

When implementing these two required interfaces, the language designer has considerable degrees of freedom: First, one can choose custom names (selectors) for the system methods. Second, one can bind either predefined or custom method implementations to these selectors. Third, upon declaring the object system by nsf::objectsystem::create, one can define custom default bindings for the system methods without exposing them as accessible methods.

```
nsf::objectsystem::create myObject myClass
nsf::method::alias myClass  + ::nsf::methods::class::create
nsf::method::alias myObject - ::nsf::methods::object::destroy

nsf::is class myObject      ; # --> 1
nsf::is metaclass myObject  ; # --> 0

nsf::is class myClass       ; # --> 1
nsf::is metaclass myClass   ; # --> 1

nsf::relation myObject class        ;# --> ::myClass
nsf::relation myObject superclass   ;# -->

nsf::relation myClass class         ;# --> ::myClass
nsf::relation myClass superclass    ;# --> ::myObject
```

The creation of an object system establishes characteristic and mutual ties between the root meta-class myClass and the root class myObject. Most importantly, myObject is defined as an instance of myClass (the class of myObject is myClass), and myClass is a subclass of myObject (the superclass of myClass is myObject). Therefore, every class is an object and inherits the general object behavior.

This relational triad between root meta-class and root class underlies any NSF object system and is automatically established by nsf::objectsystem::create. A language designer can obtain the same relational setting by declaring the relations explicitly, using the NSF primitive nsf::relation.

Listing 3: System Methods Specification for the NX Object System

```
namespace eval ::nx {

  nsf::objectsystem::create ::nx::Object ::nx::Class {
    -class.alloc {alloc ::nsf::methods::class::alloc}
    -class.create create
    -class.dealloc {dealloc ::nsf::methods::class::dealloc}
    -class.objectparameter objectparameter
    -class.recreate {recreate ::nsf::methods::class::recreate}
    -object.configure configure
    -object.defaultmethod {defaultmethod ::nsf::methods::object::defaultmethod}
    -object.destroy destroy
    -object.init {init ::nsf::methods::object::init}
    -object.move move
    -object.unknown unknown
  }

}
```

NSF defines a set of about 30 primitive commands in the `::nsf` namespace for further defining the object system. For application developers, however, the necessary functionality offered by the NSF primitive commands is exposed by the object system (e.g., the `info` method for introspection) directly.

The NX object system (see Figure 2) is entirely defined using these language-programming primitives. Listing 3 depicts the relevant script fragment for creating the NX root objects (`nx::Object`, `nx::Class`), as well as for tailoring the provided system method interfaces.

The NX Concrete Syntax

Scripted Init-Blocks - Defining Objects Block-wise

In the tradition of nesting evaluable Tcl scripts as definition units (e.g., proc bodies, looping constructs, namespace scripts), NX objects can evaluate scripts in their context upon request or upon initialization. The scripted init-blocks are evaluated at the end of object initialization and are typically used for defining variables, properties and methods. A block-wise notation helps avoid redundancy (i.e., tediously repeated object names) and allows for grouping related declaration statements.

Consider a bare example. Instead of defining a class and its structural features (i.e., relations, properties, and methods) via separate Tcl commands ...

```
nx::Class create ASuperClass
nx::Class create AClass

AClass superclass ASuperclass
AClass property aProperty
AClass public method aMethod {} {...}
```

one can specify a script for every object/class definition which is evaluated in the context of the newly created entity:

```
nx::Class create ASuperClass

nx::Class create AClass -superclass ASuperClass {
   :property {aProperty 0}
   :public method aMethod {} {...}
}
```

The `create` method accepts the name of the entity to be created (here `AClass`) and optional, non-positional parameters for configuring the entity; referred to as *object parameters*. After the object parameters, an optional script might be provided which is called the *init script*. In this example, all commands in the init script are prefixed by a single colon, which means that they denote methods dispatched on the current object (here `AClass`). This is achieved by using a special-purpose command resolver [3].

Scripted init-blocks are equally available for declaring all kind of objects, i.e., direct instances of `nx::Object` or instances of arbitrary application classes.To create instances of the previously defined class `AClass`, one can write:

```
AClass create a0
AClass create a1 -aProperty 10
AClass create a2 {
   :public method foo {} {...}
}
```

While the instance `a0` is created without object parameters (using just the defaults), the instance `a1` is initialized by object parameters, and `a2` uses a scripted init block for defining an object-specific method `foo`.

The Colon Prefix - Shortcutting Self Calls and Self-Variable Access

By leveraging Tcl's variable and command resolver infrastructure, NSF introduces colon-prefixed names for referencing instance variables and for specifying method calls with implicit receivers for little syntactic overhead. The colon prefix refers to the current object for the scope of scripts evaluated in an object's context (e.g., in init scripts or in method bodies).

```
AClass create a2 {

   set :x 1; # set an instance variable named "x"

   :public method foo {} {
       set x 1    ; # set a method-scoped variable
       set :x 1   ; # set an instance variable
       set ::x 1  ; # set a global variable
       incr :x    ; # access an instance variable
       puts "var x value ${:x}"; # refer to value of an instance variable
   }

   :foo
}
```

In the above listing, each colon-prefixed variable reference resolves to an instance variable named `x` stored with the object `a2`. When requesting instance variable substitution, the dollar sign must be preceded by the colon-prefixed variable name protected by a pair of curly braces, for example: `${:x}`. A colon-prefixed command name (such as `:public`) corresponds to an invocation of a method of the same object. For example, `:foo` corresponds to `my foo` in XOTcl.

Slim Method Set - Easing API Learning

Each NSF object system provides a core API through its base classes. The perceived usability [2] of APIs is affected by various cognitive properties, including the API's conceptual chunks needed for frequent programming tasks (e.g., introspection) and the penetrability of an API. An ultimate design goal was therefore to keep the core interface of NX as concise and as consistent as possible. As a result of this design effort and new implementation techniques being available (e.g., extensible method ensembles), the NX core API consists of only 44 methods, as compared to 124 in XOTcl, while exhibiting a functional superset of the XOTcl core API.

Table 1. Comparison of the Number of Predefined Methods in NX and XOTcl

	NX	XOTcl
Methods for Objects	20	51
Methods for Classes	3	24
Info-methods for Objects	15	25
Info-methods for Classes	6	24
Total	**44**	**124**

In addition to the reduced interface sizes, the NX core APIs also benefit from the capacity of creating method interfaces in a hierarchical manner. The figure below sketches the tree-like structure of the `info` introspection available for all instances of `nx::Object`. Each sub-level of the hierarchical interface (e.g., `callable`, `has`, `filter`, and `mixin`) groups introspection operations which relate to the same language construct to be introspected (e.g., mixins or filters) or which identify a particular introspection scope. For example, `info callable` refers to the methods dispatchable on a given object rather than the ones defined by it (`info methods`). Hierarchical method interfaces allow the language or application developer to define working frameworks [2] within an API. At the same time, the hierarchically organized interfaces can still be extended and refined by standard means of method combination (e.g., mixin classes) at each sub-level. This API structuring technique is the result of using method ensembles(find details below).

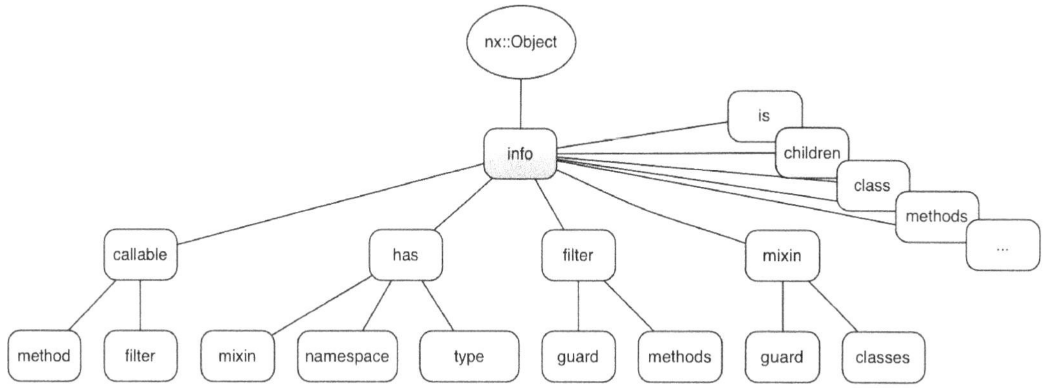

Figure 4. Hierarchical Method Interfaces: An Excerpt from the 'info' Method Ensemble

Parameter Types and Parameter Options - Constraining and Transforming Parameter Values

Tcl provides the command `string is` to check whether a provided string has certain properties, i.e., whether it can be converted into an internal representation with a certain value format. NSF extends this value checking for specifying method parameters and method return values, as well as object interfaces. A method is specified by a method signature, i.e., the number of method parameters (in/out), their names, and value constraints defined over the permissive arguments. An object is configured by object parameters.

Value constraints for method and object parameters can be specified with built-in and custom defined parameter type checkers. They apply to both positional and non-positional parameters. The range of built-in constraints includes object-type checks and predefined Tcl value classes. Table 2 below presents selected examples of parameter types and options. Additionally, custom defined value checkers can be provided by defining special-purpose methods.

For all types of value checkers, parameter options can be specified to define the multiplicity class and the optionality of the parameters. Moreover, parameters can be turned into method and forwarder dispatches, using disposition parameters. For multivalued object parameters, an incremental getter/setter API is available, offering the per-element operations `add` and `delete`.

These provided value checkers can also be used to perform representational transformations on parameter values (e.g., normalizing values). This syntactic value checking can be en- or disabled for the scope of an interpreter; in the sense of an optional representational "type system" [1].

Listing 5: Parameter Types for Arguments and Return Values

```
nx::Class create C {

  # Define method "set" with an optional positional parameter "value":
  :public method set {varName value:optional} {
    # ....
  }

  # Define method "foo" with a non-positional parameter "opt" having a
  # default value and a positional parameter "x" with the value
  # constraint "integer":
  :public method foo {{-opt true} x:integer} {
    # ....
  }

  # Define a method "bar" with a non-positional
  # parameter "objs" carrying the value constraint "object" under the
  # multiplicity class "1..n" and a positional parameter "c" with value
  # constraint "class" for a multiplicity of "0..1":
  :public method bar {-objs:object,1..n c:class,0..1} {
    # ...
  }

  # Bind the Tcl command ::incr as a method (an alias) to the class and specify
  # that it always returns an integer value:
  :public alias incr -returns integer -frame object ::incr

  # Define a forwarder that has to return an integer value:
  :public forward plusOne -returns integer ::expr 1 +
}
```

Value checking is fully integrated with the argument parser and the error handler for scripted and for C-implemented methods. For C-implemented methods, value checking provides the internal representations (e.g. integers, boolean, objects, classes, etc.) as arguments to the underlying C functions [3]. This greatly helps implement C extensions, such as the MongoDB binding described later in this paper.

Table 2. Thumbnail Descriptions of Common Parameter Types and Parameter Options

Parameter type/option	Description
	Value constraints
integer	The argument must be a 32-bit Tcl integer (`string is integer`).
boolean	The argument must be one of the acceptable Tcl boolean values, e.g. `0`, `1`, `true`, `false` (`string is boolean`).

Parameter type/option	Description
object ? type=className ?	The argument must refer to an existing object (i.e., an instance of the root class `nx::Object`). If the `type` option is provided, the object's class must correspond to an existing class *className*.
class ? type=metaClassName ?	The argument must refer to an existing class (i.e., an instance of the root meta-class `nx::Class`). If the `type` option is provided, the class' meta-class must correspond to an existing meta-class named *metaClassName*.
	Multiplicities
0..*, 0..n	Specifies that the argument can be either an empty list (i.e., `""` or `[list]`) or a list with any number of elements (unbound cardinality). If the argument is a non-empty list (element cardinality > 0), each element is then tested against the value constraint specified.
0..1	Specifies that the argument can either be an empty list (i.e., `""` or `[list]`) or a list with exactly one element (cardinality: 1). If the argument is a non-empty list (element cardinality > 0), the element is then tested against the value constraint specified.
1..*, 1..n	Specifies that the argument must be a non-empty list with an unbounded number of elements (cardinality > 1). Each element is then tested against the value constraints specified.
	Requiredness/Optionality
required	An argument for the parameter must be provided. Note: Positional parameters are considered required implicitly.
optional	An argument for the parameter may be omitted in the arguments vector. Note: Non-positional (named) parameters are considered optional implicitly.
	Disposition
alias ? method=methodName ?	The parameter specifies a method dispatch to a method identified by the parameter name or, if the `method` option is provided , to a method *methodName*. An unqualified name resolves to a method for the scope of the called object.
forward method=forwardSpec	The parameter specifies a forward dispatch, according to the mandatory `method` type which contains the forward specification *forwardSpec*.
	Various
switch	The parameter is specified as a flag, i.e., a non-positional parameter which does not accept an explicit argument. If the flag is provided, the default value (`0` for `false`) is toggled. The default value can be set explicitly to change the toggle direction.
incremental	The object parameter representing a multivalued instance variable should be mutable through per-element ("incremental") setter methods, including methods for adding and deleting single elements.

Object Parameters - Configuration Interfaces for Objects

Like method signatures declaring positional and non-positional parameters with default values and value constraints, NX provides parameters for initializing and configuring objects and classes. The parametric object interfaces are derived from the class definitions. In conventional OO languages, object creation and initialization are realized by chained constructor methods, risking unwanted interactions in classification hierarchies (e.g., common constructor anomalies [9]). The less ambiguous object initialization through object parameters and scripted init-blocks complements the use of constructors.

Recall the classic example of a compositional anomaly resulting from pairing constructor chaining and dynamic method binding in a class hierarchy. The following code listing reproduces an example for creating partially initialized objects for XOTcl, adopted from [12].

```
xotcl::Class create A
A instproc init args {
  # 2) Invoke method "m", dispatching to B.m()!
  my m
}
A instproc m {} {
  # ...
}

# A subclass, possibly defined by a different module (e.g., Tcl package)
xotcl::Class create B -superclass A -parameter {b}
B instproc init {s} {
  # 1) Pass control to the superclass constructor
  next    ; # dispatching A.init()
  # 3) Initialize and define the instance variable "b"
  my instvar b
  set b $s
}
B instproc m {} {
  # 4) Returning instance variable 'b', which is expected to be
  # already initialized and defined
  my instvar b
  return $b
}

B create b1 "ZAP!"; # --> can't read "b": no such variable while executing "return $b"
```

The numbering of the comments (1, 2, 3, and 4) reflects the "intended" unfolding of the control flow during the creation of an instance of B. The anomalous behavior manifests in terms of step 3 effectively occurring after step 4. This is due to the dispatch to *m*, which is contracted by the superclass constructor `A init`, causing an preemptive attempt to access of `B`'s instance variable `b`, yet to be initialized and defined in the subclass constructor `B init`.

This is only one example of various kinds of constructor anomalies discussed in [9]. A further critical kind of anomalies is that construction protocols, though automatically inherited down a class hierarchy (at least in NX and XOTcl), can be easily breached — maybe intentionally, maybe accidentally — by simply omitting a `next` in a subclass constructor. NX, as well as XOTcl, are even more vulnerable to such anomalies due to the considerable degrees of freedom during object configuration (e.g., dispatching to `init` or accessor methods in arbitrary orders) and due to the compositional complexity incurred by mixin classes and transitive mixins.

The object parameter facility in NX relaxes this vulnerability to constructor-based parametrization anomalies considerably. Rewriting the above example in NX yields, for example:

```
nx::Class create A {
  :method init {} {
    :m
  }
  :public method m {} {
    # ...
  }
}

nx::Class create B -superclass A {
  :property b:required
  :public method m {} {
    return ${:b}
  }
}

B create b1 -b "ZAP!"
B create b2; # --> required argument 'b' is missing, should be: ::b2 configure -b ...
```

Object parameters provide means for discriminating between four separated stages when constructing objects:

1. *Creation:* This is a class-side event, with the operations for allocating a memory store etc. being performed in the scope of the instantiating class.
2. *Parametrization:* At this stage, the argument vector passed to the object creation procedure (i.e., `-b "ZAP!"`) is evaluated against the object parameter specification of the newly created instance. This specification represents the concatenation of all object parameters (e.g., `A property b:required`) going up the entire inheritance path of the instance's class. The parameter specifications can also contract the mandatoriness or value ranges of parameter values, along with default values etc.
3. *Setup by Init Script:* After having completed the parametrization stage, the object is fully initialized as stipulated by the object parameter specification. The evaluation of the init script block is performed to allow for continued set-

up of the newly constructed object. This step can only be performed once, i.e., at construction time, as the init script is not preserved.

4. *Setup by Constructor:* Finally, the chain of `init` methods provided is invoked upon. Note that in NX, the `init` methods do not receive any intermediary results of previous object construction or residuals of the initial vector of construction arguments as input arguments. In NX, constructor methods are therefore not equipped for initializing the initial state of an object. Still, they serve as important extension points during object construction.

Object Variables and Properties - Defining Object State

NX supports defining instance variables with and without accessor methods. While internally accessible instance variables are defined via the method `variable`, externally accessible instance variables are equipped with accessors (setter/getter methods). In addition, so accessible instance variables can also be exposed as object parameters by the object interface. Instance variables with accessors are created using the `property` keyword. Value checkers can be specified for instance variables defined via `variable` and via `property`. Properties can also be accessed through an incremental getter/setter interface (`add`, `delete`). The following listing gives three showcase examples, including the specification of default values and parameter types with `property` and `variable`, respectively:

```
nx::Class create AClass {
  :property {aProperty:integer 0}
  :variable aVariable:integer 0
  :property {multiProperty:1..*,integer,incremental 0}
  :create a1
}

#
# property plus setter/getter methods
#
::a1 aProperty; # returns "aProperty" (0) through the so-named getter method
::a1 aProperty 1; # sets "aProperty" through the so-named setter method

#
# variable without setter/getter methods
#
::a1 aVariable; # no getter method: ::a1: unable to dispatch method 'aVariable'
::a1 aVariable 1; # no setter method: ::a1: unable to dispatch method 'aVariable'
::a1 eval {set :aVariable}; # internally, the instance variable is accessible/mutable

#
# property with incremental setter/getter methods
#
::a1 multiProperty; # returns 0
::a1 multiProperty delete 0; # removes an element from the list
::a1 multiProperty add 1; # adds an element to the list and returns 1
::a1 multiProperty add 2 end; # adds another element and returns "1 2"
```

Methods

Like XOTcl, NX offers open class and open object definitions. This means, for example, that it is possible to define a class or an object without methods and to add methods dynamically at runtime. NX supports scripted and C-implemented methods. Scripted methods are defined via a predefined keyword `method`. When `method` is applied on a class, an instance method is defined (i.e., a method applicable to instances of the class); when `method` is applied on an object, an object-specific method is defined. The method definition can be refined by modifiers such as `public` and `protected` to request call protection and by the keyword `class` to refer explicitly to the class object. One can use `class method` to define methods applicable to the class object. Such methods are sometimes referred to as "class" or "static" methods. Similarly, one can use `class variable` or `class property` to define variables and properties for the class object.

Aliases and Forwarders - Method-Level Reuse

In addition to defining scripted methods as outlined above, NX supports reusing preexisting method definitions for a class or for an object by means of method aliases and method forwarders. For aliasing a method, NX provides the method `alias`. Aliasing means registering a method by a distinct name with an object. This method alias can refer to the implementation of a method of another object/class, a Tcl proc, or even a Tcl/C command.

In NX, the idea of assembling the base class interfaces from a set of core C-implemented commands [3] is extended to a general-purpose aliasing mechanism in NX (not to be confused with Tcl's interp aliases). Method aliases are one foundation of traits and method ensembles (we go into more details in later sections). Aliases serve for bootstrapping an object system and are an essential instrument for object system developers (as presented earlier in Listing 1).

Listing 6: Method Aliases and Method Forwarders

```
nx::Class create C
  :property {a 0}
  :public alias incr -returns integer -frame object ::incr
  :public forward plusOne -returns integer ::expr 1 +
}

C create c1     ;# create instance c1
c1 incr a       ;# increments instance variable "a" to 1
c1 incr a       ;# increments instance variable "a" to 2

puts [c1 a]     ;# outputs 2
```

```
puts [c1 plusOne [c1 a] * 100] ;# outputs 201
puts [c1 a]     ;# outputs 2
```

The `alias` statement in Listing 6 are taken from Listing 5. It defines a public instance method named `incr` of the class `C`, which reuses the implementation of the C-implemented Tcl command `::incr`. The parametrization by `-frame object` has the effect that variable names provided as arguments to the newly defined method `incr` refer to instance variables. Note that all arguments provided to a method alias are always passed unmodified to the underlying command implementation.

A *method forward* is somewhat similar to a method alias except that one can extend and rewrite the provided argument vector. The definition of the method `plusOne` reuses the Tcl command `::expr` and adds `1 +` at the front of the provided argument vector to complete the Tcl expression.

In general, a method forward is more flexible than a method alias, but less efficient. Apart from efficiency, method aliases have another important property: For a method alias, introspection returns the method parameter specification of the alias target (if available). Parameter introspection is not possible for a method forward.

Method Ensembles - Implementing Hierarchical Method Interfaces

The capacity of objects to act as message receivers [3] has been further refined into the concept of ensemble objects and method ensembles. Resembling Tcl's idiom of sub-commands and namespace ensembles, ensemble methods establish hierarchical and compound method names in an extensible fashion. From the perspective of a method client, not only a single but multiple Tcl words are the selectors of a method implementation. As for the method provider, a complex protocol (e.g., introspection through info) can be organized into several related ensemble method implementations.

Central to the compositional feature of ensemble methods is the idea of breaking up otherwise monolithic methods with heavy conditional branching (e.g, extensive switch threading) into distinct units, i.e., ensemble methods [11]. At the same time, the ensemble methods remain grouped by a parent method selector. Consider the following example:

Listing 7: Definition of Ensemble Methods without Language Support

```
Object create o {

  # Define method "foo", the parent method selector:
```

```
  :public method foo {sub args} {
    #
    # Define sub-methods behavior via "switch" statement
    #
    switch -exact -- $sub {
      sub1 {
        # ensemble method 'foo sub1': provide a custom parser for "args"
      }
      sub2 {
        # ensemble method 'foo sub2': provide a custom parser for "args"
      }
      default {
        # unknown handling
        set m "[current method]: unknown sub-method '$sub'. Available: sub1 sub2"
        return -code error $m
      }
    }
  }
}

o foo sub1 arg1 arg2; # OK
o foo sub2 -np1 arg1 -np2 arg2 arg3; # OK
o foo sub3; # --> foo: unknown ensemble method 'sub3'. Available: sub1 sub2
```

While this switch-threaded method implementation certainly mimics sub-commands (i.e., `foo sub1` and `foo sub2`) to a certain extent, there are considerable limitations, potentially affecting code evolution and maintenance tasks:

1. *Homogeneous vs. Heterogeneous Signatures*: To begin with, there is a tension between providing heterogeneous signatures for ensemble methods and reusing the built-in parameter processing infrastructure. In the above example, the intention is to constrain `foo sub1` to requiring two positional parameters only, while `foo sub2` accepts two non-positional parameters. The parent method `foo` effectively shares its method parameter specification with its children, with the variable argument vector (`args`) not enforcing any further parameter constraints on behalf of the ensemble methods. This leaves the developer with the only option to enforce the signature constraints specific to each ensemble method in the respective switch branch by providing for custom argument parsing.
2. *Blinded introspection*: The built-in object introspection is not aware of the very existence of the ensemble methods nested under `foo`, nor their possibly deviating method parameter specifications. For example, `o info methods foo` and `o info callable methods` won't reveal the two ensemble methods `foo sub1` and `foo sub2`. As one of the consequences, introspection cannot be leveraged to implement ensemble methods. In the above example, the list of available ensemble methods must be maintained explicitly for generating the unknown error message.

3. *Nesting level limitations*: Any implementation variant based on conditional control structures (e.g., switch threading) risks adding further complexity with each further nesting level added to an ensemble method hierarchy (e.g., `foo sub1 sub4`). As each nesting level turns into a nested conditional, e.g., scattered across several switch threads in the example above, the implementation suffers from extra complexity due to dealing with parameter specifications and unknown handling for ensemble methods.
4. *Unknown handling*: The built-in unknown handling of NX is an important meta-programming vehicle. The native unknown handling is sidetracked by the requirement for the switch-local unknown handling. That is, the `default` switch branch replaces the otherwise responsible `unknown` method for objects. Also, unknown handling must be implemented for each and every method ensemble repeatedly; unless facilitated by a piece of meta-programming. Adding nesting levels further complicates this form of ensemble-specific unknown handling.
5. *Method combination*: Combining ensemble methods with refining ensemble methods provided by intrinsic (superclasses) or by extrinsic classification (mixin classes) is hindered. First, the scope for combining methods is the parent selector only. In our example, refining methods can only hook onto the selector `foo`, without further specifying an ensemble method as its refinement target. Second, using `next` chaining in a linearized order of refining `foo` methods becomes non-obvious and error-prone as the scope of `next` calls is the top-level method only.
6. *Method reuse*: The type and the implementation of ensemble methods cannot be reused. This is, to a large extent, due to the limitations of method combination (see the previous item). However, ensemble method implementations based on conditionals are also not accessible to other composition techniques, most importantly method aliases.

Besides, the effects of excessive tangling throughout conditional blocks (e.g., the "Switch Statement Smell" in [10]) and the non-orthogonal extensibility for method ensembles are the consequences. To overcome these limitations, NX supports ensemble methods natively. Ensemble methods are implemented by an advanced form of object delegation hierarchies. A variant of method objects [10], referred to as ensemble objects, are recorded as methods with a registration object. In the above example, `o` acts as the registration object for an ensemble object `foo`, so that `foo` becomes dispatchable as the method member `o foo`. To avoid common pitfalls of method objects, in particular self schizophrenia, special dispatch semantics apply: First, exclusively per-object methods of the ensemble objects provide the leaf methods in a method ensemble hierarchy. Second, the dispatch to an ensemble method is bound to the self-object context of the registration object. With some syntactic sugar, which effectively hides the declaration ensemble objects and the building of their delegation hierarchies, NX allows one to rewrite the example from Listing 7 as:

Listing 8: Definition of Ensemble Methods with Language Support

```
Object create o {
  :public method "foo sub1" {p1 p2} {
    # ...
  }
  :public method "foo sub2" {-np1 -np2 p3} {
    # ...
  }
}

o foo sub1 arg1 arg2; # OK
o foo sub2 -np1 arg1 -np2 arg2 arg3; # OK
o foo sub3;
# --> Unable to dispatch sub-method "sub3" of ::o foo; valid are: foo sub1, foo sub2
```

Such method ensembles can be incrementally extended, indirected by mixins and filters, and easily shared between objects through method aliasing. To complete the support for ensemble methods, object introspection is fully aware of ensemble methods. One can resolve the entire method path, for which a given ensemble method is registered, from within the ensemble method (via `nx::current methodpath`). Also, introspection makes the unfolded method paths available for querying by method path patterns (using e.g. `/obj/ info methods ?-path? … ?pattern?`).

Public, Protected, and Private - Module Encapsulation versus Method Combination

A primary reason for putting units of code (i.e., object, classes) into relation (e.g., instance-of, superclass/subclass) is to establish various kinds of reuse between these code-units. These relations establish ways of accessing, using, or mutating structural and behavioral features (primarily instance variables and methods) of these units. For example, by method combination (using the `next` primitive) a subclass may use the methods of its superclasses. A similar reuse can be achieved by mixin classes, by traits or, at the method level, by method aliases and method forwards.

When reusing complex units of code (e.g. deep class hierarchies), which have possibly been developed by different teams and which have been constantly refactored, one danger arises from unwanted interactions, such as the accidental shadowing of methods. The example of a constructor anomaly given earlier falls into this category of unwanted interactions.

The more relations between code-units are established and the more bloated object interfaces become, the more likely unwanted interactions will occur. To manage such interactions, it is important to define explicit and strict module interfaces [14]. The literature employs the notion of *module encapsulation* for describing means to regulate the accessibility, the use, and the changeability of module features by other modules [13].

NX supports stronger means for module encapsulation than XOTcl. The design goal of NX was to encourage encapsulation by language constructs rather than prohibiting access at all. For example, denying any access to an object's state would make serialization of objects from the scripting language impossible since the serializer needs access to all internals. NX adds the following means of module encapsulation:

1. In NX, the object state (instance variables) is better protected than in XOTcl by not providing any publicly available, built-in accessor methods to all instance variables. XOTcl, on the contrary, exposed the methods `set` and `unset`; or, the general variable importer `instvar`. The *access to instance variables* from within instance methods is encouraged in NX via Tcl's variable resolvers and the colon prefix.
2. The redefinition of behavioral object features (in particular methods and properties) can be restricted by declaring the object features *redefine-protected*.
3. NX provides a fine-grained mechanism to establish method *call-protection* between objects and classes. An object can expose three different method sets at the same time:
    a. The `public` method set is usable by any client object, without restrictions. The methods of this set can be targeted by self-calls (e.g., `:bar` in the example below), next-calls, and command-calls (i.e., when specifying the object's Tcl command name as receiver: `a1 foo`).
    b. The `protected` set restricts the method's use to self-calls and next-calls. That is, calling upon the method set through the command reference of the object is forbidden.
    c. The `private` interface is restricted to self-calls and to call sites defined for the same class or object scope as the called method.

```
nx::Class create A {
  #
  # Public interface of class "A"
  #
  :public method foo args {
    :bar             ; # invoke protected method of current object
  }

  #
  # Protected interface of class "A"
  #
```

```
  :protected method bar {} {
    : -local baz     ; # invoke private method of current object with "-local" flag
    # ...
  }

  #
  # Private interface of class "A"
  #
  :private method baz {} {
    # ...
  }
}
A create ::a1
```

In the above listing, the method modifiers `public`, `protected`, and `private` are used to add methods to these three method sets. If omitted, the default call protection in NX is `protected`. This default can be altered by configuration. From within methods of the instance `::a1`, the protected and the private method sets can be effectively used. The method call statement `:bar` represents a self-call to the protected method set. The invocation of a private method is performed via `: -local baz`. The flag `-local` indicates to call only methods from the private method set. The flag `-local` at the call site makes the intention clear to use only a method declared for the same class context. It cannot be invoked from within methods of subclasses (as the following example shows), nor from methods of superclasses.

However, when the methods `foo`, `bar`, and `baz` are called from the "outside" (i.e., from instances of other classes, or from the top-level namespace), neither the protected, nor the private methods of `A` are callable:

```
a1 foo; # command-call to public interface --> OK
a1 bar; # command-call to protected interface --> ::a1: unable to dispatch method 'bar'
a1 baz; # command-call to private interface --> ::a1: unable to dispatch method 'baz'
```

Let us now introduce a superclass/subclass relation between the classes `A` and `B`, with the sublcass `B` defining its own public method set consisting of the methods `bar` and `baz`:

```
nx::Class create B -superclass A {
  :public method bar {} {
    next     ; # next-call to protected interface --> OK
  }
  :public method baz {} {
    next     ; # next-call does not reach the private method
  }
}

B create ::b1
b1 bar; # command-call to public interface --> OK
```

The public method `B bar` shadows `A bar`. Because `B bar` can be called unrestrictedly, it can be invoked from the outside. Since protected methods are available for next-calls, `A bar` can be reused via `next` in this context.

The method `B baz` is part of the public interface of class `B` and defines a next-call. While `A baz` is a candidate target for this next-call, however, since private methods are not available to next-calls, the invocation of `next` behaves exactly like `A baz` would not have been defined.

The redefinition protection and the call protection in NX are implemented by a set of properties assignable to method implementations through NSF primitives. Based on these property assignments, the language runtime regulates the modification of the method implementations (redefinition protection) and determines the availability of method implementations as message receivers depending on the caller context (call protection). This low-level interface allows the NSF language developer to specify custom redefinition and call protection schemes. For example, for XOTcl 2.0, the default call protection mode is so implemented as `public`.

To summarize, discriminating between `public` and `protected` methods provides for defining explicit object interfaces (i.e., intended ways of having classes and objects reused by client objects). The `private` modifier helps hide implementation details and helps avoid unwanted method combinations due to name clashes in, e.g., mixin classes or traits.

Support for Advanced Feature Composability: Traits

NX supports the concept of per-object, per-class, and transitive per-class mixins [7]. In addition to mixins, NX adds a variant of traits [6] as a scripted language extension. Traits realize a composition mechanism for the reuse of methods. Contrary to other forms of reuse (e.g. inheritance of methods in a class hierarchy or via mixin classes), the methods defined in traits are materialized in the target objects and classes. For the implementation of the traits, method aliases provide the necessary implementation infrastructure. Every method inherited from a trait can be modified, deleted etc. by subsequent method definitions for a given class. This gives more fine-grained control over the reuse of methods and overcomes the "total composition ordering" limitation of mixins [6]. Consider the following example of a simple trait called `tReadStream` which provides the interface to a stream:

```
package require nx::trait

nx::Trait create tReadStream {
  #
  # Define the methods provided by this trait:
```

```
    #
    :public method atStart {} {expr {[:position] == [:minPosition]}}
    :public method atEnd {} {expr {[:position] == [:maxPosition]}}
    :public method setToStart {} {set :position [:minPosition]}
    :public method setToEnd {} {set :position [:maxPosition]}
    :public method maxPosition {} {llength ${:collection}}
    :public method on {collection} {set :collection $collection; :setToStart}
    :public method next {} {
      if {[:atEnd]} {return ""} else {
        set r [lindex ${:collection} ${:position}]
        :nextPosition
        return $r
      }
    }
    :public method minPosition {} {return 0}
    :public method nextPosition {} {incr :position 1}

    # This trait requires a method "position" and a variable
    # "collection" from the base class. The definition of the trait is
    # incomplete in these regards.
    :requiredMethods position
    :requiredVariables collection
  }
```

Define a class ReadStream with properties position and collection which uses the trait. The method require trait checks the requirements of the trait and imports the methods of the trait into the class ReadStream:

```
  nx::Class create ReadStream {
    :property {collection ""}
    :property {position 0}
    :require trait tReadStream
  }
```

One can now create an instance of the class ReadStream ...

```
  ReadStream create r1 -collection {a b c d e}
```

to test the behavior of the composed class:

```
  % r1 atStart
  1
  % r1 atEnd
  0
  % r1 next
  a
  % r1 next
  b
```

NX supports simple and composite traits, with a composite trait definition inheriting from another trait.

MongoDB Mapping

The NSF development toolkit features a Tcl/C-API generator and Tcl_Obj type converters for developing NSF/C extensions. By using these helpers, we developed a MongoDB binding for NX. The C-implemented part of this extension integrates with the C client library of MongoDB. The extension also provides an NX/Tcl package for integration of NX objects with MongoDB.

The MongoDB extension provides both a low-level interface and a high-level, object-oriented interface based on NX. By using this high-level API, one can create NX classes and objects which are equipped with additional capabilities for defining (`property`, `index`), retrieving (`find`), and storing (`save`) objects in MongoDB. The example below shows an excerpt from the *"Business Insider"* data model, a frequently cited MongoDB showcase [16]. The listing depicts the entity definitions for postings, authors, comments, tags etc. Using the parameter option `embedded`, one can created embedded (nested) documents with the required multiplicity. In this example, we also use the `incremental` setter interface for creating tags.

```
package require nx::mongo

nx::mongo::db connect -db "tutorial"
#
# Create the application classes based on the "Business Insider" data
# model. Note that instances of the class "Comment" can be embedded in
# a posting (property "comments") as well as in a "Comment" itself
# (property "replies"). All comments in this example are multivalued
# and declared "incremental" (i.e., one can use slot methods "... add
# ..." and "... delete ..." to add/remove values of the multivalued
# attributes).
#
nx::mongo::Class create Comment {
  :property author:required
  :property comment:required
  :property replies:embedded,incremental,type=::Comment,0..n
}

nx::mongo::Class create Posting {
  :index tags
  :property title:required
  :property author:required
  :property ts:required
  :property comments:embedded,incremental,type=::Comment,0..n
  :property tags:incremental,0..n
}

# Create a Posting
set p [Posting new -title "Too Big to Fail" -author "John S." \
          -ts "05-Nov-09 10:33" -tags {finance economy} \
```

```
        -comments [list \
             [Comment new -author "Ian White" -comment "Great Article!"] \
             [Comment new -author "Joe Smith" -comment "But how fast is it?" \
               -replies [list [Comment new -author "Jane Smith" -comment "scalable?"]]] \
             ]]

# We add an additional comment at the end of the list of the comments
# using the incremental operation "add" ...
$p comments add [Comment new -author "Gustaf N" -comment "This sounds pretty cool"] end

# ... and we add yet another tag ...
$p tags add nx

# ... and save everything
$p save

# Now fetch the first entry with the tag "nx"
set q [Posting find first -cond {tags = nx}]
....
```

Infrastructure and Toolkit

For developing object systems and programs in NSF/NX, a rich development environment is available. Monitoring the runtime performance is possible through a DTrace binding and a native measurement facility. Detecting skewed refcounts is facilitated by a built-in monitoring facility for Tcl_Objs which complements Tcl's `memory` command. For defining Tcl/C APIs based on the uniform parametrization infrastructure of NSF, an API generator based on a declarative API specification language can be used. Functional tests can be managed using the `nx::test` environment, a documentation generator (`nxdoc`) takes Javadoc-styled Tcl comment blocks as input and outputs to various templating backends (e.g., YUIDoc markup documents or wiki pages).

The following listing shows a D script for DTrace which turns DTrace probes on and off during a script run. The D script measures (when activated) the time spent in methods called on `nx::Object`. Finally, it provides a graph produced by the DTrace `quantize` aggregator function.

```
/* -*- D -*-
 *
 * Quantize time between method-entry and method-returns for calls on nx::Object
 *
 * Activate tracing between
 *    nsf::configure dtrace on
 * and
 *    nsf::configure dtrace off
 *
 */

nsf*:::configure-probe /!self->tracing && copyinstr(arg0) == "dtrace" / {
```

```
    self->tracing = (arg1 && copyinstr(arg1) == "on") ? 1 : 0;
}

nsf*:::configure-probe /self->tracing && copyinstr(arg0) == "dtrace" / {
    self->tracing = (arg1 && copyinstr(arg1) == "off") ? 0 : 1;
}

/*
 * Measure time differences on method calls on nx::Object
 */
nsf*:::method-entry /self->tracing && copyinstr(arg1) == "::nx::Object"/ {
    self->start = timestamp;
}

nsf*:::method-return /self->tracing && copyinstr(arg1) == "::nx::Object" && self->start/ {
    @[copyinstr(arg1), copyinstr(arg2)] = quantize(timestamp - self->start);
    self->start = 0;
}
```

The snippet below shows how DTrace can be applied to monitor the evaluation of a NSF/NX test script, as well as how the result is rendered (showing here just a small part of the output). The NSF distribution contains some more examples for using DTrace with NSF/NX.

```
% sudo TCLLIBPATH=. dtrace -F -s dtrace/timestamps-q.d -c "./nxsh tests/object-system.test"
....
  ::nx::Object                                        eval
           value  ------------- Distribution ------------- count
            4096 |                                         0
            8192 |@@@@@@@@@@@@@@@@@@@@@@@@@@@              2
           16384 |                                         0
           32768 |@@@@@@@@@@@@@                            1
           65536 |                                         0

  ::nx::Object                                        vars
           value  ------------- Distribution ------------- count
            2048 |                                         0
            4096 |@@@@@@@@@@@@@@@@@@                       4
            8192 |@@@@@@@@@@@@@@@@@@@@@@                   5
           16384 |                                         0
```

A Synthetic Performance Evaluation

This section presents a first performance comparison between NX and XOTcl 2.0, on the one hand, and XOTcl 1.6.0, on the other hand. The measurement design is comparable to the one presented in [3]. The data for NX, XOTcl 2.0, and XOTcl 1.6.0 were gathered running on top of the same Tcl versions (especially Tcl 8.5.10 and Tcl 8.6b2) and using the same machine (3.33 GHz Intel Core 2 Duo) under Mac OS X 10.6.8. All C-programs and Tcl libraries were compiled with gcc 4.2.1 and identical compiler flags (in particular, `-O3`).

The first probes used to gather execution times were adopted from the methcall benchmark of the OO shootout (http://wiki.tcl.tk/2428). By doing so, the results can be related to previously published benchmark reports for other Tcl object systems.

In addition, probes for object creation and object deletion times are included. To be precise, we measured the average execution time to create and to destroy a single object while creating/destroying 100.000 objects.

Table 3. Comparison of the OO Shootout Benchmark, Object Creation and Deletion

	NX 2.0 Tcl 8.5.10	NX 2.0 Tcl 8.6b2	XOTcl 2.0 Tcl 8.5.10	XOTcl 2.0 Tcl 8.6b2	XOTcl 1.6.0 Tcl 8.5.10	TclOO 0.6 Tcl 8.5.10	TclOO 0.6.3 Tcl 8.6b2
OO Shootout: methcall (n=30.000)	0.57	0.79	2.07	2.78	2.61	1.40	2.07
Object create (n=100.000)	35.63	40.19	39.71	45.46	56.77	48.56	49.85
Object destroy (n=100.000)	20.95	23.21	20.97	22.89	25.77	269.70	257.98

The first table row gives the OO shootout methcall timings. It reports the average timing for 30.000 iterations of the method call probe. The second and third rows show the timings for object creation and deletion. The timing measure is the average execution time per operation in micro seconds (hence, smaller values indicate a better performance).

Figure 9 visualizes the measurement provided in Table 3 in terms of performance improvements relative to XOTcl 1.6.0 (index: 100). The higher the indices, the more substantial is the relative improvement. The chart shows that NX is 4.5 times faster than XOTcl 1.6.0 for the OO Shootout methcall probe, both running Tcl 8.5.10. The methcall performance of NX 2.0 under Tcl 8.6b2 slightly decreases. Despite this, both NX probes give the best result. The methcall script used for XOTcl 1.6.0 and for XOTcl 2.0 are the same (i.e., the new language features of XOTcl 2.0 are not used). For Tcl 8.5.10, XOTcl 2.0 is about 26% faster than XOTcl 1.6.0. The object creation and object deletion probes draw a similar picture. NX is the fastest under Tcl 8.5.10. TclOO appears to be especially slow on destroying objects, both under Tcl 8.5.10 and Tcl 8.6b2.

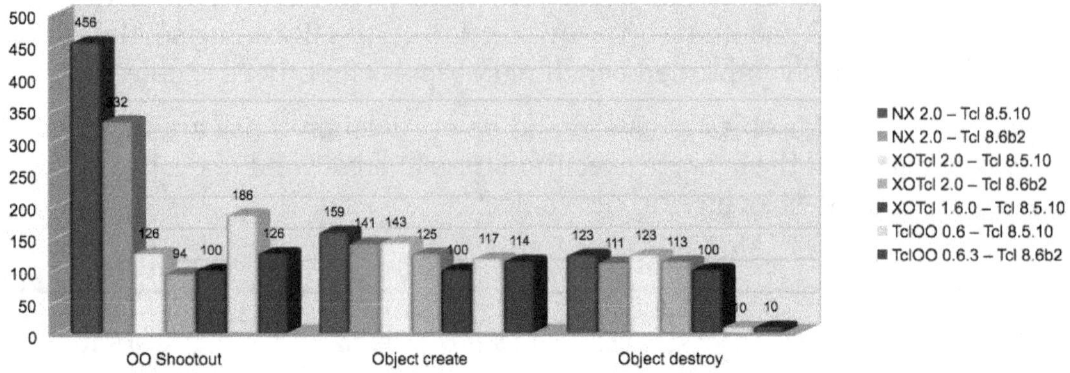

Figure 9. Performance Improvements (relative to XOTcl 1.6.0) on the OO Shootout Benchmark, Object Creation and Deletion.

The second set of measurement probes aims at capturing the execution timings of method dispatches for different parameter handling and argument parsing tasks. The method implementations used as probes have trivial bodies (no-ops might be treated differently by the byte-code compiler). The first probe, `args0`, is a method without parameters. The method `args3` specifies three positional parameters, `np2` expects two non-positional parameters and `np2args3` has two non-positional and three positional parameters. None of the parameter specifications in these probes contains parameter value constraints, which would have to be scripted in XOTcl 1.6.0 and TclOO, inducing a considerable performance penalty.

```
nx::Class create C {
  :public method args0 {} {return 1}
  :public method args3 {x y z} {return $x}
  :public method np2 {{-a 10} {-b 100}} {return $a}
  :public method np2args3 {{-a 10} {-b 100} x y z} {return $x}
}
#
# Measuring the following method invocation on instance "c1" of class "C":
#     c1 args0
#     c1 args3 1 2 3
#     c1 np2
#     c1 np2args3 -a 20 -b 200 1 2 3
```

Table 4 presents the collected probe throughput in terms of calls per seconds (higher numbers are better). The results are illustrated as a chart in Figure 7. XOTcl 2.0 is not reported separately in this test since it builds upon the same parameter/argument handling infrastructure as NX. The NX timings apply to XOTcl 2.0. Also, the comparison for non-positional parameter handling does not cover TclOO, since it does not feature a built-in implementation for non-positional parameters. A pure Tcl implementation would be substantially slower.

Table 4. Calls per Seconds on Method Dispatches

	NX 2.0 Tcl 8.5.10	NX 2.0 Tcl 8.6b2	XOTcl 1.6.0 Tcl 8.5.10	TclOO 0.6 Tcl 8.5.10	TclOO 0.6.3 Tcl 8.6b2
args0	3,074,463	2,113,561	1,360,003	2,499,743	1,942,890
args3	2,609,651	1,815,349	1,175,925	2,069,303	1,711,060
np2	2,198,836	1,553,550	481,428	n.a.	n.a.
np2args3	1,440,079	1,116,283	250,525	n.a.	n.a.

Figure 10 provides a graph with values of Table 3 illustrating the performance index against XOTcl 1.6.0 (which has for every test a performance index of 100). These tests show that especially for non-positional argument handling NX improves substantially over XOTcl 1.6.0, by factors of up to 5.75. NX shows the best performance profile for all parameter handling tests. Similar to the methcall probes above, when NSF is compiled against Tcl 8.6b2, the parameter handling performance degrades significantly as compared to the same NSF version built against Tcl 8.5.10.

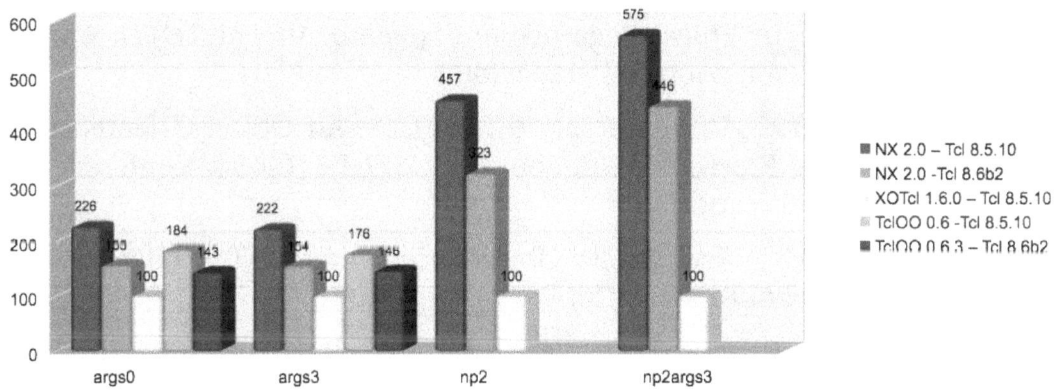

Figure 10. Performance Improvements on Method Dispatches (as compared to XOTcl 1.6.0)

Summary and Availability

For this paper, we were motivated to present a comprehensive overview of the features of the Next Scripting Toolkit, and the Next Scripting Language (NX) in particular. We gave a first insight into advancements for the NX concrete syntax (i.e., init blocks and the colon prefix) and discussed the basics of object and method parameters. The overview was completed by walking the reader through the enhancements for defining behavioral features of objects, i.e., method aliasing, method ensembles, and method call protection. The interplay of these features was demonstrated by introducing NX traits as an important composition technique. We concluded by hinting at developer support tools (e.g., DTrace) and at first libraries realized for NX, most importantly a MongoDB binding for NX.

NSF, NX and XOTcl 2.0 will become publicly available at the time of the Tcl/Tk 2011 Conference from http://next-scripting.org/.

References

- [1] Bracha G. (2004): Pluggable Type Systems. In Proceedings of the OOPSLA'04 Workshop on Revival of Dynamic Languages (RDL 2004).
- [2] Clarke S., Becker C. (2003): Using the Cognitive Dimensions Framework to evaluate the usability of a class library. In Proceedings of the 15h Workshop of the Psychology of Programming Interest Group (PPIG 2003), Keele, UK (pp. 359—336).
- [3] Neumann G., Sobernig S. (2009): XOTcl 2.0 — A Ten-Year Retrospective and Outlook. In Proceedings of the Sixteenth Annual Tcl/Tk Conference, Portland, Oregon, 2009. Tcl Association.
- [4] Neumann G., Zdun U. (2000): XOTcl — An Object-Oriented Scripting Language. In Proceedings of the 7th USENIX Tcl/Tk Conference (cl2k), Austin, TX, USA, 2000.
- [5] Fellows D.K. et al. (2008): Object Orientation for Tcl. TIP#257, finalized in September 2008. URL http://www.tcl.tk/cgi-bin/tct/tip/257.html.
- [6] Ducasse S., Nierstrasz O., Schärli S., Wuyts R. , Black A. P. (2006): Traits: A mechanism for fine-grained reuse. ACM Trans. Program. Lang. Syst. 28(2): 331-388 (2006).
- [7] Zdun U., Strembeck M., Neumann G. (2007): Object-Based and Class-Based Composition of Transitive Mixins, Information and Software Technology, 49(8) 2007.
- [8] Fowler M. (2009). Language Workbenches: The Killer-App for Domain Specific Languages? http://www.martinfowler.com/articles/languageWorkbench.html, last accessed: July 7, 2009, 2005
- [9] Cohen T., Gil, J. (2007): Better Construction with Factories. Journal of Object Technology, 6(6), 103—123.
- [10] Fowler, M. (2003): Refactoring - Improving the Design of Existing Code. Boston, MA, USA: Addison-Wesley Longman Publishing Co., Inc.

[11] Renner P., Rauschmayer A. (2005): TUBE - Structure-Orientation in a Prototype-Based Programming Environment. In Proceedings of the 2005 International Conference on Programming Languages and Compilers, PLC 2005, Las Vegas, Nevada, USA, June 27-30, 2005 (pp. 194-200). CSREA Press.

[12] Fähndrich M., Leino, K. R. M. (2003): Declaring and Checking Non-null Types in an Object-Oriented Language. In Proceedings of the 18th Annual ACM SIGPLAN Conference on Object-Oriented Programing, Systems, Languages, and Applications (OOPSLA 2003), Anaheim, California, USA, New York, NY, USA, 2003 (pp. 302-312). ACM.

[13] Schärli N., Black A. P., Ducasse S. (2004): Object-oriented Encapsulation for Dynamically Typed Languages. In Proceedings of the OOPSLA'04. ACM.

[14] Buschmann, F. & Henney, K. (2003). Explicit Interface. In Proceedings of EuroPLoP 2003, Irsee, Germany, 2003.

[15] Sobernig, S., Gaubatz, P., Strembeck, M., & Zdun, U. (2011). Comparing Complexity of API Designs: An Exploratory Experiment on DSL-based Framework Integration. In Proceedings of the 10th International Conference on Generative Programming and Component Engineering (GPCE'11), Portland, OR, USA, 2011.

[16] White, I. (2009). How This Web Site Uses MongoDB, URL: http://www.businessinsider.com/how-we-use-mongodb-2009-11, last accessed: October 8, 2011.

Tcl 2011
Manassas, VA
October 24-28, 2011

Tcl Google Summer of Code 2011

Tcl/GSoC 2011

Andreas Kupries ActiveState Software Inc. 409 Granville Vancouver, BC CA
andreask@ActiveState.com

ABSTRACT

As in previous years the Tcl Community took again part in Google's Summer Of Code[1], under the auspices of the Tcl Community Association[2].

1. OVERVIEW

Google's Summer Of Code[1] (short: GSoC) is a global program that offers student developers stipends to write code for various open source software projects. The Tcl Community participated again this year, for the fourth time in a row. As in previous years this participation was managed by the Tcl Community Association[2] (short: TCA) as the mentoring organization, the same organization which runs the US Tcl Conferences, like this one.

The main entrypoint to the program for the community itself can be found on the Tcler's Wiki [8].

2. PAST

Starting in 2007, we applied five times, and were accepted four times, with only our very first application not getting accepted by Google. This year was our fifth application and fourth participation.

Through negotiations by previous program administrators we usually got just shy of 10 slots for our projects[8], with our usual argument the fact that the Tcl Community Association[2] acts as an umbrella for smaller organizations with Tcl related projects. An example for this is the aMSN chat client[3]. This dropped a bit last year. The full statistics for the past years[4] are shown in table 1 below.

	2006	2007	2008	2009	2010
Students	630	950	1125	1000	1026
Organizations	102	>130	175	150	150
Average	6.18	<7.31	6.44	6.66	6.84
Tcl	-	-	9	9	7

Table 1: Statistics of past four years

3. PRESENT

Matthew Burke[6], our program administrator of the past years served as a backup this year, with me moving from backup to the main position.

In the slot allocation game/roulette we got seven slots, the same as last year, and a similar tick above the average, as can be seen in table 2 for the final statistics[4] below.

	2011
Students	1115
Organizations	175
Average	6.37
Tcl	7

Table 2: Final statistics for 2011

Our projects for this year are listed in table 3 [1] on the next page, with larger descriptions in the upcoming sections. The overall timeline we followed is shown in table 4.

3.1 W3C Widgets Compliant Content Packaging for XoWiki/OpenACS

[10] by Michael Aram Mentor: Gustaf Neumann

Content packaging has the purpose to provide a platform and renderer-independent interchange format for a set of resources (content). Content packaging has high relevance for content exchange, i.e. for reusing and sharing content among different platforms. In the area of learning management systems content packaging has a long tradition, where a range of standards has evolved over the last years and decades (for example the SCORM or Common Cartridge, which both profile a generic packaging format). Although content packaging is getting increasingly more important as evermore learning resources become available, the e-learning community is rather small compared to the overall web development community. With the rise of rich Internet applications and mobile apps, several alternative approaches for rich content distribution have been developed outside of the e-learning communities: small, web-based applications/web-content packages commonly referred to as "widgets". One reason for the high interest in widgets is that major vendors developed user agents integrated into operating systems and web-based platforms. However, compared to the respective standards in the e-learning world, these new packaging standards are in several respects even more restricted, i.e. less powerful. On the other hand, they

[1]The same table can also be found at[9]

Student	Project	Mentor
Michael Aram	W3C Widget Packaging Standard Compliant Content Packaging Infrastructure for OpenACS	Gustaf Neumann
Krzysztof Kwasniewski	Debugging tools for NRE	Miguel Sofer
Michal Poczwardowski	Tcl Plugin for Netbeans	Arnulf Wiedemann
S. M. Saurabh	Extending and Evolving CRIMP	Kevin Kenny
Lars Hellstrom	stasher: Tcl_Obj intRep as cache also at script level	Donal Fellows
George Andreou	Create a binding to the Hwloc library	Andreas Kupries
Saurabh Kumar	Micro-benchmarking extension: access to CPU performance counters	Edward Brekelbaum

Table 3: 2011 Projects, Students, and Mentors

	January 24	Program announced.
Organizations	February 28	Organization application window opens.
	March 11	Deadline for organization applications.
	March 14-17	Submission review.
	March 18	Publication of accepted organizations.
Students	March 18-27	Discussion of ideas between students and organizations.
	March 28	Student application wind opens.
	April 8	Deadline for student applications.
	April 10-21	Organizations rank and review student applications.
	April 22	Ranking/scoring deadline. Mentor sign-up deadline.
	April 25	Publication of accepted students.
Coding		Community bonding sudents to mentors.
	May 23	Coding period starts.
	July 11-15	Mid-term evaluations.
	August 15	Soft-end of coding. Scrub code, test, document.
	August 22	Hard end of coding period.
Post-Mortem	August 22-26	Final evaluations.
	August 29	Final results announced.
	August 30	Students can begin submitting the require code samples.
	October 22-23	Mentor Summit at Google.
	October 24-28	Tcl Conference At Manassas

Table 4: 2011 Timeline

provide some aspects, which the e-learning standards have not tackled at all yet (e.g. Device APIs). In sum, the investigation of the overlaps and differences between these worlds seems to be worthwhile.

In general, the content packages described so far are typically deployed as a single (archive) file and hold some form of configuration / manifest file describing the content. In addition to that, the packaged content might be allowed to use some form of API provided by the run time environment. Hence, from a technical perspective, there is a range of aspects within this "content packaging field" that could be abstracted from the different standards into a generic implementation. As a consequence, the standard specific content packages could be generated by specializations of this universal component.

The main goal of the project was to write an OpenACS package for generating W3C widgets out of learning materials that reside within OpenACS and its major content authoring tool XoWiki. Moreover, the package aims to provide means to also generate content packages adhering to other important (vendor specific) formats. As a result, the OpenACS package "xocp" has been created in the course of the GSoC. In a nutshell, the xocp package provides an infrastructure for generating content packages that comply with various specifications, for example "W3C Widgets", "Opera Widgets" or "SCORM". In general, "xocp" acts as a "backend" API to be used by other packages or by developers. In particular, "xowiki" is considered to be the main authoring environment for end users and a focus is put on the packaging of XoWiki-based content (e.g. wiki text books).

3.2 Debugging tools for NRE

[11] by Krzysztof Kwasniewski
Mentor: Miguel Sofer

The Tcl core has become a lot harder to debug since NRE's adoption. The problem is intrinsic to the nature and goals of the NRE: C keeps a stack of “who called me” frames, NRE does its best to replace it with a stack of “who do we call next” callbacks. But

1. Most debugging tools like gdb are designed for C.
2. Bug analysis requires understanding the path that leads to failure, not so much what would have happened after that.

Tcl on the other hand is a lispy language built onto C - a 100procedural substrate. The NRE is a mechanism that enables features like coroutines and proper tailcalls.

All's well when all's well, but when things go boom in the night the tools designed for C get lost too. Today the only way to understand what is happening is a tedious manual inspection of the NRE stack, which allows the deduction of the execution history if there were no intervening tail-calls. It is hard work that requires a lot of concentration and knowledge of the internals.

The extension to Gdb developed over the summer has the following capabilities:

1. Allows inspection of the NRE stack in a way more less similar to what Gdb offers for the C stack.
2. Parses and displays Tcl_Obj structures as strings. When a Tcl_Obj has its string representation, that one is used, however sometimes only the internal representation is present and in that case for the most common Tcl_Obj structures the string representation is created on the basis of the internal representation.
3. Displays the contents of the Tcl_HashTable structure.
4. Currently the best way of extending Gdb requires using Python and that is why my extension was developed with that language. Many Gdb users would however much rather use another languages of their choice for developing extensions to Gdb, like Tcl. For that reason I have also developed IO channels enabling a user to extend Gdb with virtually any programming language.

For more information on the capabilities and limitations of my project, please read the documentation available in the project's repository [12].

The code will be maintained until at least the end of the next edition of the GSoC program unless earlier many significant changes are introduced to the extension by someone else, in that case I may not be able to maintain the code. During the time of the maintenance I will fix all the bugs found in the extension.

I will try to commit some time for adding new functions to the extension providing I get any ideas for further development from the community - in this sense the future of this extension also depends on the Tcl community. The exact amount of time spent on the further development is hard to assess.

To sum the above up - I will try to support this extension for at least a year and providing someone will use and need it, this period may be extended.

3.3 Tcl Plugin for Netbeans

[13] by Michal Poczwardowski
Mentor: Arnulf Wiedemann

Tcl is available as a plugin for Eclipse, it would be helpfull to also have the same functions within netbeans.

The student would research how to write a plugin for netbeans and how to use available features like execution trace to drive debugging for Tcl within netbeans.

Netbeans for Tcl has been successfully brought to version 1.0, which can be downloaded from the netbeans plugin page. The student (Michal) has proposed to do further work on the Plugin, especially for Itcl which is not really functioning yet. And he will do bug fixes. Additionally he plans to add autocompletion for editing and maybe other features like debugging for itcl in javascript.

3.4 Extending and Evolving CRIMP

[14] by S. M. Saurabh
Mentor: Kevin Kenny

CRIMP, aka "C Raster Image Manipulation Package", is a package for image processing with Tcl. While it already provides the most basic algorithms it has not much of advanced or very advanced algorithms.

This project aimed at extending the package with more algorithms.

The project resulted in the addition of edge detection algorithms (Canny Sobel/Deriche), noise generators of various types, Wiener-based denoising, and the beginnings of FFT/LPT-based affine image registration. As part of the latter we got implementations of the log-polar transform (LPT) and a new image type for "complex" images, with associated operations.

Next up are the completion of the image registration functionality, and working on integrating the new pieces with the changes coming from my own work with the not-yet-released critcl v3.

3.5 stasher: Tcl_Obj intRep as cache also at script level

[15] by Lars Hellström
Mentor: Donal Fellows

The aim of this project is to make Tcl's internal mechanism of dual-ported Tcl_Obj's (which cache information about a value for fast access) available at the script level.

The stasher package has reached a point of being fully functional and stable. It is possible that further development will happen, in particular concerning making use of TclOO classes, but first more experience should be gathered of using the current interface; it may well turn out to be sufficient for what one would do in practice. The immediate focus will instead be on producing utility commands that make use of stashers to accelerate argument parsing.

3.6 Create a binding to the Hwloc library

[16] by George Andreou
Mentor: Andreas Kupries

This is a larger idea spun out of the idea for extending CRIMP, notably the ticket proposing to enhance the package's performance through parallelization and/or threading. As a foundation for that we need some introspection into the machine Tcl runs on, i.e. number of processors, cores per processor, threads per core, etc.

The HWloc library, aka "Portable Hardware Locality" provides all this information, and more. As such it is natural to create a Tcl binding for it to lift the information it provides up to the level of scripts.

The project was successful, creating a draft binding to the most important pieces of hwloc's functionality, i.e. creating, reading, and writing of topologies, navigation, plus CPU and memory binding of threads and processes.

Currently still left is the writing of proper documentation and test suite before a 0.1 release can be made. When that is done people working with the Thread package, thread pool implementations and the like should start working with the binding, to determine if the API as is is useful to them, like for sizing a thread pool to the available resources or multiple thereof, pinning threads of the pool to processing units, etc.

3.7 Micro-benchmarking extension

[17] by Saurabh Kumar
Mentor: Edward Brekelbaum

The goal of this project is to design and implement a Tcl extension with commands to interact with the CPUs harware counters. Initially the goal is to code an extension that works under Linux using its infrastructure for performance counters.

If time permits, we will research the possibility of porting the extension to Windows and/or OSX. This will entail finding out about interfaces analogous to the Linux Performance Counters, (possibly) redesigning parts of the extension's C-code so that it can be configured to work with the three different APIs, and coding a portable extension.

The project was a success and the support for the Linux and Windows operating systems is in working condition. For Linux, the "Performance Application Programming Interface" library [18] has been used to gain access to the CPU counters and the results are very precise and accurate for the latest Linux kernels. The support for Microsoft Windows is based on the "Performance Inspector" [19] and is not as accurate as the Linux version. The typical events which can be traced using the extension include various cache events, number of different type of CPU instructions, total number of CPU cycles etc.

Currently we do not see an obvious way to implement the utility for Mac OS and we will try to find a way to go about it in future. We will also try to make the output data for Windows OS more precise.

4. FUTURE

For a mentoring organization Google's Summer Of Code[1] is pretty much a year-round operation. Simply look back at the timeline (Table 4 on the previous page).

Next up in this cycle is starting the preparations for 2012, i.e., updating our application[7], restarting the collection of project ideas, and reaching out to prospective students and mentors in general. The last point is one of the more important things to do, not only for us as a mentoring organization, but for the Tcl community at large too, to make a general effort of spreading awareness of Tcl and its community as a viable (and fun) scripting language which doesn't has to hide.

APPENDIX

A. REFERENCES

[1] Google, GSoC. http://socghop.appspot.com/

[2] Tcl Community Association. http://www.tclcommunityassociation.org/

[3] aMSN. http://www.amsn-project.net/, http://wiki.tcl.tk/12783

[4] GSoC Statistics. http://code.google.com/p/google-summer-of-code/wiki/ProgramStatistics

[5] Andreas Kupries. http://wiki.tcl.tk/26

[6] Matthew Burke. http://www.seas.gwu.edu/~mmburke/

[7] Tcl Org Application 2011. http://wiki.tcl.tk/27864

[8] Google Summer Of Code on Tcl'ers Wiki. http://wiki.tcl.tk/25801

[9] GSoC 2011 Executed Projects. http://wiki.tcl.tk/28291

[10] W3C WPS Compliant Packaging Infrastructure for OpenACS, Michael Aram. http://wiki.tcl.tk/28188 Idea, http://wiki.tcl.tk/28538 Execution

[11] Debugging tools for NRE, Krzysztof Kwasniewski. http://wiki.tcl.tk/28091 Idea, http://wiki.tcl.tk/28334 Execution

[12] NRE Source Repository http://chiselapp.com/user/krzykwas/repository/nredebug1/index

[13] Tcl Plugin for Netbeans, Michal Poczwardowski. http://wiki.tcl.tk/28110 Idea, http://wiki.tcl.tk/28292 Execution

[14] Extending and Evolving CRIMP, S. M. Saurabh. http://wiki.tcl.tk/27866 Idea, http://wiki.tcl.tk/26953 Execution

[15] stasher: Tcl_Obj intRep as cache also at script level, Lars Hellstrom. http://wiki.tcl.tk/28288 Idea, Execution

[16] Create a binding to the Hwloc library, George Andreou. http://wiki.tcl.tk/28167 Idea, http://code.google.com/p/tcl-hwloc Execution

[17] Micro-benchmarking extension: access to CPU performance counters, Saurabh Kumar. http://wiki.tcl.tk/28157 Idea, http://code.google.com/p/tcl Execution

[18] Performance Application Programming Interface http://icl.cs.utk.edu/papi

[19] Performance Inspector http://perfinsp.sourceforge.net

Tcl 2011
Manassas, VA
October 24-28, 2011

Applications II

A Novel Method for Representing Hierarchies in a Relational Database Using Bignums and SQLite

Stephen Huntley
stephen.huntley@alum.mit.edu

Abstract

I introduce a method of using a rapidly-converging infinite series to generate integer values which, when stored in relational database table rows, act as tags allowing each row to be interpreted and queried as a node in a hierarchy. To overcome integer precision limitations, I use Tcl 8.5's Bignum feature and tcllib's math::bigfloat package. I use SQLite's ability to store arbitrary binary data in its BLOB data type to manage overflow precision digits. The resulting code provides a fast and efficient way to store and query tree-structure data of theoretically unlimited size.

1. Introduction

It is natural for beginners as well as for experienced computer programmers to wish to organize and store information in the form of hierarchies, or tree structures. The filesystem on every modern computer is the most straightforward and ubiquitous example. Most users grasp and appreciate the utility of hierarchical file storage immediately.

Power users are also generally familiar with the frustration of trying to find particular files or file types in a directory structure, only to be faced with long waits as the computer grinds through a recursive search of the directory space.

The tree-structure data type is widely used for a variety of computer data-processing tasks beyond file storage. LDAP, OLAP, XML, 3D scene graphs, and network spanning trees are a few examples of technologies which organize data into hierarchies. The sizes of the datasets utilized by means of these technologies have typically grown enormously over the past several years, a trend consistent with datasets of nearly every type. What has not grown is the efficiency of algorithms used to query and retrieve information in these datasets. The approach still used in the overwhelming majority of cases is recursive search. Recursive search is a viable method for querying small to medium-sized datasets, but the technique does not scale, and performance of such searches on very large databases is becoming unacceptable even on the most advanced hardware.

This paper introduces a new method for parametrizing, storing and searching hierarchical information that eliminates the need for recursive approaches for the most common search query types applied to trees. I also present details of a prototype executed with the help of advantageous features of Tcl 8.5 and the relational database extension TclSQLite.

Certain techniques described in this paper are covered by US patent #7,769,781, granted to the author.[1]

2. Hierarchies and Relational Databases

Although the method herein described is generally applicable to any linear or tabular data storage method, this presentation and the prototype focus on application to the problem of storing tree-structure data in a relational database.

The conundrum of storage and querying of tree-structure data in RDBMS programs has been a topic of persistent interest for many years.[2] The relational database is, generally speaking, the most powerful and flexible tool available to the mainstream programmer for dealing with large datasets. The presumed advantages of using a SQL-powered RDB package in this field have seemed self-evident for decades, but implementation issues have bedeviled almost everyone who has tried it for sizable datasets.

The obvious approach is simply to assign a unique number to each record in a database table that represents a node in the hierarchy, and define a "parent" field in the table schema to contain the unique number of the node linked one level up in the hierarchy from the node represented by the record. Thus finding a node's "children" is simply a matter of querying all records whose "parent" field contains the identifying number of the node of interest.

The problem comes when one wants to search all the linked nodes on the levels below a given node, an entire sub-tree. In that case, it's necessary first to retrieve all of a node's children, then all of those children's children, and so on recursively. A single complete search of this type might require thousands of individual read actions on the database, which is likely to take an unacceptably long time.

To get around this problem, the concept of "nested sets" was devised in the early nineteen-nineties. To use this method, each node is assigned an "entry" integer and and "exit" integer. The range of these numbers defines the set of integers lying between them. Every descendant of a given node is assigned entry and exit numbers which lie within the range of the given node's set. With these parameters defined for each node, querying all descendants of a node is then a simple matter of finding all nodes whose entry and exit numbers lie within the given node's defined range, which can be done with a single properly-crafted SQL statement.

This approach proves impractical, however, unless the tree structure is completely defined in advance and is expected not to change, or change very little; because adding a node to the hierarchy requires recalculating and rewriting some of the other nodes' entry and exit numbers. In a worst case most or all of these parameters may need to be rewritten, and the performance cost of so many write actions to a database is likely to be unacceptable.

One may hit upon the solution of using non-consecutive integers in entry and exit integer numbering; e.g., using multiples of five. There would then be room to add up to three more children to any given node before forcing the need for a recalculation and rewrite. But this simply delays the reckoning.

Over the past two decades a number of proposals have been made to generalize the nested sets approach with more sophisticated means of generating entry and exit intervals, using complex parametrizing equations. None has proved workable or popular in practice for a number of reasons; including insufficient capacity to describe very large sets of nodes within available precision of integers storable in database table fields, and difficulty in expressing the necessary math in the form of SQL queries.

3. Solution Parameters

Existing solutions impose performance and/or capacity limitations on the size of hierarchies that can be stored. The bottlenecks they impose may have been considered manageable with the small to moderate-size datasets typical of the past, but they quickly become unacceptable when trying to deal with contemporary data processing challenges involving very large dataset sizes.

Hardware and supporting software limitations will always make it impossible to store or process hierarchies of perfectly unlimited size, but a near-optimal improved method would impose minimal additional bottlenecks. The performance of the method would thus be close to the performance limitations of the underlying RDBMS itself.

An improved method would impose minimal performance penalties on adding nodes to a tree structure that will inevitably grow and change in the course of real-world use. It would also preferably be relatively simple to implement and to design SQL queries that put it into action.

The solution proposed here, in addition to approaching the above goals, has the additional advantages of not requiring complex schemas or extra record-keeping tables, and of employing simple integer parameters that can be indexed in a straightforward fashion using well-known database management practices.

4. An Infinite Series for Generating Hierarchy Tags

To tag records in a database table as nodes in a hierarchy, I employ an infinite series specially crafted to converge very quickly; by assigning a term of the series in increasing order to each node descending down the tree, each branch of the hierarchy defines a unique partial series subset of the infinite series, and each node can be assigned a value representing the sum of terms of itself plus its ancestors in the partial series it belongs to.

Since the infinite series is designed to converge very quickly, the sums assigned to all nodes in a given branch of the tree can be guaranteed to fall between all the sums of nodes in adjacent branches. The quick convergence ensures that the limits of partial sums of the series can be strictly ordered according to the size of the first term of the partial sum; that is, the sum of a partial series will never overlap any value of another series whose first term's sum is greater, no matter how many terms are added to the initially lesser sum.

The greatest difficulty in designing this method was finding an infinite series that converged fast enough to guarantee non-overlap of values in adjacent partial series. At the same time the series needed not to converge so fast that the precision of the sum parameter was exhausted before a sizable tree could be defined. In the end I could not find a suitable simple series with a standard linear-progressing index value.

Ultimately I had to design a double-indexed infinite series and use traits of the nodes themselves as indexes for the element function. That is, one of the indexes of the series is the depth level of the node in the hierarchy, and the other is the node's place in the count of its "siblings" (nodes with the same parent).

This approach ensures that available precision is doled out suitably depending on whether a child or a sibling is being added to a given node, always allowing for appropriate room for growth of the tree overall.

As far as I am aware, incorporating actual traits of the node as inputs into the interval-generating function is an innovation unique in the field.

The equation, expressed in standard form, is shown in Equation 1:

$$\sum_{m=0}^{\infty} \sum_{n=1}^{\infty} \begin{cases} m = 0 & 0 \\ m >= n & 0 \\ m < n & 1/2^{(\sqrt{(n-1)} * \sqrt{(3m-2)})} \end{cases}$$

Eq. 1

In Equation 1, the index m represents the node's level, and n represents the node's place in the sibling count. (More precisely, n is an "inheritance count," the first child of a node gets the node's n value plus one, so the count always increases as children and additional descendents are added to the tree.)

Since there is no general method for calculating the limit of convergence for an infinite series with transcendental terms in the element function, the conclusion that Equation 1 will always converge with sufficient speed is purely heuristic. Extensive testing has shown this always to be the case in practice.

When a node is added to the hierarchy, Equation 1 is used to calculate a term value for the node. Neither index value need be globally unique, so the term value may not be either. What is unique for the node is the sum of its term value together with the values of its ancestor nodes. It is this sum that is stored in the database record as a numerical tag uniquely descriptive of the node's place in the hierarchy.

A column of hierarchy tags so generated in a database table makes searching a sub-tree quite simple. An ancestor node's descendents are identified simply as nodes whose tag value is greater than the ancestor and less than the ancestor's nearest older sibling ("older" meaning having a smaller inheritance index number). The SQL query to accomplish this is simply a single-pass search for numeric values that fall within a defined range. No special joins, views or caches need be employed. This is just about the fastest kind of search a relational database can perform, and of course the column of tag values can be indexed for maximum speed.

Adding nodes to an already-established tree is straightforward as well. One simply needs to know the level of the parent to receive the new node as a child, and the inheritance number of the current youngest child of the parent. Equation 1 automatically produces a value which, when added to the parent's node sum, produces a new node sum that can be written directly to the database table and is guaranteed to conform to the existing hierarchy scheme.

5. Prototype

In order to test the capabilities of this method, I developed a prototype program using Tcl 8.5 and the TclSQLite extension.[3] Tcl and SQLite were good complimentary choices to form a platform on which to build the prototype. SQLite is both easy to use and fast, and can handle very large datasets. SQLite also has the ability to store and process integer values of up to sixty-four bits in length -- that much available precision makes it possible for numbers generated by the method to describe very large sets of nodes. And given that calculation of numbers of such bit lengths made extra-precision mathematical calculations necessary, Tcl 8.5's new feature supporting native bigints in the core proved very useful, both directly for integer calculations and indirectly via its utilization in the tcllib::bigfloat package.

5.1 Implementation Example

Figure 1 illustrates a small sample hierarchy showing eight numbered nodes along with their level and inheritance number parameters in parentheses (m,n).

```
1. (0,1)
    2. (1,2)
        3. (2,3)
        4. (2,4)
            5. (3,5)
    6. (1,3)
        7. (2,4)
        8. (2,5)
```

Fig. 1: Sample hierarchy

The process of preparing this hierarchy for storage in a SQLite database table starts with feeding each node's (m,n) parameters into Equation 1 to produce a term value to associate with the node. The term values clearly need not be unique.

```
t(1)= 0
t(2)= 0.5
t(3)= 0.1407857163281744654
t(4)= 0.0906152944101931834
t(5)= 0.0255328320537928796
t(6)= 0.3752142272464817736
t(7)= 0.0906152944101931834
t(8)= 0.0625
```

Fig. 2: Term values

Each node's term value is then added to the term values of its ancestors; e.g., node 5's value is added to the values of node 4 and node 2. The result is a unique numerical tag for each node which is unambiguously descriptive of its place in the hierarchy. For example, node 5 is known to be a child of node 4 because its node sum is greater than node 4's but less than node 3's. Because Equation 1 converges so rapidly, one could create unlimited descendents in this way for node 5, and those descendents' node sums would always be less than node 3's sum.

In order to take advantage of fast integer processing, the floating-point node sums are converted to integers by taking their fractional parts (with suitable precision-preserving zero-padding) and storing those in fields of a SQLite database table.

```
s(1)= 0
s(2)= 0.5
s(3)= 0.64078571632817447
s(4)= 0.59061529441019318
s(5)= 0.616148126463986
s(6)= 0.3752142272464817736
s(7)= 0.465829521656674957
s(8)= 0.43771422724648177
```

Fig. 3: Node sums

If then for example one wanted to retrieve all the descendents of node 6, one could use a simple SQL statement looking something like (sums truncated for clarity):

```
SELECT sum WHERE sum>3752
AND sum<5000
```

Clearly this query would return the sums associated with nodes 7 and 8, as desired.

6. Handling Node Distribution Limitations

With sixty-four bits of precision to work with, this method can easily be applied to hierarchies of tens of millions of nodes. It should be able to accommodate just about any data tree one is likely to come across in practice.

But the limited precision of integer storage in SQLite tables does impose some limitations in how nodes in a tree can be distributed. For example, no more than thirty-seven levels of depth can be described using this method before available precision runs out. In practice one is unlikely to encounter a tree with more than thirty-seven levels. But there may be pathological instances where this is the case. One would not wish to invest the time bringing this program into a real-world application only to find out in the midst of importing that ones dataset could not be accommodated. And what of the likely characteristics of the datasets of the next generation?

In order to eliminate inherent barriers to use of the prototype program for arbitrary hierarchies, I added a feature that makes it possible to encode and store any conceivable tree-structure dataset, up to the performance limitations of the database itself.

6.1 Overflow Precision Storage

SQLite has a BLOB (Binary Large Object) datatype which allows storage of arbitrary binary data. In order to accommodate trees of theoretically any size or node distribution, the prototype program adds a field to its table schema of the BLOB type, which is used to store extra precision digits in the form of binary data where necessary, without limitation as to length.

The Tcl code, when calculating the node sum for a new child, detects whether 64-bit precision has been exhausted by checking if the child's node sum is identical to the parent's. If this is the case, a global precision parameter is increased and the node sum is recalculated. The sum is divided into a part which can be stored using 64 bits, and a part containing all excess digits. The excess digits are converted into hexadecimal form as SQLite prefers them and are written into the BLOB-format field at the same time the integer part is stored in the integer sum field as described above.

Thenceforth, search queries which potentially require the extra precision to give complete results are done with a slightly more complex

SQL statement that incorporates comparison of the BLOB fields alongside integer value comparison of the sum fields. SQLite does comparisons of BLOB fields via binary byte-by-byte comparisons from the beginning of the field value to the end (analogous to Tcl's `[string compare]` command option). So precision of a calculated sum can be extended without limit by appending extra digits to a parent's overflow value stored in its BLOB field; and if use of overflow precision grows by multiple increments, binary values of varying lengths can be meaningfully compared just as varying length string comparisons are done.

I anticipate that in practice overflow precision storage will be rarely needed and employed chiefly in pathological situations, so impact on performance is expected to be minimal.

6.2 Separating Branch and Leaf Nodes

In the great majority of tree datasets, there will be many more leaf nodes (nodes with no children of their own, which terminate a branch) than branch nodes (which have one or more children). For example, in a hierarchy in which each node is assigned eight children up to a limit of a million nodes, only 62,500 branch nodes are required.

In practice, there is no reason to expend available precision and CPU resources calculating node sum values for leaf nodes. For querying purposes, leaf nodes can share the node sums of their parent branch nodes, as long as there is some established means of identifying the leaf nodes as such.

In the prototype program, a separate table is created for storage of leaf nodes solely. This table defines fields for a unique node ID, the parent node sum, and the parent overflow BLOB value in case it's necessary.

When a leaf is added to the tree, the node ID and parent sum information are written to a row in the leaf table. If a leaf node subsequently acquires a child of its own, Tcl code is first called to calculate a unique node sum of the leaf's own, and the node with its new sum is migrated to the branch table. Then the new child node is added to the leaf table complete with the reference to the newly-created branch's node sum value.

By granting unique node sums only to branch nodes, the capacity of the node sum-calculating method to describe and store large hierarchies is greatly increased. Splitting the total data into two tables also helps keep table sizes tractable, deterring the onset of any database-related maximum table-size capacity issues. It also helps SQLite maintain efficient caching and indexing states. I believe these advantages outweigh the performance penalty of requiring two separate queries on the database to ensure a complete search of a given sub-tree.

7. Performance

In truth it has been difficult to test the maximum capacity of the prototype program. It handles queries on databases containing in the tens of millions of nodes with little difficulty, even though minimal performance tuning has been done.

By way of comparison, probably the most widely-used tool for storing and querying large hierarchies is OpenLDAP, which in its most common implementations utilizes a Berkeley DB (BDB) backend for storage. Discussion in online forums suggests that the maximum capacity limit for practical operation of an OpenLDAP server with a

BDB backend (after extensive expert configuration tuning) is on the order of ten to fifteen million records.[4]

The chief performance difficulty is in initially populating the database from a large tree-structure dataset given for input. Calculating node sums and writing them to table rows can take hours for hierarchies containing millions of nodes. This of course would be impracticable in applications requiring close to real-time loading of data; such as, for example, reading and examining large XML files in an XML editor. In such cases the performance difficulties could be partially overcome by pre-calculating large template hierarchies with node sums already included. A suitable template hierarchy could be matched with an input dataset and imported with it, leaving custom calculations only for instances where the node distribution of the dataset of interest does not fit within the template exactly.

8. Future Developments

The prototype program was successful in demonstrating the basic validity of this novel method for encoding hierarchies, and in producing evidence that the limitations of the method are bounded chiefly by the inherent limitations of the underlying tools used to construct the program rather than by newly-introduced bottlenecks. Tcl and SQLite proved very useful in developing the prototype.

But it is to be expected that the next generation of computing challenges will present even larger datasets and more complex computing environments, and I believe that it is in meeting future challenges that this new method, and the particular advantages of Tcl and SQLite, will prove exceptionally valuable.

8.1 Parallelization

The prototype, despite its early state of development and minimal performance tuning, already performs well enough to handle very large hierarchical datasets which are typically handled only with difficulty by existing solutions. As the next generation of larger datasets arrive, I believe it will be possible to expand the capacity of the prototype greatly by introducing the ability to execute queries in parallel.

A strong advantage of the method described above is that partitioning a tree by node sum ranges without foreknowledge of the structure of the tree is a conceptually straightforward task. Thus SQL statements could be designed in advance to search sub-sections of the tree.

SQLite has no built-in client-server or parallel query-processing features. But it does make use of shared memory on operating systems that offer it for loading tables into RAM.. Thus multiple independent processes or threads that attempt to open a single database are all accessing a single in-memory set of tables.

With that feature in mind, SQLite's lack of multi-processing features can be well-compensated by Tcl's advanced event looping, socket networking and threading features. These features would be well put to use by expanding the prototype to include the ability to execute separate sub-queries in independent processes or threads, and collecting results via event loop polling.

As growing dataset sizes push the limits of a computer's ability to host a single database containing an entire hierarchy, the ability to partition trees and index the partitions by node sum also makes the concept of calving off sub-trees into separate tables appealing. These tables could be moved to separate computers, thus efficiently sharding that database. Tcl's networking features could be used to distribute and collate queries and their results across a cluster.

The rapid development of multi-core processors and clustering technology in the commodity computer market suggest almost unlimited scalability in application of this method to hierarchical search.

8.2 Disconnected Hierarchies

Related to the ability to partition a tree into sub-trees is the ability of the method to add nodes to a parent without global information about the tree: only the traits of the parent node itself are required to calculate values for child node values (namely parent node sum, level and inheritance number). Thus if a sub-tree is moved to a separate computer, it can be updated and grown independently, without loss of ability to coordinate, or even re-merge, with the original tree. This ability distinguishes the method from most competing approaches for handling large-size hierarchies.

This feature is potentially useful for scaling and sharding databases for a single server application. But it also makes possible the concept of distributed filesystems or similar hierarchical information systems. In short, node sums calculated via this method could be used as universally valid hierarchical position identifiers (UHI:// ?).

Whereas in the Internet Protocol the concept of hierarchy is imposed arbitrarily on an undifferentiated 32-bit range of numbers, node sums used for network host identification would be meaningful within themselves, and thus potentially make tasks like routing as well as searching more efficient (at the cost of maximum node capacity in a given number space).

The version control system git is a conceptual example of a tool that organizes project files into hierarchies, and lets individuals check out subsections of the main project for disconnected development, with changes re-merged to the main project later. If one were to imagine a future iteration of the git concept which managed thousands or millions of entities in a project (rather than the now-typical few dozen files), assigning node sums to each entity would be a useful way to ensure consistent classification and search capabilities throughout the development cycle.

Various other tools for sharing information in discontiguous and dispersed usage patterns continue to appear and evolve into widespread use, from the old (e.g. Usenet) to the new (BitTorrent).

Advances in mobile computing and the spread of computer networks into the less-developed parts of the world have spurred interest in ad hoc and disconnected networking.

These and many other use cases could conceivably benefit from a globally valid yet locally editable hierarchy tagging protocol. The great diversity of environments and platforms encompassed by these use cases make the portability, compactness and power of the combination of Tcl and SQLite highly attractive for future development of applications which make use of this method.

References

[1] Huntley, S. "Method for labeling data stored in sequential data structures with parameters which describe position in a hierarchy." US Patent 7,769,781, issued August 3, 2010.

[2] A comprehensive treatment of the state of the art can be found in: Celko, J. *Joe Celko's Trees and Hierarchies in SQL for Smarties,* Morgan-Kaufmann. San Francisco, CA, USA, 2004.

[3] TclSQLite - http://www.sqlite.org/tclsqlite.html

[4] See for example: http://www.openldap.org/lists/openldapsoftware/200611/msg00051.html

An efficient text mining application for log file analysis in an emulation environment using Tcl/Tk with C

Mishra, Shyam
Mentor Emulation Division,
Mentor Graphics Corp.

Abstract

Text mining refers to the process of deriving high quality information from text files. Hardware emulation is the preferred way for verification of multi-million gates SOC designs. Text mining can be applied for log file analysis of huge log files that get generated in an emulation based design verification flow. Typically an emulation based verification flow consists of two discrete steps, namely compile and runtime. During the compile stage, a HDL design is prepared for emulation. The compile tools generate log files and other reports. The emulation based verification flow is used typically for largest of design databases, and the mapping to hardware involves multiple complex compilation steps. This makes it imperative to have intelligent debug systems with advanced data mining capabilities. Text mining is applied to extract useful information from these log files and reports in order to help the user detect errors and warnings in compile that might affect the emulation. Logs and reports generated during emulation runtime are also similarly analyzed.

Using Tcl/Tk , a GUI is developed to use text mining methods on very large emulation databases for log file analysis. Main considerations for design for such text mining application has been that interactive user response remains fast, the parent Emulation control and Debug GUI is able to interact and work with the text mining widget with fast response time, in unblocking manner, and with minimal overhead to the parent Emulation control and Debug GUI. Besides design ensures search operations are fast, the application memory image is low, and the application provides host of ease of debug utilities like GUI based linkages to user RTL source, informative help from the messages in log files. To achieve this intelligent partitioning of functionalities between C and TCL code is done. The application makes use of a C/C++ based shared object for efficient retrieval of information from the huge log files generated by the emulation tools. The application GUI makes use of the latest Tcl/Tk features to provide an easy to use interface to give the users a rich debugging experience.

1. INTRODUCTION

Hardware emulation is the preferred way for verification of the next generation multi-million gates SOC designs. In a typical emulation flow, the user design is compiled and prepared for configuration on the emulator hardware.

In the process, the user code which consists of RTL and transactor level models is compiled by a set of compilers to generate the model which can be configured on the emulator.

The compile flow is quite complex .The error, warning and other messages generated by the compilers provide important information to the user, which can help understand the changes or modifications required in the user code in order to perform the emulation. During design emulation at runtime also advanced debug and log file analysis capabilities are required to understand any functional mismatches. Often the clues to a bad design behavior at runtime or a compile failure are hidden in the log files and the reports generated by the tools.

The user can manually check the log files and the reports to locate the cause of such failures.

However, manually browsing through a huge database, locating all the log files generated by the different compile and runtime tools and checking the information present therein can be time consuming. Besides, the user might be unable to

locate the relevant information.
Therefore text mining methods are applied to allow the user access the relevant information from the log files and the reports without losing precious time.

Text mining refers to the process of deriving high quality information from text. Text mining usually involves the process of structuring the input text (usually parsing, along with the addition of some derived linguistic features and the removal of others, and subsequent insertion into a database), deriving patterns within the structured data, and finally evaluation and interpretation of the output. 'High quality' in text mining usually refers to some combination of relevance, novelty, and interestingness. Typical text mining tasks include text categorization, text clustering, concept/ entity extraction, production of granular taxonomies, sentiment analysis, document summarization, and entity relation modeling (*i.e.*, learning relations between named entities).
(Reference : http://en.wikipedia.org/wiki/Concept_mining)

In the following sections we will discuss how an efficient text mining tool was developed using Tcl/ Tk 8.5 with C.
The text mining tasks which are computationally intensive are implemented in C. The Tcl/Tk makes calls to the C functions as and when required. Display is managed entirely by Tcl/Tk side.

2. C based library for text mining

A C based database manager is developed to store the information related to the tools and the corresponding log file paths.
C functions are implemented to access interesting information from the log files.
Those functions efficiently extract the requested information from the log files and provide it to the caller code.
The C functions are embedded inside a shared library which registers Tcl commands on a Tcl interpreter. The Tcl commands can be called from any Tcl/Tk based GUI that loads this shared library. Internally, those Tcl commands are mapped to the C functions.
Searching through the large database of log files can be time consuming, so C is preferred over Tcl. Besides, C can be used to implement an efficient parser that parses the log files on demand to retrieve the requested information for the user.

The command interface between the Tcl/Tk GUI and the C shared library is designed to be backward compatible. Thus, the GUI can be modified without requiring a recompile of the shared library and conversely, the shared library can change the implementation of its parser and search functions without necessary build of the GUI, as long as the interface is maintained intact.
Assuming that the C library is named "libloganalyze.so", the Tk gui makes the following call:

load <path to libloganalyze.so>
The load call passes the Tcl interpreter handle to the C library. Commands are created on this interpreter for use by the subsequent GUI queries.

3. GUI display of tools and log files: text categorization

The GUI is designed to have a tree view for the tools and log files hierarchy.
For example, a hierarchy looks like this : tool → log files → messages. Under a tool such as "HDL compiler" , there could be logs such as "hdl_compile.log", "hdl_compile.report". Further, the hdl_compile.log node can be expanded to display the "Errors", "Warnings", "Note", "Status" and other categories of messages.
The ttk treeview widget is used for this purpose. It provides the user a convenient way to view the various messages occurring for the different tools in a single window.
Whenever the user expands a node of the tree, a query is generated for the C shared library. The query is executed in C code and the relevant information is fetched by the GUI.
GUI side : Treeview->Expand (node)
Calls C function : loganalyze -get_child_nodes –queryString <queryString>
GUI gets the results of the C call and changes tree display / log file view as applicable.

For example, if the user expands a tool node, then the result of the C function call will return the log file names associated with the tool.
Similarly, for an individual log file node, the C function will return the message types as the child nodes and also the text to display as the contents of

the given log file in the text view widget.
The text mining operation is carried out in the C function and the results are displayed in the Tcl/Tk GUI.

4. Search results display using text clustering

The text display clusters messages of a particular type based upon the type. For example, the warnings are displayed clustered together, as are the other message types.
If the search is based upon some pattern, the pattern is highlighted in the search results.
For example, if the user searches for "simulation mismatch", the clause "simulation mismatch" will be highlighted in the search results displayed in the text view.
For example :
Warning [100] : Net top.a has been removed from the design.
Warning [100] : Net top.b has been removed from the design.
……………………………………………………………
SimWarning [200] : Net top.c has multiple drivers, this may cause a simulation mismatch.
SimWarning [200] : Net top.inst.q has multiple drivers, this may cause a simulation mismatch.
…………………………………………………………….

5. Concept / entity extraction

To display file names, line numbers and net names in the text view, the file names are extracted and displayed with hyperlink tags. The hyperlink is programmed to open the corresponding file and line number in an editor such as vi or emacs, as specified by the user , upon right mouse button click.
For example a message could look like this :
Warning [101] : File *design.v*, line 11, syntax error near "=".
In the above message, the file path "design.v" will be hyperlinked.

Code snippet :
```
set textWidget $mainWidget.logFileDisplay
  $textWidget tag configure hyperlink -foreground royalblue -underline true
  $textWidget tag bind hyperlink <Double-Button-1> { clickALink %x %y %W}
     $textWidget tag bind hyperlink <Return> {clickALink %x %y %W}
```

Search for all the file names and tag those as hyperlink.

```
proc clickALink {x y w} {
set i [$w index @$x,$y]
 set range [ $w tag prevrange hyperlink $i]
 set url [eval $w get $range]
sourceViewFile $url
}
```

The procedure sourceViewFile opens the specified url in the editor selected from the user environment.

A separate display canvas is provided for the design statistics , such as the design size, compile status of the tools and various performance / capacity related metrics.
This information is obtained via a call to the C library at start up.
GUI call : loganalyze –get_design_stats
C function : loganalyzer->GetDesignStats().
Returns the design stats after mining the log and reports database.
During startup, a list of predefined phrases is also searched in the database and those are displayed in a different view as the "Analysis Report".
The analysis report allows the user to browse to the relevant phrase in the log files spread across the emulation database using hyperlinks.

GUI side : loganalyze –queryString <get statistics for important messages>
C side : loganalyzer->GenerateReport()
Returns the statistics for the important messages in all the log files and reports.
This call returns the statistics of all the important messages in which the user might be interested, right at the start up.

6. GUI architecture for multiple views

The three log file related views : namely the text view, the design statistics canvas and the analysis report view are implemented as tabs in a ttk notebook widget.
The text display changes for each and every text file, so the text view tab has sub-tabs for each and every log file that is opened for search.

Using some customization using ttk::style, the sub tabs are provided with a X icon at the right top corner to allow the user to close the view for a particular log file.

Code snippet :[Ref : wiki.tcl.tk]

```
image create photo closeImage -file $::closex.gif
ttk::style element create ButtonNotebook.close
image closeImage
ttk::style layout ButtonNotebook {
    ButtonNotebook.client -sticky nswe
}
 ttk::style layout ButtonNotebook.Tab {
    ButtonNotebook.tab -sticky nswe -children {
        ButtonNotebook.padding -side top -sticky
nswe -children {
        ButtonNotebook.focus -side top -sticky nswe
-children {
     ButtonNotebook.close -side right -sticky n
     ButtonNotebook.label -side left -sticky {}
        }
       }
    }
}
```

It can be reopened later on if required, using the appropriate node in the tree view.

7. Query generation interface

The log file analyzer GUI provides a versatile query editor. The user can select the type(s) of message(s) to display and can specify the scope of the search in terms of the tools or the log files.
The user is also allowed to input text patterns for search including regular expressions. Search is possible with and without case sensitivity. The query editor is implemented using check buttons and text entry fields.

Code snippet (query creation)

```
proc CreateQueryString {} {
  Get all check button status
  Get search entry
  Get regular expression or not
  Get case sensitive or not
   Create a query string for loganalyze command
call.
}
```

The user can also use the tree widget to specify the scope of the search.

GUI side : loganalyze –queryString <queryString>
C function : loganalyzer->Search(queryString)
Returns the search results for the specific query.

The search results are displayed in a categorized form in the log file text view tab which is embedded in the ttk notebook widget.

8. Sentiment analysis : comparative analysis of log files

Often the user likes to compare the number of warnings generated in the current compile with the numbers generated in a prior compile of the same design.
For this purpose, the tool allows the user to save a given set of log files in a compact form. After re-compiling the design, the user can load the older set of log files and do a comparative analysis based upon the types and contents of the messages generated in both the older and the newer compile sessions.
This allows the user to check whether the number of warnings has increased or reduced, whether the area requirements have changed and whether or not a better performance can be expected from the new compile. It also allows the user to know if new bugs have crept into the design in compile flow, possibly leading to erroneous behavior later, during emulation run.
GUI side : loganalyze –compare <project 1> <project 2> -queryString <query string>
Returns the results for the comparison to GUI.
Display categorization is managed by the GUI.

9. Online help system

For the log file analyzer to be useful, it must not only display the relevant messages or search results , but should also provide some tips to the user for the various errors or warning messages.
The log file analyzer extracts the message mnemonic or id and searches the available documents and web resources for relevant help. The user can make use of this online help functionality to understand the cause of an error or a warning or just the significance of a status message.
GUI side : loganalyze –help <search phrase>
C function: loganalyzer->HelpDatabaseQuery(searchPhrase)
Returns the help string for display in the GUI.

10. Design debug using the parent emulation debug gui

The log file analyzer GUI maintains a socket based connection with the parent emulation debug GUI. Through this connection, the extracted name of a signal or a module can be passed to the GUI, where it can be browsed in the design path viewer.
Thus the user can understand the reason for a typical warning message such as "Net is dead logic" or "Net has multiple drivers" by browsing the design in the emulation debug gui.
The sequence of actions done by the user would look like this :

a) Search for "multiple drivers" in compiler logs.
b) Results are displayed categorized in the text view.
c) Visit any particular interesting message and click on the hyperlink for the net name.
d) The net name is displayed in the emulation gui path viewer.

Similarly, the log file analyzer allows the user to view the waveforms for an interesting net where those are available with the emulation debug gui.
GUI side : "Send Parent GUI command : Add net to path viewer".
Parent GUI : Receives and parses the command and calls appropriate command : "add pathviewer <net name>".

11. Summarization of area and performance reports

Area reports are generated at compile time. Performance reports are generated at runtime.
The log file analyzer can display the modules that consume the most of the design area. The user can focus on the relevant modules and remodel the HDL code to optimize the area requirements.
The number of simulation cycles consumed , the design frequency, the number of transaction calls made and the time taken are available in performance reports.
A summarized display of those allows the user to optimize the test bench and the design quickly without having to browse through the reports manually and undertaking the effort to interpret them.

12. Cost , limitations and future work

The text mining techniques applied here make use of the standard messaging format used by the emulation tools.
In case there are third party tools which generate huge log files in an unknown format, the log file analyzer is not able to apply text mining techniques for those.
The current implementation can be made more intelligent to accept a user defined messaging format to analyze any log file database generated by any product.
If the log files are very large in number, the volume of information extracted can be quite huge. In such cases, the user has to do selective searches and not go for generic pattern searches which could become time consuming.

13. Conclusion

A text mining tool using Tcl/Tk and C for emulation databases has been described here.
It makes use of text mining techniques such as text categorization, entity/concept extraction, text clustering, document summarization and sentiment analysis for analysis of log files and reports.
It makes use of the efficiency of C to quickly analyze and retrieve useful information from the emulation database. A Tcl/TK 8.5 based GUI interfaces with the C shared library to provide a rich and interesting debugging experience to the emulation users.
The concept can be extended in the future to any system where the log files are generated in a predefined messaging format and the debug functionality can be made configurable for the relevant system.

REFERENCES:

[1] http://en.wikipedia.org/wiki/Text_mining
[2] wiki.tcl.tk

Maintainable, Shareable and Easily Creatable & Updateable toolbar, menubar, statusbar - pillars of any GUI application.

Tarun Goyal

Abstract – This paper presents a novel approach to efficiently manage, update and share the *toolbar, menubar & statusbar* widgets that are integral to any TCL/TK based GUI application. However, considering that any GUI would have different windows performing variety of tasks and be dependent on the overall tool state, the solution should effectively support context sensitivity with respect to windows, selected object in its constituent windows and tool status.

Fig: Typical Menubar/Toolbar in a GUI

Summary - It has been observed that in any GUI application the onus of creating/updating the widgets inside the toolbar, menubar or statusbar lies with the developer responsible for creating a component [or window/frame] in the GUI with everyone creating their own "versions", resulting in code duplication and raising maintainability issues. However, considering that same widget [e.g. button, menus etc.] might perform similar function in various windows and/or the same real estate could be utilized to create different widgets for different windows, necessitates a functional requirement to have centralized *toolbar, menubar & statusbar* managers [or *smart widget managers*] that helps one to easily register widgets and update them dynamically based on the current window [or the element therein] in focus. Essentially, following are the desired features of these centralized "managers".

1. Each manager should be structured in a way so as to provide a centralized mechanism for creating/updating [e.g. enabling/disabling/setting a value] the widgets.
2. Ability to create a variety of widgets – e.g. a *checkbutton* or *menu* in a *menubutton*, *text-widget* or *button* in a *toolbar* or *progress-bar* or a *labelframe* in a *status-bar*.
3. Make the same widgets as reusable as possible – e.g. a "cut" button can be used to cut a text item in one window whereas could be used to cut a schematic element in another.

The following sections captures the pseudo implementation interface [written in *incrTcl*] of various managers, the central repositories that will entertain requests received from any window/component. Please note that only "major" interface functions have been mentioned here and the managers may contain some other methods from implementation perspective. For the complete implementation, please refer the supplied TCL source code.

TOOLBAR MANAGER

```
itcl::class ToolBarManager {
    #variable list
    set dock_bars( std, tree, browser, schematic, dataview)   ## dockbars of tool-bar
    set dock_bar_widgets (copy, cut, paste, find ........... )    ## widgets in the dock-bar

    ## widget_prop store the properties of the widget  - e.g. label, underlying index etc.
    set widget_prop[std, copy] = { icon_name, default_callback}
    ## default_callback is the method to call on  "invoking" this widget
```

```
    # Tool Bar associated with a window:
    set windowToolBar(windowName) = {toolBarObject}

    # this will store the global tool-bar object of the main framework
    private  variable  globalToolBarObject

    # Register_Window::  This  function enables a window to register associated docbar and
    # the widget
    private method  Register_Window   { windowName, docName, widgetName }

    # Unregister_Window:: This function deregisters the given window from relevant dockbar
    # lists
    private method  Unregister_Window {windowName }

    # Update_ToolBar :: This proc is the updates the respective toolbar based on the window
    private  method Update_ToolBar   { windowName }

    ## Update_DocBar :: This function updates the requested dock-bar, with the latest-status
    ## of the widgets residing inside the dock-bar.
    private method  Update_DocBar { docBar_Name }

    # Create_DocBar :: Create a dock-bar with a given doc-bar-name..
    private method  Create_DocBar { docBarName }

    #  Create_Widget :: Create a widget in the specified doc-bar, with the given widget-name
    private method  Create_Widget { docBarName  buttonName }

    # this will handle the call-backs, smartly finds the current window object and calls it
    # method.
    public method CallBackHandler { widgetName  docBarName}

    #  this  method  changes the state of buttons  depending  upon the current selection inside
    # a window
    public method updateState { windowName  docBarName widgetName }
}
```

The Toolbar manager is instantiated in the constructor as follows-
set globalToolBarObject [mtiwidgets::dockbar $_vars(debug_win).$toolBarName -relief sunken -borderwidth 1]

Some of the salient features, among others, of the toolbar manager are as follows-

1. Only those *dockbars* [*dockbar* is a subunit of a "toolbar"] that are registered with current set of visible windows shall be shown and the widgets inside these *dockbars* are enabled/disabled as per the window requirements. Further the *dockbars* are added/deleted incrementally as windows are shown/hidden in the tool.

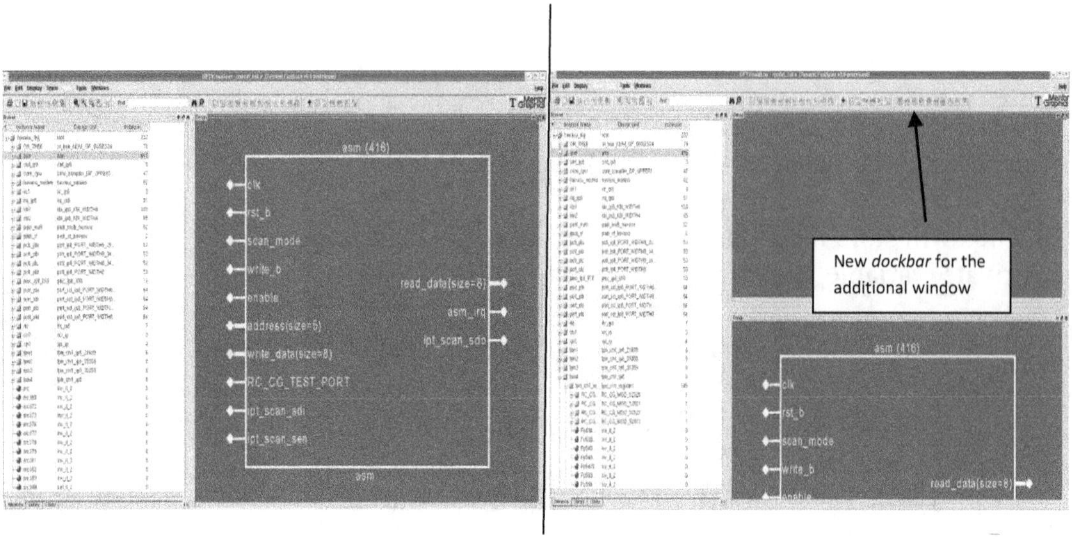

Fig: Tool in 2 different states on opening a new window

2. As per our present tool requirements, the currently supported widgets are – *buttons*, *entry*, *combobox*, *checkbutton*, *radiobutton*. The manager can easily be enhanced to support more widgets.
3. The manager also supports placing the window specific widgets in the undocked state i.e. in case user undocks [i.e. does a "*toplevel .$windowName*"] the window from the tool, only the widgets that are registered with that window comes in the undocked toplevel window. A separate instantiation happens for the toolbar inside the undocked window.
set windowToolBar($windowName) [mtiwidgets::dockbar "[$frameworkHandle getPaneManager].$windowName.toolbar" -relief sunken -borderwidth 1]

MENUBAR MANAGER

Similarly, the Menubar manager looks as follows:

```
itcl::class MenuBarManager {
 # Following data-structures are maintained by Task-Manager internally storing the dock-button
 # related properties
 private variable globalMenuButtons, menuButtonMenus, menuProps, menuButtonProps

 # List of created menu-buttons are maintained as ::
 # createdMenuButtons {} = { std, .................... }
 private variable  createdMenuButtons {}

 # Array which tells us about the status of a menu-button ::
 # menuButtonStatus (std) = { "Enable" } ..............
 private variable  menuButtonStatus

 # Global list of registered menu-buttons and menus ::
 # Reg_WindowMenuButton (docName) = {  windowName, ...........}
 # Reg_WindowMenu (docName, ButtonName) = { windowName, ........................}
 # Reg_WindMenuCallback(docName, ButtonName) = {  CallbackFunction , ........... }

 # this list will store the menus that you want to create dynamically
 # at each update. e.g. display->marking menu (format = [list "menubutton,menu" ..])
```

```
  private variable menuIsDynamic

  private variable  windowMenuBar ; # windowMenuBar(windowName) = {menuBarObject}
  # Register_Window:This  function enables a window to register associated doc-Name and
  # button-Name
  public method  Register_Window  { windowName menuButtonName menuName
callBackFunc }

  # Unregister_Window:: This function deregisters the given window from the
  # both the lists :: Reg_WindowMenuButton and Reg_WindowMenu.
  public method  Unregister_Window {windowName }

  # Update_MenuBar :: This proc  is called from a centric place and  depending on the
  # "windowName" updates the respective menu-bar. Showing/hiding the menu-bar is also
  # handled here.
  public method Update_MenuBar  { windowName Docked {forceTag "no"}}

  # Update_MenuButton :: This function updates the requested menu-button, with the  latest-
  # status of the menus residing inside the menu-button.
  private method  Update_MenuButton { menuButtonName object windowName
menuBarObjState {forceTag "no"}}

  # Create_MenuButton :: Create a menu-button with a given menuButtonName..
  private method  Create_MenuButton { menuButtonName menuBarObj Docked {enterTag 0} }

  # getUndockedMenuBarObj  :  This proc creates the object for undocked menu-bar with all the
  # contents that goes into the Undocked Window. This proc is called as soon as the window is
  # undocked.
  public method GetUndockedMenuBarObj { windowName  }

  # this will handle the call-backs
  public method CallBackHandler { menuName menuButtonName }

  # this  method  changes the state of menus  depending  upon the current selection inside a
  # window
  public method UpdateState { state windowName menuButtonName { menuName "" } }

  # this method handles tool-bars when a window is maximized
  public method maximizeWindowMenuBars { windowName }

  # method creates deleted menu-item
  private method Create_DeletedMenuItem { menuButtonName menuName menuObj \
insertIndex  Docked windowName {enterTag 0}}

 # function to test for the validity of menu-item in "data" menu-button for "design & debug"
  public method MenuItemValidForData { args }
```

```
  # this function sets the widget value to the instructed "value"
  public method setWidgetVal { windowName menuButtonName menuName value }

  # this function returns the value stored in widget
  public method getWidgetVal { windowName menuButtonName menuName }

  # this function sets the key index array
  public method setKeyIndex {menuNameList }

  # this function returns the key Index
  public method getKeyIndex { menuName }
}
```

The Menubar manager is instantiated in the constructor as follows-
set globalMenuBarManager [iwidgets::menubar $_vars(debug_win).$menuBarName –font $_fonts(helvB:12) -helpvariable helpstr]

Some of the salient features of the menubar manager are:

1. The menus are created/deleted on the fly and are dynamic in nature in that they can be created at run time. This is accomplished by various functions talking to each other in parallel - *Create_DeletedMenuItem* is called from *UpdateMenuButton* for each registered menu with the window with *Create_DeletedMenuItem* checking the validity of the menu by calling *MenuItemValidForData*. The "runtime" menus are stored in a special variable called *menuIsDynamic*, which is checked every time a menu-item is created.
2. Menubar manager supports widgets such as *menubutton*, *menuitem*, "*cascade*" [no limit], *checkbutton*, *radiobutton*, *sepators* and can be enhanced to support more widgets easily.
3. As with toolbar manager, menu-bar manager has also been implemented in a way so as to show the registered menubuttons with the undocked window in the toplevel window. Each window gets its own menubar manager object as follows-
set windowMenuBar($windowName) [iwidgets::menubar "[$frameworkHandle getPaneManager].$windowName.menubar" -font $_fonts(helvB:12) -helpvariable helpstr]

STATUSBAR MANAGER

```
itcl::class StatusBarManager {
  # Following data-structures are maintained by Task-Manager internally
  private variable statusBarWidgets ; ## all the widgets in the status bar
  private variable widgetProps ; ## widget related properties


  # Global list of registered doc-bars and buttons ::
  # Reg_WindowWidgets = {  windowName, ...........}
  # Reg_WindowWidgetCallback(widgetName) = {  CallbackFunction , ........... }
```

```
  private variable  Reg_WindowWidgets
  private variable  Reg_WindowWidgetCallback

  # public methods

  #  Methods that will be used by the tool windows
  # Register_Window::  This  function enables a window to register associated status bar widget
  public method  Register_Window  { windowName widgetName  {callBackFunc ""}}

  # this method return the value stored in the widget variable
  public method getWidgetVal { windowName widgetName }

  # this method sets the widget's variable value to "value", with "progressBarVal" is an
  # optional argument that will be valid in the case of "progressBar" widget.
  public method setWidgetVal { windowName widgetName value {progressBarText ""}}

  #  this  method  changes the state of widgets depending  upon
  # the current selection inside a window
  public method UpdateState { windowName widgetName State}

  #  Methods that will be used by framework
  # Update_StatusBar :: This proc  is called from a centric place and  depending on the
  # windowName updates the status-bar
  public method Update_StatusBar  { windowName Docked }

  # getUndockedstatusBarObj  :  This  proc will return object of the statusbar, that goes into the
  # Undocked Window.
  #This proc is called as soon as the window is undocked.
  public method GetUndockedStatusBarObj { windowName }

  # private methods
  # Create_StatusBar :: Create a status-bar with a given status-bar-name..
  private method Create_StatusBar { widgetName windowName }

  # this will handle the call-backs
  public method CallBackHandler { widgetName }

  # this function initializes the various status-bar related Lists
  private method initializeLists {}
}
```

The Statusbar manager is instantiated in the constructor as:

set globalStatusBarObj [frame $_vars(debug_win)._bottomFrame]

As can be seen, statusbar is a frame widget and we are packing the widgets it.

Statusbar manager is similar to the above managers [mostly toolbar manager] and works in a similar fashion. Some salient features are:

1. Statusbar manager supports widgets such as – *"progressbar"*, *entry*, *label*. We have created our own progress bar and have instantiated it inside the status bar. The function *"setWidgetVal"* handles the update process of the progress bar accepting %ages and/or text as an argument. Including progress bar has helped in creating significant value for our customers especially for operations that take time to complete.
2. As with other managers, *statusbar* manager created a separate instantiation for all the undocked windows and places the registered widgets inside that window. Each window has its own "status bar manager *frame*" in which the widgets are packed.

USAGE

A single object of each of the managers is instantiated inside the constructor of the respective class . This object could then be accessed and used by various windows to manage their *dockbar, menubar & statusbar* items, as captured in some ways below.

1. *Register a variable*: registering any widget with the toolbar [or statusbar] manager is easy. The client needs to call the following:
$toolBarManObject Register_Window $windowName $dockBarName $widgetName "CALLBACK FUNCTION"
Above has the syntax as – {Window/Component Name registered with widget, DockBar within the toolbar, Widget Name, method that will be called on "invoking" the widget}

In the toolbar manager, the following would be done for initializing it.
widgetProps($dockBarName,$widgetName) { "Print ...." , "print.gif", "Print", "button" }
Above has the following syntax – {Widget ToolTip, Icon, Widget text,Type of Widget (e.g. button, entry etc)}

As for menubars, the cascading menuitems within a menu-button would be supported as follows:
*$toolBarManObject Register_Window $windowName $menuButtonName *
"$firstlevelMenubuton,$secondlevelMenubutton, $menuItem" "CALLBACK FUNCTION"
there is no limit to upper the number of levels of cascading

For a normal menu-item that is not cascaded should be captured while specifying the widget properties.

set widgetProps($menuButtonName,$widgetName) {"Test-Setup....", "0", "normal", "MenuItemValidfor Data Test_Setup"}
Above has the following syntax – { Widget Text, Underlying Alphabet Index, State[**normal, cascade**], Function to be called for widget validity [optional]}

In order to support dynamic creation widgets the *widgetProps* has special item that checks whether the widget needs to be created under the present set of conditions.

2. APIs provided to return/set the current value in the widget [*GetWidgetVal/SetWidgetVal*] :: The onus is on managers to set the value/return the current value residing inside a widget. That

will save the various windows the burden of managing the variables themselves. Here you just need to pass the "dock-bar-name" [or menubutton-name for menubar manager], "window-name" and "widget-name" to get the value.

```
set Val [$toolBarManObject getWidgetVal $windowName $dockBarName $buttonName]
set Val [$toolBarManObject setWidgetVal $windowName $dockBarName $buttonName Value]
```

It is important to mention here that the managers first find the state of the window and set or get the value of the widget associated with that window appropriately. So the "text" widget, for example, that is registered to the particular docked window(s) [or *global* text widget] can take values independently of the "text" widget that is registered to another window but in undocked state [or *local* text widget]. However, when this undocked window is docked, the local "text" widget is destroyed and the undocked window starts using the *global* text widget. We can see a good example here as to how sharing helps in managing the widgets better and in better utilization of precious GUI real estate.

3. *Initializing the value*: The widget can be initialized to some set values based on the window/context while invoking an application. An example could be a *checkbutton* that is "registered" to 2 different windows. One component wants the state of this "*checkbutton*" as "1" whereas the other as "0". So, we read in this initial value in "ToolBarManager" and set the state of the widget accordingly. It shall be handled in ToolBarManager as

```
set internVar ::$windowName::$widgetVal
```

4. *Dynamically updating the "managers" on the fly*: The "managers" provide methods that can be called on the fly to update the state of various widgets that are present inside the *toolbar, menubar or statusbar*, including creation of new widgets dynamically. Such an operation would enable/disable certain widgets and/or create new widgets such as menu items for certain *menubuttons* are created if it is valid under the present situations. These optimal-ties help in the maximum utilization of the real estate, avoiding clutter, and share-ability among the various component of the GUI.

It is important to mention here that the managers have been written modularly in that they could be adopted easily by any GUI application, with minor modifications. Further, such "managers" can be added into the existing set of TK widgets, in case of need.

Bibliography

TCL/TK wiki, http://wiki.tcl.tk

Tcl 2011
Manassas, VA
October 24-28, 2011

Multitasking Techniques

Efficient Communication Strategy of Enterprise TCL/TK Application with Multi Process System:-A Study

Kumar Gaurav, Tushar Gupta, Madhur Bhatia

Mentor Graphics Corporation

Abstract

The GUI tool of Veloce emulation system is a TCL/TK based application. The Veloce software has a complex multiple process distributed architecture. The Inter-Process-Communication (IPC) within the software components involves frequent and bulky data transfers between the processes. VeloceGUI on one hand needs to update its state very frequently based on responses from some of the software components and emulation runtime system, and on the other hand needs huge on demand data transfer from other set of servers.

The paper elaborates how to use different communication methods to get maximum performance with minimum memory utilization. The paper also discusses how the TCL/TK based GUI interacts with larger client-server ecosystem, communicating with each other, using a sophisticated message passing system

Glossary

GUI – Graphical User Interface

IPC – Inter Process Communication

RDS – RTL Data Server

WDS – Wave Data Server

1. Introduction

There are two types of communication mechanism used by VeloceGUI: –

i) TCL Sockets
ii) Message passing library built over C-Sockets

Socket Communication consists of two steps:

i) Exchanging of data
ii) Processing of data

Exchanging and processing of data between client and server through socket communication, involves lot of challenges such as optimization of time, speed, memory and maintaining backward compatibility. Processing of data requires, parsing of data to find the actual command, that client has passed to the server for processing. Parsing of data may take significant amount of time if the frequency of communication is high; however this can be optimized to get fast response from the server

VeloceGUI communicates with RTL-Data Server (RDS) and Wave Data Server (WDS) processes through raw socket interface using the TCL library functions, as these involve bulk data transfers, of rtl design connectivity information and waveform data. This interface is optimized for data transfer efficiency, as the volume of data is huge. The frequency of communication is generally on demand and numbers of commands are lesser between GUI application and RDS/WDS. Thus the time overhead of command parsing is minimal and therefore bulk data is transferred in most efficient way. At the same time most of the intensive databases loading and data processing tasks are out-sourced to the servers, reducing the overall memory foot-print and response time for VeloceGUI application.

For interactive emulation control and communication, VeloceGUI uses C/C++ API interface (also called VeloceAPI), which is a shared library system. The VeloceAPI system interacts with other components of Veloce runtime system, using a message passing system (called messaging systems) built over C-sockets. This communication interface is mainly designed for fast interactive response, as the number of command and communication frequency is larger between GUI and Veloce runtime system. The design eliminates time spent in parsing the command level data through interface definition mechanism. The messaging system also takes care of maintaining backward compatibility within different servers/clients. The Messaging System sockets are registered in the TCL Event Loop to enable continuous polling on the messaging system sockets without blocking the GUI.

In this paper, we will discuss the various aspects of communication of GUI with RDS/WDS using TCL raw sockets and Veloce runtime system using message passing system built over C-sockets. We will also discuss the issues that were resolved during the development.

2. Communication between GUI and RDS/WDS over raw sockets

RDS and WDS are rtl-data-server and wave-data-server. These servers are meant for storing large databases corresponding to RTL design hierarchy and their waveform data.

Our emulation GUI shows the RTL design hierarchy and waveform data in hierarchy/signal browser and wave browser respectively. For the population of hierarchy/signal tree and waveform data, Veloce GUI communicates with RDS and WDS through raw sockets. GUI initiates the socket connection between itself and RDS/WDS process when the need arises i.e. when the first query arises for the RDS/WDS. Until then there is no connection between these processes. After the connection is set, GUI creates different commands and send them to RDS/WDS. These commands are used to populate the RTL design tree structure for hierarchy/signal browser and waveform data for wave browser. As the command reaches the RDS/WDS, it parses the command, process and fetches the corresponding data and provides the data to GUI. GUI remains in blocking state till the processing is completed by RDS/WDS. As the data reaches the GUI end, GUI populates its corresponding database and displays the results in hierarchy/signal browser if provided data is from RDS, or in wave browser if provided data is from WDS.

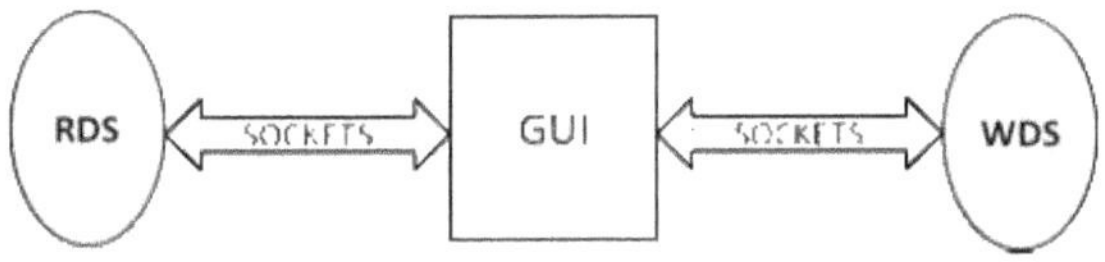

1.a *Communication of GUI with RDS/WDS using Sockets*

The code snippet shown below illustrates, how the connection establishes between GUI and RDS/WDS

Adding signal to wave window.

```
$wave_data_obj add_to_wave $hierarchy
```

This proc will first check that the connection is established between wave data server and GUI or not. If not then it will connect both the servers and then will send the command.

```
itcl::body
wave_data_server::add_to_wave  {args} {
if {$d_wave_server_id} {
  if {[catch {eval $this wave_server \
    $args} msg]} {
      return "error $msg"
    }
  } else {
    if {[catch {wave_server_connect} \
      mesg]} {
        return $mesg
      }
      set d_wave_server_id $mesg
      if {[catch {eval $this \
        wave_server $args} msg]} {
          return "error $msg"
      }
  }
}
```

In the code above when the first query arises for the wave server i.e. add signal to wave, then before sending the command to the corresponding servers, GUI checks for the server id, if it exists then GUI sends the command otherwise it establishes the connection between itself and the server and then executes the command.

The communication between GUI and RDS/WDS is a blocking communication, it means that GUI will have to wait till RDS/WDS processes and provides the data. When a user submits a request, he has to wait for that request to complete. As RDS and WDS are dedicated database servers serving the GUI only, so providing the data to GUI does not take much time. When user submits the tasks, GUI creates its corresponding command and sends to these servers. These servers fetch the data and send the results back to GUI without taking much time.

These are the list of tasks, which need communication over raw sockets with RDS/WDS

- Expanding any hierarchy in design hierarchy tree.
- Searching all the signals of a module.
- View designs in schematic and netlist graphical view.
- View waveform of signals in wave window.

When user gives any such task to GUI, then user does not want to wait for the notification from the GUI- about finishing of the tasks, but user wants to see the results immediately and will not mind if he is blocked from submitting new requests for the small time interval during which the request will be served.

The frequency of communication and number of commands are lesser between GUI application and RDS/WDS. These servers are created only to entertain the user tasks, for which user want to see the result immediately. The syntax of these commands is also simple, thus the time overhead of command parsing is minimal, therefore bulk data is transferred in a most efficient way. RDS/WDS read big intensive databases so their loading time and data processing time remain outside GUI bring up time, reducing the overall memory foot-print and response time of VeloceGUI application.

3. Communication between GUI and Veloce Runtime System using Message Passing System

Veloce Runtime System interacts with VeloceGUI using C/C++ API interface (also called VeloceAPI), which is a shared library system. VeloceAPI system interacts with other components of Veloce runtime system, using a message passing system built over C-sockets.

Emulation GUI, apart from displaying design hierarchy and waveform, also does many critical tasks, which are generally required from the GUI of Emulation product. These tasks involve

- Compiling the RTL design
- Keeping the GUI state updated
- Running the Emulation
- Downloading the Emulation database
- Downloading the Memory in the design
- Downloading and Updating the Trigger into hardware
- Getting and Setting the value of the register
- Adding break points in the design

For executing these tasks GUI communicates with Veloce runtime system through VeloceAPI, which is dynamically linked shared object library. GUI access Veloce runtime system through a message passing system (Messaging System) built over C sockets. The communication APIs are generated using a sophisticated compiler and socket management is done internally inside the messaging system library. The messaging system library provides the mechanisms to register the messaging system sockets to the event loop of GUI developed in TCL/TK. As these sockets get registered in TK event loop, then all the functions in Veloce runtime system can be accessed through VeloceAPI interface by the GUI and through the Messaging System interface by the VeloceAPI. All the calls to access the VeloceAPI functions are asynchronous calls. The VeloceAPI manages the launching/terminating of Veloce runtime system. The VeloceAPI uses a predefined protocol with the GUI to unblock while it is waiting for the data from the Veloce runtime system. Thus the GUI does not wait till the processing of the task is done by Veloce runtime system. GUI can be used for other purpose, till the time callback comes from Veloce runtime system. GUI remains in non blocking state.

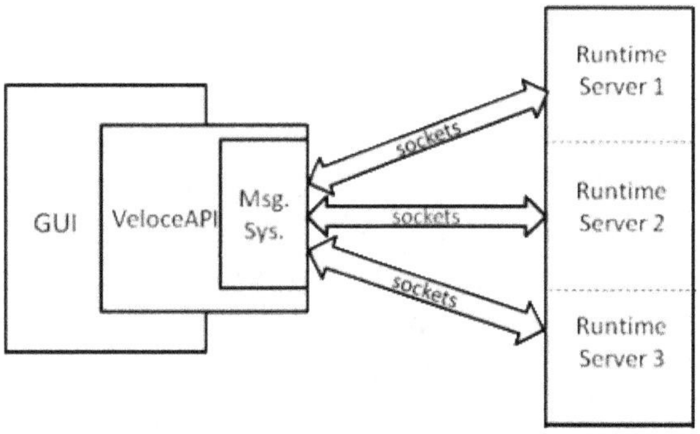

2.a *Communication of GUI with Veloce Runtime System using Messaging System*

The code snippet shown below illustrates, how GUI communicates with Veloce runtime system using VeloceAPI message passing system

// VeloceAPI Interface Code

```
int    RTS_evalcmd    (ClientData    cld,
Tcl_Interp  *intrp,  int  argc,  char**
argv) {

    ........................
    ........................
    sts = RTS_eval (argv[1]);
    RTS_WaitForCallbak(wait);
    If(wait == true){
      Tcl_SetVar(intrp,hastowait,"1",
        "TCL_GLOBAL_ONLY");
    } else {
      Tcl_SetVar(intrp,hastowait,"0",
        "TCL_GLOBAL_ONLY");
    }
    ........................
    ........................
    Return sts;
}
```

TCL CODE

```
incr task_queue 1
set retval [RTS_evalcmd $cmd]
if{$retval !=0}{
    return -code error $retval
    incr task_queue -1
}
if {$retval == 0 && $hastowait == 1}
    wait_for_callback
    release_prompt
} else {
    incr task_queue -1
}
```

In the code above, the GUI process invoked the commands of VeloceAPI with the task that needs to be processed in Veloce runtime system. VeloceAPI interface just sends the task to Veloce runtime system. The Veloce runtime function accepts the task and sends the acknowledgement for the acceptance. A callback function is registered which is being called when the processing of task is being done by the Veloce runtime system. If the processing of the task requires time then TCL global variable "hastowait" is set by the VeloceAPI interface. After the status is being returned back to GUI then GUI just checks the return status and value of "hastowait" variable. If it is set then GUI called the proc wait_for_callback and releases the prompt. Now polling is started at the GUI sockets. The wait_for_callback proc does vwait on the variable which is being reset in the callback function. The prompt is released and can be used for other tasks.

The list of tasks which is allocated to the Veloce runtime servers are of the category for which user can wait for their completion. These tasks are run in the background without hindering user interaction with the GUI. User can use the GUI for other purpose like exploring the rtl hierarchy and looking at the waveforms, while these tasks are being processed in the background. The processing of these tasks should not block the GUI.

The processing of these tasks is in background but it does not mean that user can wait for long to see the results. User wants a quick response and notification from these servers. The number of commands and communication frequency are larger between GUI and Veloce runtime system thus for optimizing the time, our design eliminates the time spent in parsing the command level data through interface definition mechanism. This communication interface is mainly designed for fast interactive response.

4. Issues taken care during development

During the development of the GUI, we encountered number of issues. Two of the major issues were

i) Maintaining backward compatibility

ii) Optimizing the time and memory for blocking servers.

Maintaining backward compatibility is the major issue which needs to be handled carefully. Any change in the interface part of the GUI results in breaking the compatibility. There should always be synchronization between the servers and the GUI process. But if the forward and the backward compatibility are to be maintained between the servers and the GUI process, then instead of synchronizing the GUI and the servers, you also need to support the parsing of the older commands by the new server and parsing of the older data from the new GUI process. This is the important point that needs to be taken care of.

Communication between GUI and RDS/WDS server is blocking. The GUI will be in hung state till the RDS and WDS servers are processing the data. The busy state of the GUI increases the impatience in user. So it is the important task of the developer to optimize the processing and fetching time of the data. RDS and WDS are database servers. These servers just parse the command, fetch the corresponding data and send it back to GUI. As frequency of commands are lesser thus the time spend in the parsing is minimal. Developer should concentrate on minimizing the fetching time of the data. The fetching time can be minimized, if the data is stored in a proper container, which decreases the complexities during the search. Decreasing the complexities by using the proper container, increase the response time of the servers.

5. Conclusion

Performance of the GUI can be increased by selecting the right communication methods between the processes. If the communication between two processes is less and the syntax of commands are simple then GUI can communicate with the server using raw sockets. If the frequency of communication is large then communication between the processes can be done using message passing system.

Interface compatibility between the processes also needs to be taken care of during the development. Thus any change in the server side of the interface should be reflected in the client side as well and vice versa.

A Versatile Beowulf Task Distribution Application

Clif Flynt
Noumena Corporation
www.noucorp.com
clif@noucorp.com

1 Abstract

Running faster has been the holy grail of computing since the days of the abacus. The first thing a programmer hears after "does it work" is "can you make it run faster?"

In the early days of computing, the best way to make a program run faster was to find a better algorithm or optimize the commands. After some 50 years of study, most of the better algorithms have been discovered and put into well optimized libraries.

The next way to make an application run faster is to split it into smaller applications and run them on multiple processors. Modern CPU chips do this to some extent and modern Graphics Processing Units do it to a greater extent.

Problems that can be optimized for parallel computing range from fine-grained applications in which the behavior of one thread is influenced by the computations of other threads to coarse-grained application sets that are totally separated from each other.

Fine-grained applications in which one thread influences another require tools like PVM (Parallel Virtual Machines) or CPS (Concurrent Processing System), specialized hardware with high-speed interprocess communication (often shared memory) and generally involve instrumenting the code or writing a special application to perform the processing.

In medium and coarse grained applications the behavior of one processing thread does not influence the behavior of other threads. These problems are much more approachable with simple hardware and relatively trivial care in the architecture of the processing applications.

Examples of medium-grain parallel tasks might be performing image processing in a set of strips and then reassembling the strips into a complete image, or generating a mandelbrot set as a collection of areas that are then assembled into a mandelbrot image. These individual tasks may run at different speeds depending on the resource used and the complexity of the task. When all of the data is available, a final result can be created.

Examples of coarse grained parallel tasks include running multiple simulations with different sets of data, calculating a fitness of solutions for a genetic algorithm, or performing the same analysis on multiple datasets. These applications are completely independent of each other, although the results sets may be combined for later analysis. This level of parallelization is the basis for the "Seti@home" and "folding@home" projects. The application requires a small amount of data and a large amount of independent data processing.

Beowulf clusters, sets of computer nodes with slow (ethernet-speed) interprocess communications are suitable for applications with medium or coarse-grain parallelization which require large ratio of processing time to inter-system communication.

The concept of a Beowolf cluster covers a large range of autonomous processing units from dedicated, diskless-compute nodes to standalone workstations that aren't being fully utilized. The techniques for distributing the tasks can range from direct memory access to scp/ssh interactions.

It is relatively simple to distribute a set of tasks across multiple computing resources. For a small number of nodes and tasks, the tasks can be distributed and hand-started. For a single application and a well controlled set of nodes, a simple shell or Tcl script can be used to start applications as necessary.

Creating a special-purpose control application for each application that needs to be distributed is costly in terms of human time and reduces the set of applications that can profit by being distributed. There is a need for a generic application that can be extended to handle multiple types of tasks and multiple styles of clusters.

The mythical Beowolf met Wulfgar when he first came to Heorot. Wulfgar escorted Beowulf to the king and thus provided him with his first task. Wulfgar was the person who connected a resource (Beowulf) with a task (Grendel).

This `wulfgar` is a Tcl/Tk application and framework for creating and distributing tasks across a set of resources (compute nodes). It can be used from a command line or a GUI. It can be extended for new types of projects by defining a new class and can be extended to control different Beowolf architectures by adding external applications to interact with nodes in different style of cluster.

While it would have been great fun to continue the naming motif and have `wulfgar` distribute quests across a network of castles, the references to ancient Geats and monsters ends with the application name.

2 Overview

The `wulfgar` application distributes a set of jobs among a set of computing nodes. The jobs will be run one-at-a-time on the nodes and the results will be collected into a defined location. One job is distinguished from other jobs by it's command line arguments. The arguments may be simple values (like `-x 1 -y 3`) or the name of a configuration file.

The jobs are grouped in a *project*. The project defines the executable to be used and how individual jobs are created from that project. The current version of `wulfgar` can create jobs using a single numeric loop, two nested loops, or from a set of configuration files. New project types can be created by adding a new classes with a custom constructor that creates jobs for this style of project.

The computing nodes are grouped into a ***nodeSet***. A nodeset is a collection of remote nodes which share a common access method (`ssh, rsh, shell`, shared memory, etc.) New types of nodeSets can be created by writing new access scripts.

The `wulfgar` application is written using TclOO and a Model-View-Controller design paradigm. The base classes control defining and distributing jobs and nodes and collecting the results. The GUI uses inheritance, mixins, the `info` command and the `trace variable` command to examine and attach itself to the controller elements of the application. This allows `wulfgar` to be run either from a command line or script or by interacting with a user via a GUI.

When running in a GUI mode, a running task resembles the image below. This shows a set of 16 tasks assigned to 3 nodes on an internal network. The jobs are distinguished by the `-x`, `-y` and `-out` command line values. The `-vw, -vh, -wd` and `-ht` arguments are the same for each job.

The top line shows the progress on the project - the collection of tasks. There are jobs in 3 states, success, running, and available. The three colors shown in the completion bar show the relative number of tasks in each state.

Each of the lines below shows the status of that task, either that it is complete, the percentage of completion, or that it is available and unassigned to a compute node.

Tasks that have been assigned show the node that they are running on and when they started. A completed task also displays the end time.

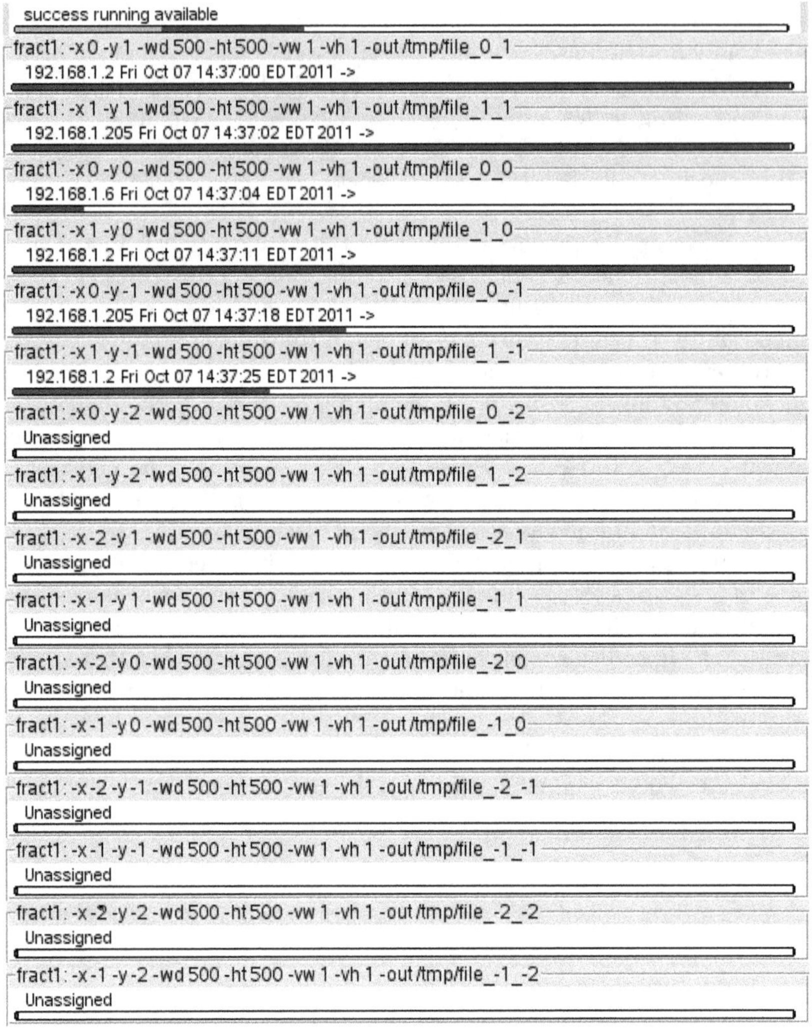

3 Internals

`Wulfgar` views the world as collections of static and ephemeral elements. The static elements are instantiated as classes which are reflected into a database (using `tdbc::Sqlite`) The ephemeral entities are implemented as memory resident classes which are created when needed and are discarded when `wulfgar` terminates.

The static elements are collections of jobs and resources. A job's non-volatile state includes the executable to invoke and the arguments to be used with the executable. A job has a volatile characteristic of whether it has been run and the final status of the run. A resource (referred to as a node) has a non-volatile state that includes the IP address, access port and a volatile attributes of online/offline status.

The ephemeral entities are the set of jobs and resources currently in use. These are grouped as a job and a resource when the job starts being executed.

A job is a single run of an executable program and a set of data. Jobs are collected into a `project`, which is a collection of jobs that use a common executable on the processing resource.

Compute resources are referred to as `nodes`, and are grouped into `nodeSets` A `nodeSet` is a collection of nodes that share a common access manner such as ssh, rsh, etc.

The `project`, `job`, `nodeSet` and `node` are relatively static entities. They have a state (available, running, completed) that is modified but otherwise they exist from the time they are created until a real-world project is complete and the database is retired.

The `project`, `job` `nodeSet` and `node` classes are shown below with their data and methods.

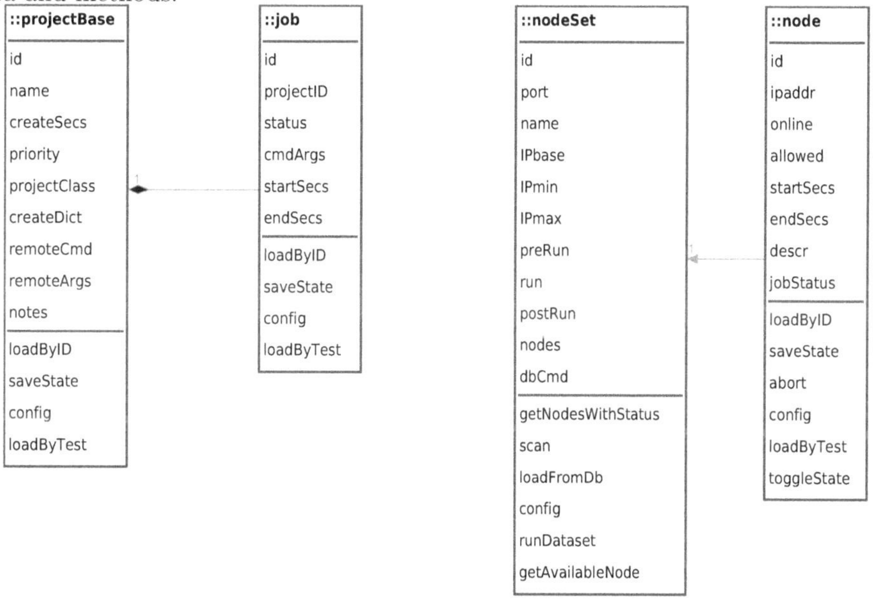

Each of the classes has an `id` variable. This is used to reflect the data to the database but is not otherwise used by the runtime system.

Each class has a `config` method. The `config` method modifies the contents of a variable and updates the modified data in the database.

The relationship between a job and a node that it is running on is ephemeral. These items are created as required and destroyed after they have been used.

The ephemeral classes in `wulfgar` are the `line` and the `piece`. The line is named for a manufacturing line. It contains a nodeSet and a project. The `piece` (for piecework) is a class with a single job and a node to run the job on.

A line has an active project and an associated nodeset. When a line is running, it creates pieces by selecting an available job and node and creating a piece object that contains the job and node. Once a `piece` has been started, it interacts with the node using the pre-run, run and post-run external applications defined by the `nodeSet`.

A `line` object contains the name of a `project` object and a `nodeSet` object and a list of the `piece` objects that it has created from the jobs and nodes in the `project` and `nodeSet`.

The next image shows the relationships between line, project, nodeset, piece, job and node.

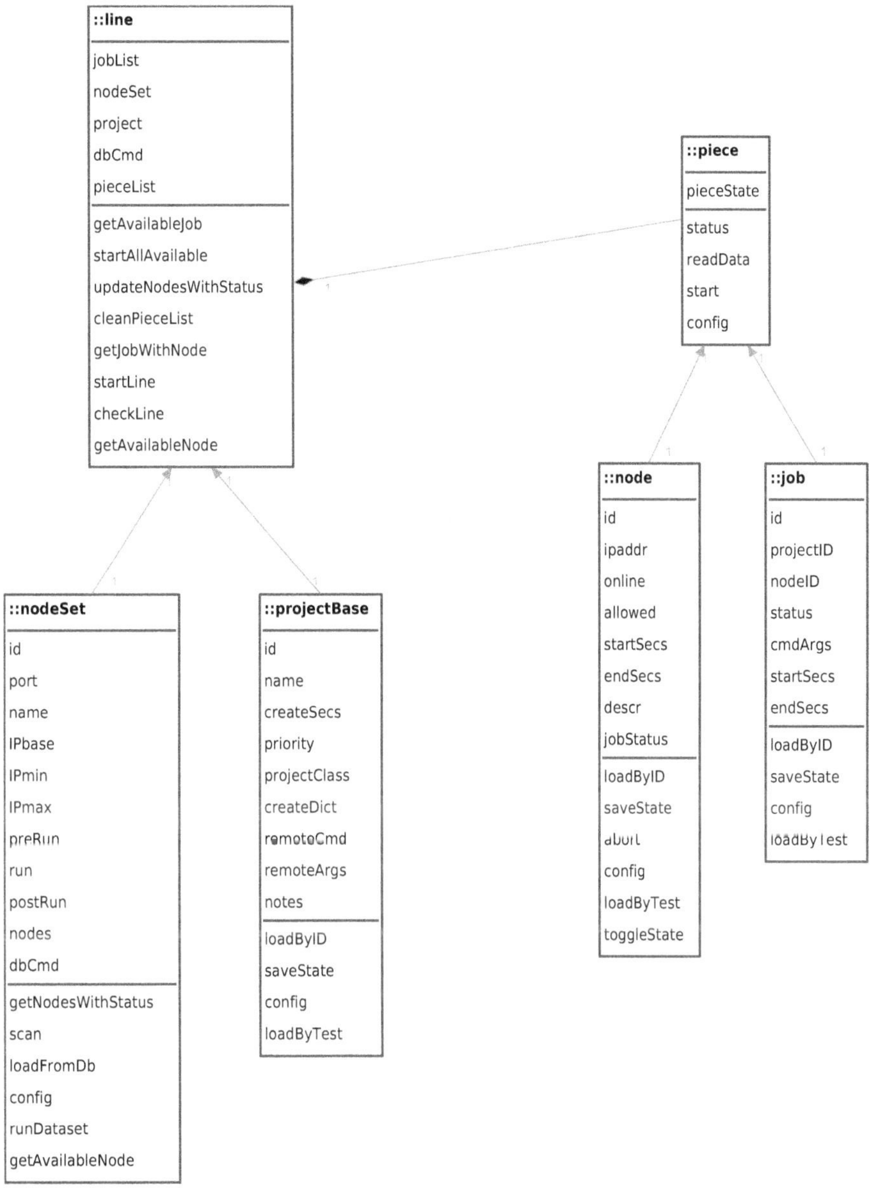

The project, job, nodeset and node objects are all reflected into an SQL database, allowing processing to be stopped and restarted as necessary at the cost of losing the work done by tasks that are currently running on remote nodes.

4 Creating tasks and jobs

When a project is created the constructor also creates a set of jobs. Different types of projects use different methods of creating tasks. As examples, tasks to model the behavior of an engine running different grades of fuel could be created by iterating through a single loop of octane ratings. A set of tasks to fill areas of a Mandelbrot set could be created with nested loops iterating over an X/Y area to define rectangles to be computed. A set of tasks to model the behavior of a complex system could be generated by iterating through a set of configuration files generated by external applications.

Support for multiple styles of creating tasks is implemented within `wulfgar` by deriving classes with type-specific constructors to create the associated jobs from a standard base class (`projectBase`). New mechanisms for creating jobs can be added by creating new project classes

The inheritance relationship between the parent class (`projectBase`) and the derived classes `countingProject`, `twoAxisProject` and `filesProject` is shown below.

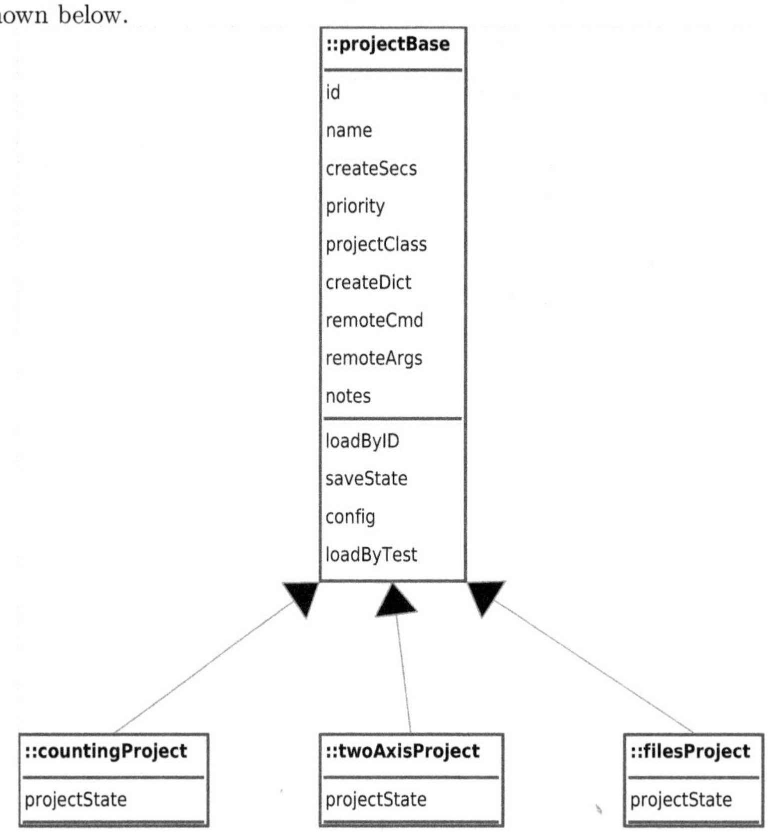

The important attributes of a project are:

`name`	Used to identify this project to a human.
`priority`	Used to schedule this project when multiple projects are active.
`createDict`	A set of key/values that are used to create jobs for this project.
`remoteCmd`	The command to run on a remote system.
`remoteArgs`	A set of patterns to use to create the command arguments for the remote task. The remoteArgs string may include tcl variables or commands which will be substituted using the `subst` command when the job object is created.

A project to generate rectangular areas of a mandelbrot set resembles this:

```
name        mandelbrot
priority    1
createDict  startX -2 startY -2 endX 2 endY 2 incrX 1 incrY 1
remoteCmd   fractal.tcl
remoteArgs  -x $x -y $y -w 25 -h 25 -vh 1 -vw 1 -out mdl_$x_$y
```

The `createDict` is used to initialize the nested loops. The loops variables are `x` and `y`, which are used (with Tcl's `subst` command) to populate the arguments to the jobs.

A job's attributes include

`projectID`	References a project's ID in the databae.
`status`	Describes the job's status: available, success, fail, abort.
`cmdArgs`	The command line arguments for this job.

An individual job within the `mandelbrot` project would resemble this:

```
status    available
cmdArgs   -x 0 -y 1 -wd 500 -ht 500 -vw 1 -vh 1 -out
          /tmp/mdl_0_1
```

5 Distributing Jobs

A classic beowolf cluster of stand-alone processors distributes jobs using `ssh/scp` or `rsh/rcp` across a network. Setting up a compute cluster using workstations is fairly cheap (by supercomputing standards) and easy. However, racks of cabinets use a lot of space and running and maintaining dozens of disk-drive based systems can chew up a lot of human time.

An economical compute cluster can be created with a set of diskless motherboards attached via an on-board network adapter to a server. The diskless nodes can be booted using the PXE environment and data transfers can be done using a NFS shared partition, the traditional `ssh` or the computationally cheaper `shell (port 514)` protocol.

A functional compute cluster can be created from castoff motherboards thumb-tacked to a cubicle wall, or as assembled into a box as crudely as shown below:

The wulfgar application can be extended to different connection architectures with external applications that are exec'd by wulfgar to transfer the client application to the target system, execute it and collect results.

These applications will receive a set of values defined for the nodeset (IP address, port, userID, password, etc) and per-job values which they must parse for more details.

The Expect extension is a very useful tool for this sort of machine control and is used in the external applications provided with wulfgar.

The example below is a sample of a post_scp.tcl application which copies a result file from the remote system to the local results folder. It receives the user and password from the values in the nodeSet's postRun attribute, and other values (-out) from the values assigned to the job's cmdArgs attribute.

```
#!/opt/ActiveTcl-8.6/bin/tclsh8.6
lappend auto_path .
package require expectTools

exp_internal 0
```

```
log_user 0

if {[llength $argv] < 4} {
  puts {post_scp.tcl -local localFolder -user loginID -pwd pwd }
  puts {From Run: post_scp.tcl -path remoteFile \
      -ip [$n config -ipaddr]}
  exit
}
puts "[llength $argv] ..$argv.."
array set av $argv

if {![info exists av(-path)]} {
  set av(-path) $av(-out)
}

if {![info exists av(-local)]} {
  set av(-local) .
}

spawn scp $av(-user)@$av(-ip):/$av(-path) $av(-local)
dialog assword $av(-pwd)
dialog 100% ""
```

The remote application on the compute node can be a single executable, or a script that invokes several cooperating applications.

6 Adding a GUI

Since `wulfgar` is an expandable, adaptable application, the GUI code needs to self-constructing and as independent of the thinking parts of the application as possible.

This is accomplished in `wulfgar` with some naming conventions and by using TclOO inheritance and mixins, Tcl's introspection (particularly `info class`) and trace facilities.

One convention is that the `config` command behaves like the Tk *widgetName* `configure` command in that it returns a list of keys and values when it is invoked with no arguments. This allows a procedure to easily retrieve a list of the attributes in an object's state array that can be assigned values.

This convention allows the GUIs that create an object to query the class for values to be used in defining the object.

The `info class` command provides access to the class state of an application. This can be used to determine how many classes are derived from another class and dynamically construct a GUI that reflects the available functionality.

The next code snippet demonstrates using the `info class subclass` command to find the classes for the specific project types and create a separate tab in the tab notebook for each class. The `configure` command is used to populate the fields with the class specific attributes and their initial values.

```
set nb [ttk::notebook $fr.nb]

foreach nm [info class subclass ::projectBase] {
  set nm [string trim $nm :]

  $nb add [frame $nb.f_$nm] -text $nm
  set f2 $nb.f_$nm

  set f3 [labelframe $f2.fs \
      -text "[string range $nm 0 end-7] Specific"]
  grid $f3 -sticky news

  foreach {k v} [$tmp config -createDict] {
    label $f3.l_$k -text $k
    entry $f3.e_$k -textvariable ::GUI($nm,cD,$k)
    set ::GUI($nm,cD,$k) $v
    grid $f3.l_$k $f3.e_$k
  }
}
```

When combined with the rest of the project GUI code an GUI like the image below is created.

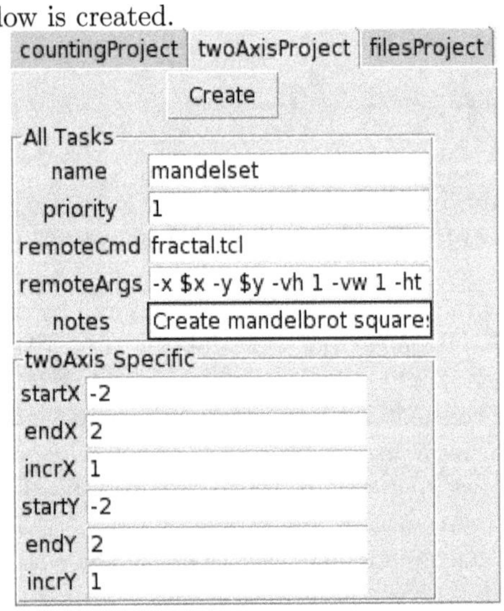

Another convention is that the external nodeState applications are named using a pattern (so that `glob` can identify them) and must return a list of arguments when invoked with no arguments. This allows the GUI for creating a nodeset to automatically expand when new nodesets are created.

A common design pattern is for a class with GUI methods to be inherited from a compute model class. This pattern is used to define the lineGui and nodeSetGui classes.

While a `line` is running, the line object creates new piece objects as it needs them. It's not convenient for a `lineGui` object to create the `pieceGui` objects, since it's not involved in the `piece` creation.

The `line` and `piece` classes interact with each other, and those interactions need to be displayed in a GUI without touching the code that controls the interactions.

The `line` class maintains a list of pieces that have been created.

The `lineGui` class inherits from the `line` class and places a `trace` on the `lineState(pieceList)` variable. This allows the lineStateGui to be updated whenever the `line` object adds or removes a piece.

As a remote task runs it should report a fraction complete message at intervals. This message is received by the `piece` object that is controlling the task and saved in the `pieceState(complete)` attribute.

Like the `lineGui`, the `pieceGui` class uses a trace on the `pieceState(complete)` variable to update the completion bar.

7 Conclusion

Controlling disparate tasks on remote systems is a solvable, but non-trivial problem. The difficulties in a generic solution are the different methods of communicating with remote nodes and automating the creation of tasks.

The `wulfgar` solution is to provide a common framework for controlling nodes and tasks, with relatively small bits of glue in the form of customized classes and external applications to allow for per-application and/or per-site customization.

Tcl's ability to exec remote tasks coupled with `expect`'s ability to interact with remote systems enables a user to tweak the control applications to match their system.

The `TclOO` support for both inheritance and mixins and the ability to load new code at runtime and introspect to find what classes can be created provides a powerful environment for customizing task creation and linking tasks with resources.

The `trace` and `mixin` facilities are a powerful tool to create a framework in which the GUI and calculation code can interact with each other without being intermingled.

www.ingramcontent.com/pod-product-compliance
Lightning Source LLC
LaVergne TN
LVHW080038210926
848481LV00011B/3227